The Principle of the Welfare of the Child

This book traces the evolution of the *welfare interests of the child* principle over the centuries in England and Wales to provide a record of the key milestones in its development. It does so by comparing and contrasting the part it has played in the public – care, protection and control – and in the private – matrimonial, adoption, etc. – sectors of family law.

By analysing the content of the principle, this book discloses the essence of what has been termed 'the golden thread running through the common law'. By considering the ways in which the legal system has shaped and been shaped by the principle, it reveals its structural influence. By identifying and assessing the significance of its operational role and functions, it shows how this principle has changed the law relating to children.

In addition to a digest of cases and legislation that tracks the evolution of this legal principle, academics and other researchers will find a wealth of information on how that evolution reflects the corresponding changes in social mores. For those interested in ethics and morality, there is much illuminating evidence on how the law has balanced this principle relative to others within both civil and criminal contexts.

Kerry O'Halloran – a professionally qualified lawyer, social worker and academic – has recently retired after 13 years as Adjunct Professor to the Australian Centre for Philanthropy and Nonprofit Studies at QUT, Brisbane. In Northern Ireland he served on the Social Care Tribunal and on an HSS Trust Adoption Panel, has advised the Irish government on law reform matters, and has served in a consultancy capacity to government bodies such as Courts Services (Northern Ireland) and to the Open University in England. Previously employed as Assistant Director (Research) at the Centre for Voluntary Action, University of Ulster in Northern Ireland, his 30 books and many other publications include *The Politics of Adoption* (4th ed., Springer, 2021), *Adoption Law and Human Rights: International Perspectives* (Routledge, 2018), *Religion, Charity and Human Rights* (Cambridge University Press, 2014) and *Child Care and Protection: The Law & Practice in Northern Ireland* (Thompson Reuters, 2003).

Children and the Law

The Principle of the Welfare of the Child
A History
Kerry O'Halloran

For more information about this series, please visit: www.routledge.com/Children-and-the-Law/book-series/CHILDLAW

The Principle of the Welfare of the Child

A History

Kerry O'Halloran

Routledge
Taylor & Francis Group
LONDON AND NEW YORK

First published 2023
by Routledge
4 Park Square, Milton Park, Abingdon, Oxon OX14 4RN

and by Routledge
605 Third Avenue, New York, NY 10158

Routledge is an imprint of the Taylor & Francis Group, an informa business

British Library Cataloguing-in-Publication Data
A catalogue record for this book is available from the British Library

Library of Congress Cataloging-in-Publication Data
A catalog record has been requested for this book

ISBN: 978-1-032-21450-4 (hbk)
ISBN: 978-1-032-21451-1 (pbk)
ISBN: 978-1-003-26851-2 (ebk)

DOI: 10.4324/9781003268512

Typeset in Times New Roman
by Taylor & Francis Books

Dedicated with love and thanks to Elizabeth.

Contents

Preface

This book lays the foundations for an exploration – to be conducted in the following books in this series[1] – of how a common law principle, forged in medieval England, came to inform the law relating to children in some of the most developed western societies in the first decades of the twenty-first century.

This principle – that the law should prioritise the welfare interests of a child, relative to all other considerations, when any decision is made that may affect his or her upbringing – undoubtedly has a place in the culture and jurisprudence of many nations. However, the record of its history, dissemination and growing importance within the family law of those sharing the common law tradition is probably unique. For that reason, the focus in the first two books of this series is firmly on the principle in a common law context, though this is subject to the caveat that account is taken of international influences, particularly those rulings of the ECtHR which have a direct bearing on the UK and Ireland. This book concentrates on the developing role of the principle in the law relating to children as it evolved over the centuries in the primary common law nation until the end of the twentieth century. It leaves to Book II a contemporary study of that law in England and Wales and in Ireland, while Book III extends the study to other leading common law nations, namely Canada, Australia, New Zealand and the United States. For purposes of contrast, further books will then profile the principle and the law in selected continental European countries, a corresponding number of Asian countries and in relation to the children of indigenous communities, relative to their non-indigenous counterparts in the CANZUS nations.[2] A final book will reflect on the impact – the centrifugal force – of the principle on family

1 O'Halloran, K., *Children and the Law: From Welfare to Rights*, Abingdon, Routledge, 2022–2029: *The Principle of the Welfare of the Child: A History* (2022); *Children and the Law: Shaping the Modern Welfare Principle in the British Isles* (2023); *Children and the Law: Welfare and Rights in a Common Law Context* (2024–2025); *Children and the Law: European Perspectives on Welfare and Rights* (2026); *Children and the Law: Welfare and Rights: Indigenous Perspectives from the CANZUS Nations* (2027); and *Child Welfare and Rights: A Contemporary Family Law Analysis* (2028–2029).

2 Meaning Canada, Australia, New Zealand and the United States.

law as a whole: on the structure of the courts and the roles of children's representatives within it; on the legal system, access to it and the separation of civil from criminal proceedings; and on the relative importance of other principles such as parental responsibility, equality, proportionality and due process. It will consider the extent to which the principle's paramountcy weighting threatens the foundations upon which family law has been constructed and contemplate the inherent complexities and, to some extent, the contradictions involved in the tensions between the legal rights of children and their welfare interests.

Arguably, such a reflection is long overdue. At a time when western nations are increasingly concerned about the numbers of children entering their public child-care systems, there is a pressing need to know what role the welfare principle plays – or should play – in their admission, care and discharge. As levels of child crime – including murder and drug abuse – continue to rise, there is every good reason for reviewing the welfare/criminal law interface. Similarly, as private family law witnesses increased rates of family breakdown, controversy over transgender matters, and as transient parenting arrangements become the new norm, there is a need to consider whether all changes to gender identity and parenting arrangements should – or can – be made subject to the welfare interests of any children involved. Across all these contexts, there is perhaps a rationale for having the same menu of hybrid court orders designed to safeguard and promote child welfare. For these and other reasons, as human rights become more deeply embedded, there is a growing need to distinguish between the welfare interests and the legal rights of children.

Introduction

The modern dilemma for family law is to strike an appropriate balance between those principles which bind and those which loosen the ties between family members. This conflict has implications as profound and uncertain for the future structure of the courts, the coherence of family law and the continued viability of some of its oldest jurisdictions as for the future of those who become the subject of family proceedings. Arguments for both camps have rested their case on the welfare of the child.

This book is in three parts, and – like its predecessor two decades ago[1] – it takes an analytical look at the meaning given to the welfare principle, its role and functions, the reasons for the controversy it attracts, and the growing legal significance attached to it. As the principle emerged from a common law context, this book naturally proceeds by tracking its development in England, the primogeniture common law jurisdiction, leaving other books in this series to consider the outcome of its transfer to and evolution in other jurisdictions. The timeline begins with the initial provisions for child welfare in feudal times and closes by taking stock of the role, weighting and effect of the principle as established by the Children Act 1989

By tracing the principle's evolution over the centuries, the book provides a record of the milestones that have shaped its development. By analysing the content of the principle, the essence of what has been termed 'the golden thread running through the common law' is disclosed. By considering the ways in which the legal system has shaped and been shaped by the principle, it becomes possible to appreciate its structural influence. By identifying and assessing the significance of its present operational role and functions, the book provides a measure of the impact of this principle on the coherence of modern family law. Finally, it provides a baseline, cohering around the 1989 Act and other legislation, that pictures the role of the welfare principle as it affected the law relating to children at the end of the twentieth century.

1 O'Halloran, K., *The Welfare of the Child: The Principle and the Law*, Aldershot, Arena/Ashgate Publications, 1999.

DOI: 10.4324/9781003268512-1

Part 1, in three chapters, examines the beginnings of the legal relationship between state, child and parents. It traces the emergence of several fundamental age-old social policy dilemmas:

- How best to set the grounds on which the right of parents to manage the upbringing of their children should give way to a public concern that they do so in a manner which does not endanger a child's welfare?
- When and how to give an appropriate weighting to the welfare of a child in the context of such other competing considerations as those of justice?
- What types of conduct, circumstances or materials are so inherently harmful to children that they should be legislatively proscribed?
- When is a parent entitled to what form of assistance from the state in support of their parenting responsibilities?
- What are the different responsibilities of first and third parties for safeguarding the welfare of a child?

These and other such issues, the integrity and challenge of which have endured across many centuries, are explored in the three chapters.

This first part of the book identifies and traces the development of key elements in the law's earliest concern for children. It provides a chronological overview of the process whereby the welfare principle came to be established in the common law. It notes the early and formative influence of the wardship jurisdiction, considers the growing leverage of the principle in a private family law context, long dominated by patriarchal interests and marital status, before it gradually acquired prominence in the public law context of child care and protection. It briefly reviews the role of child welfare in the Poor Laws era and considers the judicial and legislative contributions of the eighteenth and nineteenth centuries. It analyses the basis for the distinction made between the public and private dimensions of the principle: in particular the civil/criminal law interface. It considers the role and weighting of welfare in relation to other important principles. Finally, it provides an historical record of the emergence of the three legislative strands – private family law, public law and general social welfare law – in which the welfare principle has since evolved. In so doing it outlines the context and sets the parameters for the remainder of the book.

Part 1 aims to leave the reader with an historical outline of the principle's legal development, a clear picture of its component parts and an understanding of the different rules and proceedings through which the law gives effect to it. By identifying and differentiating between the various elements comprising the legal definition of child welfare, it sets the agenda for the book's following thematic approach.

Part 2, in four chapters, acknowledges a major development in the role played by the welfare principle in the modern law as it relates to children. Part 1 charted the principle's evolution from judicial genesis in the Court of Chancery to eventual incorporation in legislation. The principle then functioned largely as a brake to constrain an irresponsible exercise of rights by parent, guardian or stranger and as a litmus test to identify and legislatively proscribe the circumstances, conduct and materials judged to be harmful to children. Part 2 sees the principle grow from a role as determinant of the subject matter for legal processes to its present position of also governing, to some extent, the means whereby the law relates to children. It acknowledges that the principle functions not only as a factor or objective in proceedings, but is now so infused within the legal system that it shapes the appropriate structures and the roles of other principles and determines the particular statutory duties common to both public and private law.

This second part of the book examines the content and structural role of the welfare principle. It begins with a chapter that takes stock of what is meant by the welfare of the child: identifying and assessing its primary components as disclosed by caselaw. The next two chapters focus on the ways in which the legal system gives effect to the principle by providing for the identification and representation, respectively, of matters having a bearing on a child's welfare interests, with attention given to the role of the child, that of other parties and the range of professionals engaged – previously and presently – in bringing welfare interests before the court. It compares and contrasts the roles of solicitors, guardians *ad litem* and others who have the duty or the discretionary power to represent the legal and welfare interests of a child in family proceedings. The fourth chapter considers the ways in which the principle affects the legal system as it relates to children under the Children Act 1989: the jurisdiction and operation of the courts, access and the governing rules and principles. Part 2 thereby lays a foundation for Part 3, which examines the distinctive operational features of public and private family law in some detail.

Part 3, in two chapters, examines the role and functions given to the welfare principle in public and private law, respectively, as represented almost exclusively by the provisions of Children Act 1989, which governs coercive and consensual intervention by the state in matters affecting the upbringing of a child. The objective is to explore the way in which the law defines the content of the principle in each context and provides the mechanisms for applying it. Attention is given to identifying the degree of discretion available to court and local authority in their respective management of the options available to give effect to welfare interests. It also pursues themes about the balance between the welfare principle and other principles and considerations. For example, it considers the right of a parent to determine how best to rear their child and their entitlement to state support while doing so. It also considers the interface between the principles of justice and welfare and the realities of welfare in criminal and child protection proceedings.

This third part explores, firstly, the role of welfare in a public law context, dealing in turn with each of the previously identified hallmarks of the principle (care, control, protection, prevention and promotion). It examines these in the light of governing legislative provisions, the specific powers and duties involved and actual judicial and professional practice. In relation to each it identifies and assesses the different thresholds for coercive and ameliorative intervention by the state in relation to welfare matters, the rights and discretionary powers of the parties to define what constitutes such matters, and the indicators of success/failure in respect of intervention. It considers the type of authority (prescriptive, discretionary, etc.), the weighting (first consideration, paramount, etc.) and the priority (objective of, or a factor in, proceedings) relied upon to give effect to the principle. It identifies and assesses the representation of a child's welfare interests and rights in the context of coercive proceedings and when 'in care'. It considers the outcomes of the different proceedings in terms of their capacity to benefit the child concerned.

Secondly, Part 3 identifies the formal place and role given to the principle in a private family law context on matters affecting the upbringing of a child and examines the functions it performs. It deals with parenting arrangements in contested and uncontested matrimonial and separation proceedings and in adoption. For most purposes, this involves considering specific provisions of the Children Act 1989 and the powers, duties and areas of discretion which it provides to govern the choices available to the court, the parties and the children concerned. It takes each of the relevant previously identified hallmarks of the principle (direct care responsibility, contact, maintenance, etc.), considers the governing legislative provisions and assesses how they are applied in actual judicial and professional practice. This part of the book examines the changing legal balance between child welfare and parental rights with particular attention given to the growth in rights of a 'mature minor' and an unmarried father and to the rights now available to a carer, sibling, grandparent, etc. Particular attention is given to the *locus standi* of the child in private family law, their right to initiate or participate in proceedings and the significance of their consent in relation to decisions affecting their interests. An assessment is made of the differential application of the welfare principle as the basis for state intervention in private law proceedings. It explores modern developments in the balance traditionally struck between child welfare and parental rights, with particular reference to the selective application of the paramountcy principle. The difficulties inherent in ensuring that intervention is welfare related and that outcomes are compatible with welfare are examined. It analyses the change of emphasis from an adjudicative to an adjustive judicial function and relates this and the growth in influence of mediatory professions to the central problem of whether welfare factors are amenable to 'objectification' and 'one-off' decision-making processes. It raises the question as to whether judicial process is giving way to administration.

The Conclusion closes the book with reflections on the scale of the transition from the punitive regime of the nineteenth century, which saw children hanged and transported overseas, to the assertion in the Children Act 1989 of the principle that in future their welfare is to be regarded as the matter of paramount importance in judicial determinations relating to their upbringing. It considers the implications for the future role and functions of the welfare principle within the family law of the UK arising from international conventions, protocols and rulings of the ECtHR. It considers the extent to which the principle's paramountcy weighting threatens the foundations upon which family law has been constructed and contemplates the inherent complexities and, to some extent, contradictions involved in the tensions between the legal rights of children and their welfare interests. In so doing, Book I has begun a narrative and prepared the ground for an analysis of contemporary law and practice – in England and Wales, as in Ireland – which follows in Book II.[2]

2 O'Halloran, K., *Children and the Law: Shaping the Modern Welfare Principle in the British Isles*, Abingdon, Routledge (forthcoming).

Part 1

The legal origins of the child welfare principle in England and Wales

1 State recognition of child welfare

Feudalism, the common law and the Poor Laws

Introduction

Children left uncared for by parental death, absence, incapacity or destitution prompted the laying of foundations – in common law and in the Poor Laws – for the state to assume responsibility as guardian/parent of last resort. A developing common law jurisprudence, concerning the grounds justifying a voluntary or compulsory transfer of child welfare responsibilities within a family – usually from parent to parent, and in time from family to state – is recorded in a growing body of caselaw and eventually of statute law. The modern sophisticated legislative framework, regulating and differentiating the role of the welfare principle in public and private transfers of responsibility for the care of a child, has its origins in ancient caselaw concepts and constructs. This chapter sets out to identify and examine those early beginnings.

The common law and the Poor Laws

The common law of England grew out of proprietary concepts. From beginnings rooted in guardianship of the heir's interest in inherited property it gradually expanded to include a concern for the child's person. It emphasised the rights of the individual – providing for paternal rather than familial rights – and it shaped the basic law applied in the wardship jurisdiction. The constructs which came to underpin the statute law relating to child protection, such as neglect, abandonment, exposure and ill-treatment, had their origins in the common law. The approach of objectively proscribing conduct and circumstances judged to be detrimental to a child's welfare interests, setting thresholds for state intervention and determination by adjudication without recourse to discretion were all characteristics of the common law before they became assimilated into statute law.

Many of the indices of welfare interests and their parameters are also clearly traceable to the same origins. The significance of age groups, the separateness of criminal responsibility and the relevance of the 'blood tie' were established in the early days of the common law as were provision of

DOI: 10.4324/9781003268512-3

home and maintenance, education, religious upbringing, chastisement and custody of the person. Again, the importance attached to the status of the parties first emerged in a common law context, as did the obverse legal relationship between parental rights and child welfare and legal recognition of welfare as a negative rather than positive concept – only justifying action after the child concerned had suffered harm.

A rudimentary differentiation between public and private responsibilities in respect of child welfare was clearly established at common law. Respect for the privacy of the family was embedded in the doctrine of paternal rights. The concept of the state as guardian of last resort, accessed by voluntary parental relinquishment of children and given effect by residential care or boarding out, was statutorily introduced by the Poor Laws.

The common law: parental rights, duties and child welfare

The common law respect for paternal authority, itself a legacy from Roman times, was founded on the doctrine of *patria potestas* which underpinned feudal society and became absorbed into the common law. The edict of Emperor Justinian in AD 560 had abolished the doctrine and the legal concept of an autonomous patriarchal family but in Britain its hallmarks lived on. Some of the more characteristic features of this doctrine included: the private autonomous household ruled by the father; the actual or virtual ownership of children; the blood tie; filial piety; the power and limits of corporal punishment; the expectation of maintenance; and the tenuous relationship between child and state. Parents were guardians of their children as of right, a right which included a custodial authority based on ownership of the child. After Justinian's edict, parents were left with the right, and perhaps the duty, to control a wayward child by chastisement but more serious transgressions were a public rather than a private matter, and the state would intervene to bring the child before the court.

The common law, like that of ancient Rome, was essentially grounded on the rights and duties of the individual. In the context of the family, this meant that it focused on the individual with rights – the father – and then on the legal status (if any) of the others involved. The recognition given to the father with marital status was all important. The *locus standi* of this individual in common law was very powerful, that of others involved as members of his marital family were given recognition but those without status (as mistress or non-marital child) were denied any. The common law courts enforced parental authority, subject to very few limitations; it gave no recognition to a single mother or to an illegitimate child. The marital family was also denied any collective *locus standi*. Any actionable rights, in relation to his autonomous family unit, belonged to the father. For centuries, he had the right to sue a third party for the loss of services to which he was entitled as father or husband.

Paternal rights

By the middle of the nineteenth century, the doctrine of paternal rights was firmly established. At common law the *prima facie* right of a father to the control and custody of his legitimate children, subject to an absence of abuse,[1] was virtually impregnable. It was absolute as against the mother.[2] The approach of the common law was reflected clearly by the judgment of Lord Ellenborough for the Court of King's Bench in *De Manneville v De Manneville*:[3]

> We draw no inference to the disadvantage of the father. But he is the person by law entitled to the custody of his child. If he abuses that right to the detriment of the child, the court will protect the child. But there is no pretence that the child has been injured from want of nurture or in any other respect. Thus he having a legal right to the custody of his child and not having abused that right is entitled to have it restored to him.

The rationale for judicial insistence on vesting overriding authority in fathers, in respect of matters affecting the upbringing of their children, was later articulated by Cotton LJ in *In re Agar-Ellis; Agar-Ellis v. Lascelles*:[4]

> This Court holds the principle that when by birth a child is subject to a father, it is for the general interest of families, and for the general interest of children, and really for the interest of the particular infant, that the Court should not, except in very extreme cases, interfere with the discretion of a father, but leave to him the responsibility of exercising that power which nature has given him by birth of the child.

This view was endorsed by James LJ when delivering the decision of the Court of Appeal:

> The right of the father to the custody and control of his children is one of the most sacred rights.

In this judgment, which treated paternal authority as almost absolute in the absence of any misconduct, the high-water mark was reached for paternal rights. Paternal authority had evolved in consequence of the inadequacies of the feudal common law. Its principal characteristics concerned the paternal right to custody of a child and the accompanying rights to determine religious upbringing and education.

1 See *Re Thomasset* [1894] 300.
2 See *Ex parte Skinner*, 9 Moo 278.
3 (1883), 10 Vessey Junior 52.
4 (1878) 10 Ch D 49 (CA) at p 334.

THE PATRIARCHAL FAMILY

Until 1839 the custody of a legitimate child vested automatically and exclusively in the father. As head of the family he had the right to administer reasonable chastisement to his child.[5] His status was also the basis of the action for enticement.[6] Kidnapping a child was viewed essentially as an infringement of the paternal right to custody.[7] Such was the stringent judicial approach to the legal standing of the father that the courts would not permit a father to avoid his parental responsibilities by voluntarily giving up his right to custody and control.[8] No separation agreement – purporting to regulate the future care, custody, education and maintenance of his children – would be enforced by the court against a father as this was viewed as an attempt 'to fetter and abandon his parental power' and 'repugnant entirely to his parental duty'.[9] Where the welfare of a child was referred to as a factor in the judicial determination of such cases, it was only to justify judicial control of the father.

RELIGIOUS UPBRINGING

The resolve with which the courts defended the doctrine of paternal rights, created in relation to custody, was also evident in issues relating to the religion of a child.[10] A father had the right to determine questions relating to the religious upbringing of his child,[11] who had to be brought up in his religion even though, if deceased, he had left no directions to that effect.[12] In *In re Scanlan, Infants*[13] Stirling J decided that the 1886 Act made no difference to the father's right to decide in his lifetime the appropriate religious upbringing for his children or to the guardian's duty after his death to ensure that the children were trained in the father's religion. Only evidence of paternal abuse or neglect would result in judicial refusal to enforce a father's right to determine religious upbringing: the court would refuse to allow a father who was unfit to have custody the right to determine religious upbringing.[14]

5 See *Gardner v. Bygrave* [1889] 6 TLR 23 DC, *Mansell v. Griffin* [1908] 1 KB, 160, *obiter, R v. Hopley* [1860] 2F and F 160.
6 See *Lough v. Ward* [1954] 2 All ER 338.
7 See, for example, *R v. Hale* [1974] 1 All ER 1107. It was alleged that the accused had 'unlawfully secreted ... a girl aged 13 years, against the life of her parents and lawful guardians'.
8 See *St John v. St John* (1805) 11 Vessey 530 and *Vansittart v. Vansittart* (1858) 2 De Gex & Jones 249 at p 256; *Hamilton v. Hector* (1872) LR 13 Equity 511.
9 See *Van v. Van* p 259, per Turner LJ.
10 See *In re Bessant* (1879) 11 Ch D 508 and *In re Grey* [1902] 2 IR 684 at p 691.
11 See *Re Browne, a minor* [1852] 2 ICR 151 and *Hawkesworth v. Hawkesworth* LR 6 Ch 542 and *In re O'Hara* [1900] 2 IR 684 and *F v. F* [1902] 1 Ch 688 and *In re Agar-Ellis* op cit.
12 See *Talbot v. Shrewsbury*, 4 My and Cr 672; *Re Montague* 28 Ch D 82.
13 (1888) LR 40 Ch D 200.
14 See *In re Newton (Infants)* [1896] 1 Ch 740.

The duty to educate was overshadowed by the paternal right to decide on the child's religious education. Any interference with the right of the father to control his child's education met with consistent judicial approbation.[15] So strong was this right that the cases only record issues arising in relation to the religious education of children whose fathers were dead. In *Hawkesworth v Hawkesworth*[16] the court held that it had no alternative but to give effect to the Protestant father's stated wishes regarding his child's religious education, even though he had died eight years earlier, leaving no specific directions, and the child had since been brought up by her Catholic mother. In *Andrews v Salt*[17] Mellish J considered that unless the father had disqualified himself in some way, the court was obliged to give effect to his wishes. However, parental control of the child's religion – which could possibly restrict judicial endorsement of the welfare approach – failed to survive the 1925 Act.[18] Indeed, in *In re JM Carroll (an Infant)*[19] the court ruled that s1 of the 1925 Act required that in an inter-parental dispute priority should be given to the welfare interests of the child at the expense, if necessary, of either parent's views on religion.

Habeas corpus proceedings, a common law remedy, became one of the principal methods for enforcing the evolving paternal power. However, *habeas corpus* could not be used to assist a father to regain custody of a child (i.e. person below the age of 21) who had reached the 'age of discretion' (14 for boys, 16 for girls) against the latter's will.

Parental duties

The relationship between parents, their children and criminal activity was relatively uncomplicated under common law. A child would be held fully responsible and accountable for his or her criminal behaviour and like an adult could be sentenced to prison, flogging, transportation or hanging. A parent was not responsible for their child's crimes, unless as an accomplice or under the usual rules of principal and agent. In addition, however, the common law recognised a specific duty particular to the parental relationship: the duty to provide for a child. As Sir W. Blackstone stated:[20]

> The duty of parents to provide for the maintenance of their children is a principle of natural law; an obligation … laid on them not only by nature herself, but by their own proper act, in bringing them into the world.

This duty was underpinned by the criminal law.

15 See *In re Agar-Ellis* [1883] 24 Ch D 317, *In re May: Eggar v. May* [1917] 2 Ch 126 and *Hawkesworth v. Hawkesworth* (1871) LR 6 Ch App 539.
16 Op cit.
17 (1873) LR 8 Ch App 622.
18 See *In re Collins (An Infant)* [1950] Ch 498.
19 [1931] 1 KB 317.
20 See *Commentaries on the Laws of England*, Oxford, Clarendon Press, 1765.

CRIMINAL LAW, PARENTS AND CHILDREN

The common law evolved a number of criminal offences particular to children and their parents. They were focused not on the welfare of a child but on the abuse of a parental right; welfare was legally recognised only in an obverse relationship to parental right. A conviction would ensure court removal not just of custody but of all parental rights in respect of the child. These offences share the common feature of providing only for a negative recognition of the principle of the welfare of the child; not until it was irretrievably breached did the courts acknowledge the relevance of welfare. The common law was never prepared to concede that a positive welfare advantage to the child would in itself provide grounds for displacing the parental right. Parental culpability alone set the threshold for state intervention on behalf of child welfare.

Firstly, the criminal law recognised that offences of assault, neglect, murder or manslaughter could be committed against children by parents or third parties. The common law charge of assault was used by prosecutors. Thus, putting a child in a bag and leaving it suspended on palings[21] or exposing a child in inclement weather[22] was treated as assault. Any person failing to implement the duty upon them to supply the child with food and clothing so that the child died could well be guilty of murder or manslaughter.[23] The same conduct would subsequently be prosecuted as an offence of neglect under the 1933 Act, even where death resulted.

Secondly, the criminal law was used to prosecute for the offence of cruel and unnatural treatment. In practice there was a fairly close affinity between the common law offences of cruel and unnatural treatment and neglect. The latter, however, was then and remains now a fairly flexible and indeterminate offence. Cruel and unnatural treatment is a more definite concept, although it too is broad in application. There are several common law cases featuring children being beaten, left out in the cold, having cold water poured over them, etc.

Thirdly, there was the criminal offence of endangering a child. There would seem to be little doubt that it was and remains an offence at common law for a child to be treated in such a way that his or her life is endangered. Mere possibility of injury has long been sufficient. For example, in *HMA v. Jane Thom*[24] the mother allegedly threw the child from a railway carriage in motion. The charge was endangering the child's life and assault to the danger of life. The court decided that actual injury was unnecessary to establish danger to life. Such an offence was clearly intended to protect the physical welfare of the child. The genesis of the modern law relating to child protection, particularly the concept of 'likelihood of significant harm' can be traced to this common law offence and the resulting caselaw.

21 See *R v. March* (1844) 1 Carrington & Kirwan 496.
22 See *R v. Ridley* (1811) 2 Campbell 650.
23 See, for example, *R v. Bubb; R v. Hook* (1850) 4 Cox CC 455.
24 (1876) 3 Couper 332.

Finally, the last common law offence which directly protected welfare was the charge of confining and imprisoning a child. The classic instance is *HMA v Fairweather*,[25] where a child was kept for three weeks in a purpose-built wooden cage in an unheated outhouse. The child's life was endangered and she was reduced to almost total idiocy. These circumstances constituted confinement or imprisonment as well as elements of cruel and unnatural treatment, endangering life and neglect.

The flexibility and interchangeability of the common law charges are evident in the above illustrations. As has been pointed out:[26]

> The common law is not a system of rigid rules, but of principles, whose application may alter over time, and which themselves may be modified. It may, and should, be renewed by succeeding generations of judges, and so meet the needs of a society that is itself subject to change

The state as guardian of last resort

Pinchbeck maintained that 'the 20th century conception of the duty of the state towards the child has its origins, not in the reforming movement of the 19th century, but in the paternalistic policy of the Tudor state'.[27] She considered that by the sixteenth century Parliament had established principles to govern the relationship between the state and the child similar to those currently applicable. In particular she identified two such principles which seemed to be embodied in the Poor Laws:[28]

> The children of vagrant and demoralised parents were to be removed from parental control and placed in a new environment to secure their welfare. And finally, the state accepted in principle the responsibility for securing the proper treatment and training of the children thus brought into community care.

From 1572 a system of parish relief had been available for the destitute. This was extended by the Elizabethan legislation of 1597–1601 which provided for the appointment of parish overseers to work with local churchwardens and raise the funds necessary to assist all classes of destitute persons. The modern concern of the state for the welfare of children, as vulnerable citizens as opposed to young heirs, was legislatively introduced in England at the beginning of the seventeenth century with the Act for the Relief of the Poor 1601. This was adjusted by subsequent legislation and ultimately regulated by the

25 (1842) 1 Brown 309.
26 See Laws J in *C (A Minor) v. DPP* [1994] 3 WLR 888 at pp 897–898.
27 See Pinchbeck, I., 'The State and the Child in 16th Century England', *British Journal of Sociology*, 7(4) (1957), p 72.
28 Ibid at p 59.

Poor Law Commissioners under powers vested in them by the Poor Law Amendment Act 1834.

State intervention in standards of parental care

This new public concern for children, evidenced in the Poor Laws, stemmed from a state interest in avoiding bearing the cost for their upbringing. The primary characteristics of these early beginnings in state intervention on child welfare grounds were a focus on parental responsibility, a negative interpretation of child welfare and a reliance on the good offices of voluntary organisations.

The state and the Poor Laws

One of the more explicit purposes of the Poor Law legislation was to enforce, wherever possible, parental responsibility for the care and maintenance of children. Parents, with the means, were required to provide for their children. Otherwise parents were left to determine a child's welfare as they saw fit; unless they transgressed the criminal law by, for example, wilfully neglecting to provide adequate food, clothing, medical aid or lodging for them, or training them as thieves. Parenting standards that breached the criminal law would always make the future care arrangements of children a matter warranting coercive state intervention (see above).

The Poor Laws significantly extended the state interest in parenting standards by making the fact of child need itself, rather than its cause, a sufficient threshold for voluntary state intervention. Parental culpability was not a necessary prerequisite for the transfer of a child from private to public responsibility. Parents unable or unwilling to continue caring could voluntarily place their children with the Poor Law authorities. Once in care, parental rights could be assumed by the authorities under s 1(1) of the Poor Law Act 1889,[29] subject to subsequent judicial confirmation.

Poverty was most often the root cause of parental failure necessitating coercive state intervention by Poor Law guardians, to remove children from parental care and commit them to the care of the state. The destitution of whole communities resulted in a high infant mortality rate, with very many parents unable to provide adequately for their children.

29 Continued by s 52 of the Poor Law Act 1930 and subsequently by s 2 of the Children Act 1948. The Curtis Committee regarded this power as a 'very important provision' (*Report of the Care of Children Committee* (Curtis Report) (Cmnd 6922), London, HMSO, 1946, para 19), and in 1945 about 16 per cent of children in the care of Poor Law authorities had been the subject of a s 52 resolution (ibid, para 29). This was later echoed by the Houghton Committee (*Report of the Departmental Committee on the Adoption of Children* (Houghton Report) (Cmnd 5107), London, HMSO, 1972, para 153).

ABANDONMENT

Public responsibility for abandoned and destitute children had been a social problem long before the mid-nineteenth century. The Vagrancy Act 1824 was specifically introduced to address it but proved to be an ineffective legislative response to the growing numbers of children abandoned by poor parents and left to fend for themselves by begging and stealing unless rescued by charitable organisations. Many such rescued children were sent overseas or for adoption by those organisations. Abandonment was subsequently addressed in a number of statutes relating to children.[30] It eventually became a threshold requirement enabling a local authority to assume parental rights under s 2 of the 1948 Act (see, further, Chapter 3).

CHILD RESCUE

The welfare of a child, often the life of a child, was itself the criterion for state intervention and state assumption of care responsibility; parental failure was not necessarily associated with parental fault or culpable default in care standards; the transfer of parental responsibility to the state was often voluntary. But, as in the criminal law, not until a child's welfare had been impaired did the state initiate intervention and future care arrangements consequently become a matter of public rather than private law.

The influence of various philanthropic societies during the period governed by the Poor Laws laid the foundation for the development of their modern role in relation to child welfare. Most charities and other voluntary and religious organisations, particularly the Quakers, provided alms and accommodation or distributed food to the destitute without any particular regard for the separate and distinct needs of children. Not until the end of the nineteenth century did child welfare voluntary organisations make an appearance, perhaps due to the changed social conditions that accompanied the Industrial Revolution: large-scale population movements to industrialised towns; employment of young children; and the abandonment of those who had become too expensive for unemployed parents to feed. This was an era of 'street children' engaged in petty crimes.[31] Organisations such as Dr Barnardo's and the NSPCC began their current specialist services for children by developing a 'child rescue' approach to those who were abandoned, impoverished or ill-treated in the era of the Poor Laws. Their intervention, being on a voluntary rather than a

30 See, for example, the Custody of Children Act 1891, ss 1 and 3; Children and Young Persons Act 1933, s 1(1); Children Act 1975, s 12(2)(d); Adoption Act 1976, s 16(2)(d).

31 See, for example, the *Report of an Unofficial Committee of the Society for Investigating the Causes of the Alarming Increase in Juvenile Delinquency in the Metropolis* (1816), cited by Eekelaar, J., Dingwall, R. and Murray, T., 'Victims or Threats? Children in Care Proceedings', *Journal of Social Welfare Law, 4(2)* (1982), pp 68–82 at p 71.

coercive basis, was probably more acceptable than that of the state to the families concerned.

State intervention on 'child rescue' grounds often had to be followed up by a state assumption of care responsibility for the children concerned. The Poor Laws era introduced the formal role of the state as public guardian of child welfare,[32] as evidenced by the beginnings of statutory criteria for the state formally to acquire care responsibility for children, schemes for boarding-out orphans and the children of destitute mothers, and the provision of residential homes for children permanently separated from their parents.

Conclusion

The common law and the Poor Laws laid the foundations for the state to intervene – on grounds of the welfare of the child – in family affairs, which in practice and for many centuries meant intervention in paternal rights. Having intervened, the state ultimately accepted that, as carer of last resort, the question of how best to provide that welfare was a matter for it to determine and did so largely by consigning children to the poorhouse. The Poor Laws era saw the state formally assume its role as public guardian of child welfare.

This was also the time when the Court of Chancery developed the *parens patriae* jurisdiction of wardship and the responsibilities of guardianship while the High Court, exercising its statutory powers and duties, continued to adjudicate on paternal rights of custody. Chancery courts employed a flexible and discretionary approach in which equitable judgments would conform to the welfare needs of a particular child (see, further, Chapter 2). Common law courts applied precedents, adjudicated on statutorily prescribed duties and enforced their judgments by use of *habeas corpus.* This dual judicial system, in which both components dealt with matters affecting the welfare of children, continued through the eighteenth and nineteenth centuries until the Judicature Act 1873 unified the courts of equity and the common law.

32 For example, the Infant Life Protection Act 1872.

2 Judicial acknowledgment of guardianship duties

Introduction

The welfare interests of a child, as a factor in proceedings concerning his or her upbringing, rested from the outset on judicial rather than legislative initiative. This chapter examines particular judicial initiatives to recognise and further the development of the welfare principle occurring during the period framed by two statutes which, in this context, proved to be of exceptional importance: the Tenures Abolition Act 1660 and the Judicature Act 1873. The role of the Court of Chancery in relation to guardian, parent and child, where their interests are in conflict, lies at the heart of this chapter. It considers the period when the courts of common law and of equity developed separately. Particular attention is given to the degree of commonality in the principles applied by the judiciary towards guardians and parents taken in guardianship and custody proceedings, respectively. It also examines the link between welfare interests and the duty of care owed to a child by parent or guardian. The rise and entrenchment of the countervailing doctrine of parental rights – or, more accurately, paternal rights – is also considered.

Equity and the Tenures Abolition Act 1660

The Tenures Abolition Act 1660 abolished military and similar tenures and the Court of Wards and Liveries. This statute formally marked the end of the feudal system, the demise of which opened up the Court of Chancery, enabling it to entertain wardship applications in respect of children other than the young male heirs whose property rights had been so important to the maintenance of the rigid hierarchical social relationships that characterised feudalism. Until then, the jurisdiction of the Chancellor had been largely ineffective. In the opinion of Pollock and Maitland, the common law of guardianship was 'disjointed and incomplete'. The law, they indicated, 'had been thinking almost exclusively in terms of infant heirs, and had left other infants to shift for themselves … The law had not even been careful to give the father a right to the custody of his children.'[1]

1 See Pollock, F. and Maitland, F.W., *The History of English Law*, 2nd ed., Cambridge, Cambridge University Press, 1968, vol 2, pp 443 and 444.

DOI: 10.4324/9781003268512-4

After 1660 the way was clear for equitable principles to have a dramatic impact upon the legal position of children.[2] The legislative intent, underpinning s 8 of the Tenures Abolition Act 1660, was to give firm endorsement to the authority of a father in respect of the children of his marriage. It conferred wide powers on fathers but, significantly, did not refer to the powers in terms of wardship or guardianship. That section empowered a father 'to dispose of the custody and tuition of such child or children (those under 21)' with the effect that 'such disposition ... shall be good and effective against all and every person or persons claiming the custody or tuition of such child or children as guardian in socage or otherwise'. This provision, as noted by Lord Penzance,[3] authorised the father to 'dispose of the custody of the child as he thinks fit'. The year 1660 thus saw not only the end of the feudal concept of wardship but also the emerging importance of paternal rights, particularly the right to custody.

The Court of Chancery

According to Holdsworth, the generally accepted view is that the Chancellor's powers were based 'not on any inherent jurisdiction, but upon a special delegation by the Crown of its prerogative right, as *parens patriae*, of looking after their [infants'] interests'.[4] The modern duty of the state to extend protection to those incapable of protecting their own interests evolved from the ancient duty of the Crown to protect the person and the property interests of a subject who not being fully *sui juris* lacked the legal capacity of other subjects. In practice this was due to their being mentally handicapped or a child.

The parens patriae *jurisdiction*

The king was regarded as the natural protector of those without kin;[5] apparently this had a statutory foundation. Royal protection was, in particular, given to young heirs, usually orphans, during their childhood. From this prerogative right of the Crown, tied to direct knight service,[6] derived the inherent jurisdiction of the court to make a child a ward of court.

This duty in practice rested on the Lord Chancellor, who initially delegated it to the Court of Wards and Liveries until 1660, when it passed to the Court of Chancery.[7] As was stated by Lord Cranworth LC in *Hope v. Hope*:[8]

2 See Holdsworth, W.S., *History of English Law*, 7th ed., London, Methuen & Co, 1996, vol 5, p 315; vol 6, p 648.
3 See *In the goods of Thomas Parnell* (1872) LR 2P&D 379, at p 381.
4 See Holdsworth, op cit, vol 6, p 648.
5 See ibid, vol 2, p 99.
6 See ibid, vol 10, p 356.
7 Thereafter this duty fell to be exercised as follows: in 1875 it passed to the Chancery Division of the High Court; in 1971 it was transferred to the Family Division; and in 1989 it became exercisable by the family proceedings court.
8 (1854) 4 De GM & G 328, 345.

> It is the interest of the State and of the Sovereign that children should be properly brought up and educated; and according to the principle of our law, the Sovereign, as *parens patriae*, is bound to look to the maintenance and education (as far as it has the means of judging) of all his subjects.

The Court of Chancery, exercising the *parens patriae* jurisdiction, conferred the protection of wardship on its young charges and appointed a guardian to bear day-to-day care and protection responsibilities. From the outset, wardship was concerned with protecting the person as well as the property of its wards. After the 1660 statute, however, the exercise of this jurisdiction for welfare purposes became increasingly less dependent upon whether or not a ward had rights to property. The primary object of the wardship jurisdiction has always been to protect those who owe allegiance to the Crown. Hence, historically, the jurisdiction to entertain wardship applications has been based on the 'allegiance' of the child.[9]

The Court of Chancery appears to have conferred upon itself a very wide interpretational discretion in determining the grounds for intervention. Chancery judges were more inclined to intervene than were their common law counterparts. Once having intervened, the availability of prerogative powers and control of court officers enabled the judiciary to exercise direct hands-on management of a child's circumstances in a manner not achievable under the common law. The issue of a wardship order vested in the court the parental duty to maintain, protect and educate a child and was exercisable on behalf of the court by its appointed guardian. The emphasis was on preserving the *status quo* in relation to such aspects of upbringing until the infant heir attained the age of majority. This was the essence of the wardship jurisdiction over orphans. It was established as such during the era of feudalism and laid the foundation for the modern welfare approach.

Chancery also brought the added dimension of continuity because the responsibility of Chancery for its wards was a continuing one, so the welfare of a child was not simply a matter for adjudication but one that required continual reappraisal and ongoing management. The welfare of the child remained the principal if not the sole concern of the Court of Chancery in all circumstances where, for one reason or another, parental rights were irrelevant, secondary or unimportant.

CHANCERY AND GUARDIANS

Chancery had from time immemorial supervised the conduct of guardians in relation to their wards.[10] From the principle of trust underpinning 'guardianship

9 See, for example, *Hope; Re Willoughby* (1885) 30 Ch D 324; *Harben v. Harben* [1957] 1 WLR 261; *Re P (GE)* [1965] Ch 568.

10 See *Report of the Committee on the Age of Majority* (Latey Report) (Cmnd 3342), London, HMSO, 1967, para 192.

in socage' and that of a parental duty to care which grounded 'guardianship by nurture', Chancery developed firm expectations that a guardian would use his/her position of trust for the benefit of a child. Guardianship rested on parental duties rather than rights. The parent/guardian was held to be vested with the powers necessary to give effect to his or her duties. Concern for the child and his property was the basis of the guardianship concept. Prior to the eighteenth century the welfare principle took the form of a duty placed upon parents/guardians and enforced by the feudal institutions recognised by the law.[11]

The feudal concept of guardianship, founded on a sense of *loco parentis* duties and fiduciary responsibilities, can be seen as a form of public office. This accords with the role of the Court of Chancery which always had available to it not only the power of appointment of guardians but also their control and supervision, the sanction being forfeiture of the office of guardian. In *Morgan v. Dillon*,[12] for example, the issue facing the court was the power to remove a testamentary guardian. In the eyes of Chancery, if there were any abuse of trust, such as had occurred in that case (which amounted to 'any misbehaviour or ill-usage of the person of the ward'), then 'this Court could remove the person out of his custody'.

West LC decided that guardianships were intrinsically the same. The differences were not created by the method of appointing or nominating a guardian. Therefore, there was no reason why testamentary guardians should not be subject to equitable control. This view in effect overruled the earlier approach of Lord Nottingham LC in *Foster v. Denny*,[13] where he decided that equitable intervention related only to common law guardianship and therefore 'here being a Guardian by Act of Parliament, I cannot remove him or her'. Significantly, West LC added the caveat that when the interest enforceable by the wardship was 'lucrative' to the guardian rather than 'for the benefit' of the child (reflecting the distinctive purposes of guardianship in chivalry and socage), the court could not intervene. This suggests that the equitable intervention of the Chancellor was designed, at least in part, to protect the interests of the child. This was probably limited to guardianships which acknowledged the child as the beneficiary of the trust created by the wardship. Once military tenures had been abolished in 1660, such equitable intervention extended to all guardianships.

11 The first statutory description of a guardian's powers was given in the Tenures Abolition Act 1660, where it was stated that a guardian, being granted the custody and tuition of a child, was also to:

> take into [their] custody to the use of such child … the profits of all lands, tenements and hereditaments of such child … and also the custody, tuition, management of the goods, chattels and personal estate of such child … and [could] bring such action in relation thereunto as by law a guardian in common socage might do.

12 (1724) 9 Modern 135.

13 (1677) 2 Chancery Cases 237 at p 238.

The intervention of Chancery, in relation to guardians rather than parents, was significant in two respects. Firstly, while the child's welfare was not itself a ground for intervention, if there was the least suspicion of a child's interests being detrimentally affected by the guardian's conduct, then Chancery would intervene. Secondly, while recognising that the jurisdiction was exercisable for the benefit of the child, the Chancery judges were at the same time prepared to accord some weight to the views of the parents.

CHANCERY, PARENTS AND THE COMMON LAW CONCEPT OF CUSTODY

The concept of guardianship initially provided the basis on which the Court of Chancery intervened in matters affecting the upbringing of a child, including conflicts of interest between guardian and child. The principles gradually worked out in the context of a third party's duties towards a ward eventually came to be extended to the parent/child relationship. The eventual extension of this jurisdiction to include the conduct of parents was natural and one to which Chancery was able to bring a ready-formed body of principles. The concept of guardianship had been, and even throughout the eighteenth century remained, the cornerstone of the law. Until the intervention of equity in that century, custody of the child's person, as opposed to issues of guardianship, played a very minor role. Custody then emerged out of guardianship.

PARENTS AND THE 'OFFICE' OF GUARDIAN

The principal characteristic of the medieval common law had been its application of rigid rules. This, arguably, is the antithesis of the current approach. Entitlement to office, extent of the fiduciary powers and duties of the guardian, forfeiture of office: each was closely regulated. The courts limited their role to deciding on the guardian's fitness for office, establishing the grounds warranting disqualification and justifying the vesting of responsibilities in other persons. This retrospective and negative approach was to become a hallmark of future judicial intervention.

By the early eighteenth century caselaw begins to demonstrate the judicial transfer of principles, forged to govern the office of a guardian, to govern equally the responsibilities of a parent. In *ex parte Hopkins,*[14] for example, King LC alluded to the link between parental rights and a father's duties as a guardian: 'The father is entitled to the custody of his own children during their infancy, not only as guardian by nurture, but by nature.' A century later the Court of Chancery made the further step of determining that a father, like a guardian, could be deprived of his position of trust in relation to a child if found guilty of abusing that trust. As Lord Eldon LC declared in *Lyons v. Blenkin:*[15]

14 [1732], 3 Peere Williams 152 at p 153.
15 (1821), Jacob 245 at p 253.

> It is certain that the court will interfere against the acts of a guardian, if acting in a manner inconsistent with his duty; and it is equally clear that the court will control a parent if acting in a manner in which he should not.

The judiciary were viewing the duties of parents as an extension of their position as guardians. The welfare interests of the child, at least in a negative sense of preventing abuse, came to provide the justification for ultimate judicial control of the father as it had done in respect of the guardian.

Thus, the Court of Chancery in the eighteenth and early nineteenth centuries, before the era of statutory reforms, can be seen to have developed a jurisprudence in which both a guardian and a father were viewed as holders of an office of trust in relation to a child. Common grounds of disqualification for abuse of this office were slowly forged by Chancery. Those grounds were also adopted by the judiciary applying the common law jurisdiction and within it the writ of *habeas corpus*. During this period, of the two jurisdictions, the equitable jurisdiction was the one most frequently invoked. By the end of the nineteenth century, it was the caselaw of equity rather the common law which had established the welfare interests of the child as a benchmark against which continued entitlement to exercise paternal rights would be measured.[16] The judiciary in the Court of Chancery provided the foundations for the future evolution of the welfare principle: a guardian, even if a parent, held a position of trust in relation to a child; the exercise of rights inherent in such a position was conditional upon first fulfilling a basic duty of care owed by a 'guardian' to a 'ward'; failure to fulfil the duties of a guardian would justify removal of the rights even from a parent.

Custody

Custody proceedings, like those for guardianship, have always been matters of private civil law. In guardianship proceedings the Court of Chancery had been concerned mostly about the methods and purposes of intervention in the parent/child relationship. In custody proceedings, however, the focus was firmly on the grounds for intervention. A parent was deemed entitled to custody and this presumption of parental care had to be displaced before that authority could be exercised by others. This common law right of a father to the custody and control of his legitimate child was subject to the constraints of the criminal law (see, further, Chapter 1) and, eventually, to the paramount consideration of the child's welfare.[17]

16 See *In re Agar-Ellis* (1883) 24 Ch D 317, CA.
17 See *Re Thomasset* [1894] 300.

The authority of the father[18] was, as noted by Lord O'Hagan LC in *In the Matter of Meades (Minors)*[19] 'a very sacred thing bestowed by the Almighty, and to be sustained to the uttermost by human law', but he then added the qualifying condition that it was 'a trust and not a power, and the abuse of it will justify its restraint'. The courts demonstrated their reluctance to interfere with paternal authority by refusing to withdraw a father's right to custody in cases concerning cruel discipline,[20] comparative destitution[21] or 'mere incontinence or habits of intemperance'.[22] The sort of abuses justifying, at common law, the removal of a parental right to custody were 'grave moral turpitude',[23] 'abdication of paternal authority',[24] 'grievous physical abuse of wife',[25] expressing anti-religious views which were 'pernicious, noxious to society, adverse to civilisation',[26] committing an unnatural crime (homosexuality) which might cause him to 'morally contaminate' his children or cause others to 'shun their society'[27] and being a labouring man who deserted his wife.[28] According to Macpherson, the removal of the parental right to custody was permissible in two situations: failure to provide adequate maintenance (probably including desertion) and failure to provide proper education. In addition, though, the Court of King's Bench would refuse to enforce a parent's *prima facie* right to custody by issuing a writ of *habeas corpus* when 'enforcement of [the father's right] would be attended with danger to the child; and it declined to deliver the child to him, when there was an apprehension of cruelty, or of contamination, by some exhibition of gross profligacy'.[29] This reflected the view of parental power as a concession to parents merely to enable them to implement their duties. In this sense the legal imposition of duties and the powers needed to give them effect were logically dependent aspects of the same concept. The grounds for removing the power were simply failures to comply with the correlative duties. Macpherson identified one further ground for intervention:[30]

18 See Eekelaar, J., *Family Law and Social Policy*, London, Weidenfeld and Nicolson, 1984 at p 156:

> The absolute power of parents over their children was integral to the social structure. The normal protective reach of the criminal law would stop at the family's threshold. No compelling social interest existed to justify, let alone compel, its intrusion.

19 [1871] IR 5 Eq 98.
20 See *Blake v. Wallscourt* (1846).
21 See *Ex parte Pulbrook* (1847).
22 See *Re Goldsworthy* (1876).
23 See *In re Agar-Ellis* (1883) 23 Ch D 317.
24 See *Wellesley v. Wellesley* [1828] 2 BI, NS 124.
25 See *Warde v. Warde* (1849).
26 See *Thomas v. Roberts* (1850).
27 See *Anon* (1851).
28 See *Re Halliday's Estate: ex parte Woodward* (1852) 17 Jurist 56.
29 Macpherson, W., *A Treatise on the Law Relating to Infants*, London, Maxwell & Son, 1842 at pp 157 and 158.
30 Ibid at p 142.

> where his character is such that they will be in danger of personal ill-treatment or of moral contamination if they reside with him, the court has not hesitated to take the children from him, and to place them in safe custody.

Although Chancery allowed itself to be used to remedy deficiencies in the common law capacity to focus on parental duties, it was ineffective in enforcing its judgments. This was noted by Lord Eldon LC in *Wellesley v. Beaufort*: 'The courts of law can enforce the rights of the father, but they are not equal to the office of enforcing the duties of the father. Those duties have been acknowledged in this his Majesty's Court for centuries past.'[31]

DEVELOPING A LEGAL ROLE FOR THE WELFARE INTERESTS OF A CHILD

The courts were initially interested in the circumstances whereby a father could be held to have forfeited his rights by particularly reprehensible behaviour. That is to say, the courts were concerned more with applying sanctions against a father, in order to defend socially approved standards of behaviour, than with protecting or promoting the welfare of his child in pursuance of any recognition of the latter's separate legal interests. The emergence and consolidation of the common law concept of custody as the main parental right was accompanied by the corollary that a child's welfare was, in a sense, only taken into account by the judiciary *in absentia*. Not until welfare interests had been seriously infringed did they come into play as a factor capable of disentitling parent or guardian from their office of trust in respect of that child. The role played by the welfare principle was thus both negative and secondary in the context of custody proceedings.

Having determined that the father's behaviour was in breach of the law, the courts turned to examine the effect of that behaviour on the child and only then went on to consider arrangements which might safeguard the child's future welfare. The first step was court recognition that a fixed objective threshold had been breached by the father. This breach licensed the second step by which judicial discretion was exercised to take into account the welfare interests of the child concerned when disposing of the proceedings.

This profoundly negative interpretation of welfare – existing only as a measure of an abuse of rights – defined and confined the legal role initially assigned to the welfare interests of a child. But it was from this judicial approach that eventually a more positive affirmation of the separate legal interests of a child was to grow. In time the Court of Chancery expanded its supervisory role not only to protect children but also, to some extent, to play a positive role in promoting their welfare. In doing so Chancery felt bound to pay some attention to the wishes of parents and children of a certain age, alike. This created a new approach: the exercise of administrative discretion. This is probably the essence of the later statutory system.

31 [1827] 2 Russell 1 at p 23.

Equity and the Judicature Act 1873

In England, during the eighteenth and nineteenth centuries, a dual judicial system existed to deal with matters affecting the welfare of a child. Such matters might be determined by judges in the common law courts applying precedents drawn from a jurisprudence based upon the rights of the individual, adjudicating on a breach of statutorily prescribed duties and enforcing their judgments by use of *habeas corpus.* Alternatively, they could be judicially determined in the courts of equity, which would employ a more flexible and discretionary approach in which judgment would conform with the dictates of the welfare principle and, if necessary, be enforced by use of the prerogative powers. The records clearly show that in the mid-nineteenth century the majority of issues concerning the upbringing of a child were being determined in the common law courts rather than those of equity.

Background to the Judicature Act 1873

In 1839, Parliament introduced legislation designed to strengthen the position of a non-adulterous mother, relative to that of an irresponsible father, in respect of the right to custody of their child. Section 1 of the 1839 Act (Talfourd's Act) enabled a judge in equity 'if he should see fit' to make an access or custody order in the circumstances prescribed, where the infant was in the sole custody or control of the father. The judge was also enabled to attach to the access order any temporal or other regulations 'as he shall deem convenient and just'. There was no direct reference to the welfare of the child; this was incidental to the interests of the mother. These provisions conferred wide discretionary powers on the judiciary (see, further, Chapter 3).

The courts, however, continued their defence of paternal rights and failed to implement the provisions in the spirit of the legislation. Only where a father could be proven to be in absolute dereliction of his duties could a judicial challenge to his rights arise. *In re Fynn*[32] was a case where a grandmother sought appointment as guardian in place of the father who was alive and seeking his parental rights. Knight Bruce V-C explained:

> Before this jurisdiction can be called into action between them it must be satisfied, not only that it has the means of acting safely and efficiently, but also that the father has so conducted himself or has shown himself to be a person of such a description, or is placed in such a position, as to render it not merely better for the children, but essential to their safety or to their welfare, in some very serious and important respect, that his rights should be treated as lost or suspended – should be superseded or interfered with. If the word 'essential' is too strong an expression, it is not much too strong.

32 (1848) 2 De Gex & Smale 457 at pp 474–475. See also *Hope v. Hope* (1854) 4 De Gex, Macnaghten & Gordon 328 and *In re Curtis* (1859) 28 LJ Ch 458.

The father's conduct – to his late wife and towards the children – made him unfit to care for the children but did not render it essential that his right should be removed.

In *Re Halliday's Estate: ex parte Woodward*[33] Turner LJ was of the view that the purpose of the 1839 Act was to control the father's exclusive right to custody but in so doing the court should consider the father's marital duty to his wife and the interests of the children. Jessel MR in *In re Taylor, an infant*[34] considered that in deciding whether a father was to be deprived of his right to custody, 'there was to be kept in mind, first of all, the paternal right; secondly, the marital duty; and, thirdly, the interests of the children', presumably in that order (see, further, Chapter 3). Where the plaintiff was an unmarried mother or a non-adulterous mother, and the subject a young child, judicial recognition was more readily given to the welfare of the child. As Romilly MR stated in *Austin v. Austin*:[35]

> The welfare of the child is so intimately connected with its being under the care of the mother that no extent of kindness on the part of any other person can supply that place. It is the notorious observation of mankind that the loss of a mother is irreparable to her children and particularly so if young.

The Judicature Act 1873

Section 25 of this Act provided that: 'In questions relating to the custody and education of infants, the rules of equity shall prevail.' This provision consolidated within judicial practice the equitable principle that the welfare of the child should be given priority in all legal issues affecting his or her upbringing.[36] The effect of this statute was summarised by Fitzgibbon LJ in his judgment in *In re O'Hara*.[37] He then reiterated the principles stated in *The Queen v. Gyngall*:[38]

> (i) At Common Law, the parent has an absolute right to the custody of a child of tender years, unless he or she has forfeited it by certain sorts of misconduct; (ii) Chancery, when a separate tribunal, possessed a jurisdiction different from that of the Queen's Bench, and essentially parental, in the exercise of which the main consideration was the welfare of the child, and the court did what, on consideration of all the circumstances, it was judicially satisfied that a wise parent, acting for the true interests of the child, would or ought to do, even though the natural parent desired and had the common law right to do otherwise, and had not been guilty of misconduct; (iii) the Judicature Act has made it the

33 Op cit.
34 (1876) 4 Ch D 157 at p 160.
35 (1865) 34 Beavan 257 at p 263.
36 See *In re Ethel Brown* (1884) 13 QBD 614 at p 617, per Lindley LJ.
37 [1900] 2 IR 232.
38 [1893] 2 QB 232.

> duty of every Division of the High Court to exercise the Chancery jurisdiction; (iv) in exercising the jurisdiction to control or ignore the parental right the Court must act cautiously, not as if it were a private person acting with regard to his own child, and acting in opposition to the parent only when judicially satisfied that the welfare of the child requires that the parental right should be suspended or superseded.

In theory, the fusion of equity and the common law placed the High Court in a position to give a new and consistent priority to identifying and securing the welfare of a child when the latter's interests had been impaired by a parent. The overriding authority of equity was demonstrated in cases[39] where use of the common law writ of *habeas corpus* to enforce the paternal right to custody were quashed by recourse to equity when such an enforcement would be contrary to a child's welfare interests. The responsibility for safeguarding a child's welfare had been clearly vested in the state, to be discharged in accordance with the principles of equity rather than of parental rights. In practice, however, for most of the nineteenth century, the judiciary proved to be either unable or unwilling to employ and enforce equitable principles and continued to use their discretion largely to ignore the potential opportunities provided by statute to improve the relative weighting given to the welfare interests of a child when taking decisions regarding custody arrangements.

THE 1873 ACT AND IN *RE AGAR-ELLIS*

The continuing impasse reached its nadir with the ruling in *In re Agar-Ellis.*[40] The judicial rationale then presented to assert the doctrine of parental rights demonstrated the resilience of the common law approach to matters affecting the upbringing of a child. James LJ stated: 'The right of the father to the custody and control of his children is one of the most sacred of rights.' In his view, custody was simply the vehicle for giving effect to paternal duties, of which one clearly was the 'education of his children'. Education included bringing up the child in accordance with the father's wishes on religion. Cotton LJ went on to declare:[41]

> But this Court holds this principle – that when by birth a child is subject to a father, it is for the general interest of families, and for the general interest of children, and really for the interest of the particular infant, that the court should not, except in very extreme cases, interfere with the discretion of the father, but leave to him the responsibility of exercising that power which nature has given him by the birth of the child.

39 See *R v. Barnardo, Jones's Case* [1891] 1 QB 194, 210 CA. See also *Andrews v. Salt* (1873) 8 Ch App 622.
40 (1883) 23 Ch D 317 at pp 71–72.
41 Ibid at p 334.

This ruling in particular finally convinced Parliament that further legislation would be needed to require the courts to take into account matters other than paternal rights in cases where the welfare of a child was at issue.

Conclusion

By the late nineteenth century, the legal cohesion and autonomy of the patriarchal marital family unit had emerged as the central pillar of family law. From an initial interest in the property rights of young beneficiaries, the court developed its present concern to protect the welfare of a child and the power to displace a parent who abuses that welfare. The doctrine originated in the courts of equity and remained rooted there. This has allowed equity rather than statute law to lead the evolving jurisprudence based on the principle of the welfare of the child.

3 Legislative endorsement of child welfare

Introduction

A mixture of judicial obduracy and ineffectiveness characterised the role of the courts in relation to paternal rights throughout the first half of the nineteenth century. A dual judicial system existed to deal with matters affecting the welfare of a child: in the common law courts, judges applied precedents drawn from a jurisprudence based upon the rights of the individual, adjudicating on a breach of statutorily prescribed duties and enforcing their judgments by use of *habeas corpus*; in the courts of equity they would employ a more flexible and discretionary approach in which judgment would conform with the dictates of the welfare principle and, if necessary, be enforced by use of the prerogative powers. While the judgments given in the Court of Chancery continued to be flexible and balanced in their recognition of interests other than those of a father, the judiciary were ineffective in enforcing them. The judgments in the courts of the King's Bench were readily enforced but mainly concerned with defending paternal rights. By the mid-nineteenth century the majority of issues concerning the upbringing of a child were being determined in the common law courts rather than those of equity. The Judicature Act 1873 brought together both sets of courts, giving primacy to those of equity. However, the principles and precedents underpinning each continued to be evident. By the latter half of the nineteenth century, Parliament was forced to legislate to enforce recognition of the interests of mothers and children and to curb the dominance of paternal rights.

This chapter examines the forming and evolution of three separate legislative strands: private family law, public law and general public welfare and social care law. It does this in a descriptive manner by presenting an essentially historical account of developments. Beginning with private family law, the chapter deals with the statutory endeavour to curb judicial enthusiasm for parental rights, particularly paternal rights. It then considers the broadening of the public family law remit in relation to child welfare, with special regard for the steady growth in authority of the criminal law relative to the doctrine of parental rights. The third strand – the developing role of general public health and social care provision – is then outlined. The latter is considered

DOI: 10.4324/9781003268512-5

only insofar as is necessary to trace the assimilation of certain welfare-related responsibilities into the public family law domain. This approach enables the chapter to identify the legacy which the modern welfare principle owes to legislative initiatives of the late nineteenth century and their subsequent development until the Children Act 1989.

The three legislative strands

The doctrine of paternal rights owed a great deal to the common law emphasis on the rights and duties of the individual and had become evident in the proprietary frame of reference, centred on parental status, which shaped the growth of a body of private family law legislation. At the same time, the public law jurisprudence concerning child welfare was formed primarily by statutory extensions of the criminal law, itself derived from the common law. In addition and in piecemeal fashion, the broad range of civil public law was gradually extended by health and social care legislation. The latter development coalesced towards the middle of the twentieth century to form the basis of the modern 'welfare state', in which child welfare considerations were also prominent. As the general public welfare remit consolidated, the parameters of modern family law became more distinct, defining and confining the subsequent legal development of the principle of the welfare of the child. Initially, though, this third strand provided a natural context for statutorily addressing the public interest in child welfare and, as it contributed to forming the role and content of the principle, it is outlined for background purposes in this part of the book.

At first legislative intervention on behalf of children's welfare interests was concerned with conditioning the exercise of paternal/parental rights but ultimately the public interest provided the rationale for a broad framework of interventionist social care legislation in which the welfare principle was implicitly or explicitly incorporated. The Judicature Act 1873 was only the beginning, and in many ways a false start, on the road leading to the Children Act 1989.

Private family law

The Court of Chancery, in cases such as *Mytton v. Mytton*,[1] where a mother was granted custody of her five children, demonstrated its willingness to break with the doctrine of paternal rights in circumstances where not to do so would cause an injustice to the interests of other family members. The courts of the King's Bench would also occasionally refuse to use the powers of *habeas corpus* to enforce a father's rights where to do so would endanger the welfare of a child. As was then stated by Lord Denman CJ, in *R v. Greenhill*:[2]

1 (1831) Eng Rep 162; Stone, p 173.
2 (1836) 4 Adolphus & Ellis 624 at p 640.

> The court, it is true, has intimated that the right of the father would not be acted upon where the enforcement of it would be attended with danger to the child; as where there was an apprehension of cruelty, or by contamination of some gross profligacy.

At best, though, until legislative initiative demanded a more robust response, the welfare of a child continued to operate only negatively, as a judicial brake on an irresponsible exercise of paternal rights (see, further, Chapter 1). Legislative intent to interpose other considerations into judicial decision-making began to take effect towards the mid-nineteenth century in marital proceedings, custody and separation contests, guardianship, wardship and adoption.

Matrimonial proceedings

The starting point for any consideration of the law relating to child welfare in the context of marital proceedings is the Custody of Infants Act 1839, which was introduced while the matrimonial jurisdiction was still the responsibility of the Ecclesiastical Court. Known as Talfourd's Act, this legislation permitted a judge in equity 'if he should see fit' to make an access or custody order in the circumstances prescribed, where the infant was in the sole custody or control of an irresponsible father. It gave a non-adulterous mother a right to apply to the court for access to her infant, or for custody, where the child was less than seven years of age, but this amounted to no more than a discretionary judicial power to intervene in a father's rights in favour of the mother: it did not imply any specific legislative recognition of a child's welfare interests. The court's traditional defence of paternal rights was maintained, as evidenced in its rigorous enforcement of the statute's provision that maternal fault would disqualify any right to custody:

> s 4 ... no order shall be made by virtue of this Act whereby any mother against whom adultery shall be established by judgment in an action for criminal conversation or by sentence of an ecclesiastical court shall have the custody of or access to any infant.

Nonetheless, as explained in Chapter 2, the courts failed to implement the provisions in the spirit of the legislation.

The Matrimonial Causes Act 1857, however, abolished the matrimonial jurisdiction of the Ecclesiastical Court and transferred it to the newly constituted Divorce Court. Under s 35, the court was authorised in the appropriate context to make provision 'with respect to the custody, maintenance and education' of the relevant children 'as it may deem just and proper'.[3] The two principal factors influencing the exercise of this custodial provision were the rules of common law and the concept of matrimonial fault which underpinned the jurisdiction.

3 See *Clout v. Clout and Hollebone* (1861) 2 Swabey & Tristram 391.

CUSTODY

The common law approach, based on the rights of the individual and on the grounds for disqualifying an individual from exercising his or her rights, immediately reasserted itself. It was apparent in the ruling of Ordinary J in *Cartlidge v. Cartlidge*,[4] when he said of the discretionary power under s 35:

> but I think I ought to exercise that power with reference to the *prima facie* right of the father, and the petitioner must establish a case beyond the mere natural desire of a mother to have the custody of her infant child.

He decided that, there being no good reason in the interests either of the mother or of the child to do otherwise, effect should be given to the paternal right. Again, in *Chetwynd v. Chetwynd*,[5] Lord Penzance held the paternal right to custody to be forfeited because 'the common home has been broken up by the conduct of the father', but the mother would succeed only if she 'has been free from blame'. He determined that the mother was not without blame so custody of the children was awarded to an aunt and uncle. A mother found guilty of adultery would forfeit any right to custody and access.[6] Indeed, any parent responsible for the break-up of the family home would similarly be rejected for custody.[7] These cases gave rise to the so-called 'doctrine of the unimpeachable parent', the influence of which continued to be brought to bear on judicial decision-making into the second half of the twentieth century. Matrimonial fault was the basis for forfeiture of parental rights; parental fault was beside the point. The courts were more concerned with matrimonial conduct than child welfare.

The Custody of Infants Act 1873 repealed Talfourd's Act but otherwise did no more than extend the application of the 1839 Act to include custody and access orders in relation to children under 16. Whereas previously the courts would not enforce a separation agreement, to the presumed disadvantage of the father, under s 2 of the 1873 Act they could enforce it. After the introduction of the 1873 Act, the court in *D'Alton v. D'Alton*[8] felt able to reject parental claims and instead appoint a guardian. Hannen J in the court of first instance was required to choose between parents, each of whom was seeking custody in order to determine a different religious upbringing for their children. He posed the question: '[W]hat is most for the benefit of their offspring, whose interests are of paramount importance upon this application?' On appeal it was decided that neither parent should have custody; instead, this was awarded to the head of the children's boarding school.

4 (1858) 1 Swabey & Tristram 312.
5 (1865) LR 1 P & D 38 at p 41.
6 See *Bent v. Bent and Footman* (1861) 2 Swabey & Tristram 392; *Seddon v. Seddon and Doyle* (1862) 2 Swabey & Tristram 640.
7 See *Chetwynd; Milford v Milford* (1869) LR 1 P & D 715.
8 (1878) 4 PD 87 at p 88.

THE JUDICATURE ACT 1873

This was a landmark piece of legislation. It closed the book, in theory, on centuries of divided judicial practice in cases where the welfare of a child was at issue. In providing for the fusion of equity and common law, it provided also for the continuation of the *parens patriae* doctrine, its transference to all superior courts and its eventual bearing on modern child-care law. It allowed equity rather than statute law to lead the evolving jurisprudence based on the principle of the welfare of the child. Nonetheless, as was demonstrated in the *In re Agar-Ellis*[9] ruling, the courts resolutely continued to uphold paternal rights (see, further, Chapter 2).

WELFARE INTERESTS AND MATRIMONIAL PROCEEDINGS

It was not until the Report of the Morton Commission in 1956[10] that the welfare interests of children were positively asserted as an appropriate factor to be statutorily provided for in marital proceedings. The Morton Report also recommended that the courts should have the power to require a local authority to receive children into care where, in the course of matrimonial proceedings, it appeared to a court that neither spouse was an acceptable parent and no other relatives were available, willing or suitable to undertake care responsibility. The provision for mandatory assessment of child welfare interests was reviewed in 1968 (the Hall Report)[11] and found to be unsatisfactory (see, further, Chapter 6). It subsequently became subject to minor amendments, until legislatively repealed. Eventually, in *Cammell v. Cammell*,[12] Scarman J based his decision to some extent on the following proposition, which presaged its legislative articulation in the 1973 Act and proved prescient in terms of its recognition for what was to become the single most important benchmark in modern child-care law:

> In my view, however, the court in construing the statute should have regard [not only to … but also] to the policy of the law that, where in any proceeding before any court the custody or upbringing of an infant is in question, the court, in deciding that question, shall regard the welfare of the infant as the first and paramount consideration.

The Divorce Reform Act 1969, later consolidated in the Matrimonial Causes Act 1973, in theory abolished the fault-based grounds for divorce and replaced them with the single ground of 'irretrievable breakdown'. Section 41

9 (1883) 23 Ch D 317 at pp 71–72.

10 *Report of the Royal Commission on Marriage and Divorce – Report 1951–1955* (Morton Report) (Cmnd 9678), London, HMSO, 1956.

11 See, further, at: https://hansard.parliament.uk/Commons/1968-06-21/debates/e47af258-3dcd-4b8e-adaf-2d944cb9997d/Clause1.

12 [1964] 3 All ER 255.

of the 1973 Act, in keeping with the Morton Report recommendations, made the granting of a decree of divorce or nullity conditional upon court satisfaction that arrangements compatible with the best interests of any children of the marriage had been made. Given that such children formed a large proportion of all those appearing in proceedings requiring judicial determination of matters concerning their welfare, this condition was an important manifestation of the welfare principle. Eventually, the Family Law Reform Act 1987 removed the distinction between legitimate and illegitimate children, for most purposes, and also sought to substitute less stigmatising terminology.

Guardianship

The Guardianship of Infants Act 1886 made the first specific statutory reference to the welfare of the child and the modern judicial approach to children can be dated from that Act. Initially, however, little changed and the judiciary continued to defend traditional priorities. This was evident in *In re Taylor, an infant*[13] and in cases such as *In re A and B (Infants)*,[14] where Rigby J failed to acknowledge the welfare of the child as even a secondary objective of the Act. But, as Lord MacDermott later remarked in *J v. C*,[15] the Acts of 1839 and 1873 together with those of 1886 and 1891 'record an increasing qualification of common law rights and the growing acceptance of the welfare of the child as a criterion'.

Guardianship, like wardship, had its origins in the duty to protect, maintain and generally care for the child (see Chapter 2). Custody, in the sense of personal control over the child, was only incidental. During the nineteenth century this changed as custody came to be regarded as the hallmark of paternal rights and a cornerstone in judicial espousal of the related doctrine. Not until the Guardianship of Infants Act 1886 did statute law begin to redress the balance and restore the duty to respect a child's welfare interests.

Section 5 of the 1886 Act reprioritised the criteria identified by Jessel MR in *In re Taylor, an infant* (see, further, Chapter 2) and instead directed the court to have regard 'to the welfare of the infant, and to the conduct of the parents, and to the wishes as well of the mother as of the father'. This did not give a mother parity of parental rights with a father. The one substantive right created was that of a surviving mother to claim guardianship either alone or along with any guardian appointed by the father (s 2). In s 3(2) she was given a power to provisionally appoint a guardian to act with the child's father after her death and the court was authorised to confirm that appointment 'if it be shown to the satisfaction of the court that the father is for any reason unfitted to be the sole guardian of his children'. Parental unfitness could thus deprive a father of his guardianship.

13 (1876) 4 Ch D 157 at p 160.
14 [1897] 1 Ch 786 at p 792.
15 [1970] AC 668 at p 709.

THE GUARDIANSHIP OF INFANTS ACT 1925

This statute represents a landmark in the development of the law's capacity to protect the welfare interests of children. It introduced some fundamental changes: equality of parental right to custody or upbringing (s 1); equality of parental right to apply to court on any matter affecting their child (s 2); specific right of mother to apply for custody, even if still resident in the matrimonial home (s 3); equality of right of surviving parent to guardianship and to appoint a testamentary guardian (ss 4 and 5). Not until the 1925 Act did the legislative intent to assert the legitimacy of the welfare principle become unequivocally stamped on the statute books.

THE GUARDIANSHIP ACTS 1971 AND 1973

The Guardianship of Infants Acts 1886 and 1925 were consolidated in the 1971 Act, which embodied the paramountcy principle, and which was amended in the Guardianship Act 1973. The principle related to matters affecting a child's custody or upbringing and property or income. It declared:

> Where in any proceedings before any court … the custody or upbringing of a [child] is in question, the court, in deciding that question, shall regard the welfare of the [child] as the first and paramount consideration, and shall not take into consideration, whether from any other point of view, the claim of the father in respect of such custody, upbringing … is superior to that of the mother, or the claim of the mother is superior to that of the father.

This particular statutory framing of the welfare principle represented a substantive increase in its legal role and weighting. The references to 'upbringing' and to 'court' indicated that the principle was in future to be applied in equitable and statutory proceedings in relation not only to issues of custody and access but also to ancillary matters. Equality of parental rights was introduced by s 1(1) of the Guardianship Act 1973. Section 1(3) gave a parent the right to apply for a direction from the court in the event of any disagreement on a question affecting a child's welfare other than a matter of custody or access. The court was given a discretionary power to settle such disagreements 'as it may think proper'. When so doing it was directed to regard the child's welfare as the factor of paramount importance.

Wardship

Wardship was never a creature of statute. Although a species of guardianship, it has always been a distinct legal concept.[16] As Elton LJ explained in *De*

16 See *Re N (Minors)* (1973) 4 Family Law 93.

Manneville v. De Manneville,[17] this jurisdiction was one 'delegated to the Court by the Sovereign who, as *parens patriae*, has care of all persons who are unable to take care of themselves'. In that respect the court was ideally suited to protect the welfare interests of children as, being vested with the authority of royal prerogatives, it was free from legislative constraints and empowered to take and adjust such decisions as it considered necessary to meet the needs of a particular child.

The simplified procedures introduced by s 4 of the Law Reform (Miscl Provisions) Act 1949 made wardship even more attractive. It then grew in popularity as a means of solving disputes between parents and potential adopters, parents and foster-parents and even inter-parental disputes. Because it rested on unfettered judicial discretion, at least in relation to matters not already specifically addressed by statute, it permitted considerable creativity in decision-making relating to the welfare, upbringing and property of children. For the next three or four decades, until the Children Act 1989 finally barred the door on wardship as an alternative to statutory jurisdiction, exercises of judicial discretion in wardship were to play a pivotal role in developing the law as it relates to the welfare principle (see, further, Chapter 8).

Adoption

Adoption has a long history.[18] It was known to the courts long before Parliament introduced the first adoption legislation in 1926. Where the responsibility for an illegitimate, abandoned or orphaned child could be assumed within the care arrangements of a private family, instead of becoming an additional burden on public rates and the resources of the poorhouse, the courts did not interfere. The informal process whereby a natural parent voluntarily relinquished all future responsibility for the care and upbringing of a child to a third party was countenanced by the courts in circumstances where such action could not be construed as the avoidance of paternal duties. In effect this confined the practice to the relinquishment of illegitimate children by their unmarried mothers. The sympathetic approach of the judiciary was illustrated by Fitz-Gibbon LJ in *In re O'Hara*,[19] who expressed the view that:

> the surrender of a child to an adopted parent, as an act of prudence or of necessity, under the pressure of present inability to maintain it, being an act done in the interests of the child, cannot be regarded as abandonment or desertion, or even as unmindfulness of parental duty within the meaning of the Act.

17 (1804) 10 Ves. 52.
18 See, for example, Tizard, B., *Adoption: A Second Chance*, London, Open Books, 1977.
19 [1900] 2 IR 233 at p 244.

Following publication of the Hopkinson Report,[20] the Adoption Act 1926 permitted, for the first time in these islands, a formal legal procedure for the adoption of children. However, this, the most recent addition to private family law legislation, provided the proceedings that proved to be least conducive to the evolution of the welfare principle.

In 1954 the Hurst Committee[21] suggested that the 'primary object ... in the arrangement of adoptions is the welfare of the child', an approach subsequently reinforced by the Houghton Committee[22] recommendation in 1972 that 'the long-term welfare of the child should be the first and paramount consideration'. However, and for a considerable period thereafter, legislative intent consistently and resolutely maintained that the paramountcy principle did not have a role in adoption law. It was the Children Act 1975 that introduced a new part for welfare to play in the adoption process. Section 3 stated:

> In reaching any decision relating to the adoption of a child, a court or adoption agency shall have regard to all the circumstances, first considerations being given to the need to safeguard and promote the welfare of the child through his childhood; and shall so far as practicable ascertain the wishes and feelings of the child regarding the decision and give due consideration to them, having regard to his age and understanding.

This indicated that welfare was to be considered in all decisions, not just the decision to make an adoption order. The Adoption Act 1976, which came into effect in 1988, incorporated s 3 of the 1975 Act but stopped short of making adoption contingent on the agreement of the child concerned.

Public family law

The period from 1850–1940 was one of conflict between courts and Parliament, with the courts trying to enforce as far as possible the precedents that had established the parental rights doctrine and Parliament seeking to extend the role of the law in relation to children's matters. It was also a period which witnessed the beginnings of more sustained public concern for the welfare of children. This was particularly evident in the statutory reform of private family law introduced by the Guardianship of Infants Act 1886, the Custody of Children Act 1891 and the Guardianship of Infants Act 1925. It was similarly evident in the legislation dealing with public family law, notably with the launching of the 'Children's Charter' in 1889, which declared that children were entitled to protection from specific forms of cruelty. The

20 *The Report of the Committee on Child Adoption* (Hopkinson Report) (Cmnd 1254), London, HMSO, 1921.

21 See *Report of the Departmental Committee on the Adoption of Children* (Cmnd 9248), London, HMSO, 1954, p 4.

22 See *Report of the Departmental Committee on the Adoption of Children* (Houghton Report) (Cmnd 5107), London, HMSO, 1972, para 17.

criminal law relating to the punishment of parents for child abuse or neglect was gradually supplemented by civil legislation dealing with parental duties in relation to the care and protection of their children and the duties of state authorities to support families and provide alternative child-care arrangements when required to do so by parent or court. It is important to note that accountability for child abuse or neglect under the criminal law was not restricted to parents; any third party in a *loco parentis* relationship would be held responsible for criminal harm incurred by the child in their care.[23]

Criminal law

The criminal law relating to child abuse was first comprehensively addressed in the Offences Against the Persons Act 1861 in the context of general assault charges, whether committed against adult or child. Many of these offences continued to underpin the basic civic duty regarding child welfare – the responsibility to respect his or her physical integrity – throughout the twentieth century and into the post-1989 era. Child neglect was specifically addressed by s 37 of the Poor Law Amendment Act 1868, which made it a criminal offence for a parent wilfully to neglect to provide adequate food, clothing, medical aid or lodging for his children, being under 14 and in his custody, so that their health should have been likely to be seriously injured. This provision formed the basis for s 1(1) of the 1933 Act, which embedded significant protection for the welfare of children from acts of neglect by both parents and third party carers in the criminal law:

> If any person who has attained the age of 16 years and has custody, charge, or care of any child or young person under that age, wilfully assaults, ill-treats, neglects, abandons or exposes him, or causes or procures him to be assaulted, ill-treated, neglected, abandoned or exposed, in a manner likely to cause unnecessary suffering or injury to health (including injury to or loss of sight, or hearing, or limb, or organ of that body, and any mental derangement), that person shall be guilty of a misdemeanour.

To secure a conviction under this provision, it was essential to prove 'likely to cause' unnecessary suffering or injury to health in addition to providing proof of exposure or abandonment.[24] This reference to likelihood of harm has

23 See, for example, *R v. Gibbons and Proctor* (1918) 13 Cr App Rep 134, where a woman was found guilty of murder by wilfully neglecting to feed the child of her cohabitee.

24 See, for example, *R v. Whibley* [1938] 3 All ER 777, where it was held that a father had not caused his children suffering or injury to health when he abandoned them in a courthouse. See also *Brooks v. Blount* [1923] 1 KB 257, where it was held that proof of actual suffering was unnecessary; proof of likelihood was sufficient.

resonances with the prospective welfare considerations in the 1989 Act. Subsection 2(a) treats certain behaviour as neglect, such as failure 'to provide adequate food, clothing, medical aid or lodging'. These provisions list and proscribe a comprehensive range of specific types of conduct deemed to be prejudicial to the physical welfare of the child and warranting prosecution. The legislative focus was on identifying types of proscribed conduct by adults rather than the constituent elements of child welfare. The consequences of the conduct were all important; whether resulting from wilful intent, neglect or recklessness, if the conduct was intended, then responsibility for the consequences was unavoidable. For example, it was held that a considered parental refusal to consent to an operation amounted to neglect contrary to s 1 of the 1933 Act,[25] again providing resonances with modern law.

The law sets out the welfare interests of children only in relation to certain stated sources of identifiable risk. The real underpinning focus of the criminal law was on parental rights which formed the reference points for proscribed conduct. Sometimes this linkage was quite explicit, as in the offence of child-stealing. This was first proscribed by Parliament in 1814, then by ss 55 and 56 of the Offences Against the Person Act 1861 and ss 19(1) and 20(1) of the Sexual Offences Act 1950. By proscribing the removal of a child from her parents for non-sexual as well as sexual purposes, these provisions enforced parents' rights and thereby also afforded protection for the welfare of a child. The various offences of kidnapping, abduction and child-stealing all seemed to be founded on a parental rights approach, with the retention and continuity of the parental relationship presumed to be in a child's best interests.

ABANDONMENT

In the Children and Young Persons Act 1933, the criminal law and the law relating to child protection were consolidated.[26] The implementation of this legislation was examined in the Curtis Report,[27] which gave rise to the Children Act 1948. The latter established specialist children's departments under the control of local authorities and gave them such duties as:

25 See *Oakey v. Jackson* [1914] 1 KB 216. However, account must also be taken of the House of Lords ruling in *R v. Sheppard* [1981] AC 394, which held that, when determining recklessness, the standard to be applied is a subjective understanding of the circumstances as perceived by the alleged offender, not the objective assessment of the court. See also *Alhaji Mohammed v. Knott* [1969] 1 QB 1, which is authority for the view that an objective assessment must also give way to the particular values of the cultural context within which the alleged offender perceives the circumstances.

26 The Industrial Schools Act 1857 (and associated statutes) and the Prevention of Cruelty to and Protection of Children Act 1889 jointly gave rise to the body of legislation known generally as the Children and Young Persons Act (1933, 1963 and 1969), which in due course was displaced by the Children Act 1989.

27 *Report of the Care of Children Committee* (Curtis Report), London, HMSO, 1946.

- to receive children into care;
- to pass a resolution vesting in itself all parental rights in respect of a child voluntarily admitted;
- to provide comprehensive care arrangements for children whose parents could not do so;
- to give preference to boarding-out rather than residential care;
- to promote the development of children in care; and
- to provide expenses for education and training on discharge from care.

In many important respects, the provisions of this legislation foreshadowed those of the 1989 Act.

Juvenile justice

Juvenile justice also had its origins in the public family law initiatives of the mid-nineteenth century. Although the first 'reform school' was established in 1806 in Bermondsey, with several others set up in the period 1810–1830, relevant legislation was not introduced until the Industrial Schools Act 1866 (preceded by the Industrial Schools Act 1861) and the Reformatory Schools Act 1866 (preceded by the Youthful Offenders Act 1854). Reformatory schools were established for the correction of offenders, while industrial schools offered training for young 'vagrants in moral danger'. As with child abandonment, the legislative response to child offenders owed much to the initiative of voluntary organisations. The Society for the Suppression of Juvenile Vagrancy (later called the Children's Friendly Society) had been established in 1830, and the work of liberal activists such as Mary Carpenter[28] was influential in generating awareness of the problems associated with juvenile delinquency. Yet, many such children were transported overseas.

THE CHILDREN ACT 1908

This deserves to be remembered as a landmark statute in the evolution of the role of the welfare principle as it abolished the death penalty for children under the age of 16.[29] Until then, neither the welfare principle nor any other consideration differentiated the criminal law approach to the offences of children and adults, as is graphically illustrated by the fact that on one day alone in 1814 five children aged between the ages of eight and twelve were hanged in England for petty larceny,[30] establishing an iniquitous benchmark and

28 See Carpenter, M., *Reformatory Schools for the Perishing and Dangerous Classes and for the Prevention of Juvenile Delinquency*, London, Routledge, 1969 (first published 1851).

29 See Morris, A. and Giller, H., *Understanding Juvenile Justice*, London, Croom Helm, 1987.

30 Ibid at p 6.

salutary reminder of the extent to which the law has in the past abused rather than protected the welfare interests of children.[31]

This legislation also provided, for the first time, authority to remove an abused or neglected child from culpable parents to a place of safety. In addition, it provided for:

- infant life protection;
- the prevention of cruelty;
- the prohibition of juvenile smoking;
- the refining of the roles of industrial and reformatory schools;
- the creation of the juvenile courts; and
- a 'miscellaneous' division which included such provision as the banning of under-14s from public houses.

Finally, it introduced borstal institutions, which succeeded the industrial and reformatory schools as providers of residential training facilities for criminal or delinquent children.

The 1908 Act was subsequently amended and consolidated by the Children and Young Persons Act 1933, which continued the established approach of treating children brought before the court exhibiting welfare needs differently from those exhibiting criminal deeds for whom trial and punishment were appropriate. Not until the Criminal Justice Act 1948 were penal servitude, hard labour and whipping abolished in relation to children, and not until the Children and Young Persons Act 1969 did statute law give courts the power to provide welfare-oriented disposal options for children found guilty of offences[32] (see, further, Chapter 7).

JUVENILE COURTS

The introduction of juvenile courts, under the Children Act 1908, sought to provide integrated proceedings for responding to civil needs and criminal offences, on the moral basis that the legal system should treat all children, whether deprived or depraved, in accordance with their welfare needs – a jurisdiction it maintained for the rest of the century.[33] This, as the Ingleby Committee noted, required the court to perform a difficult balancing act:[34]

31 See Frost, N. and Stein, M., *The Politics of Child Welfare*, London, Harvester Wheatsheaf, 1989.

32 In response to the recommendations of the Kilbrandon Committee: *Report on Children and Young Persons (Scotland)* (Kilbrandon Report) (Cmnd 2306), London, HMSO, 1964). See also Home Office, *Children in Trouble* (Cmnd 3601), London, HMSO, 1968.

33 Dingwall, R., Eekelaar, J. and Murray, T., *The Protection of Children: State Intervention and Family Life*, Oxford, Basil Blackwell, 1983.

34 *Report of the Departmental Committee on Children and Young Persons* (Cmnd 1191), London, HMSO, 1960, p 39.

> It must try at one and the same time to protect the public, to promote the welfare of the child and to stress the responsibility and respect the legitimate rights of the parents. Finally, it must satisfy public opinion that justice is being done.

Following the Committee's recommendations, the Children and Young Persons Act 1969 reaffirmed that policy by authorising the juvenile courts to operate a dual jurisdiction – children charged with criminal offences being heard in separate proceedings from those who were the subject of care and protection issues – until this was ended by the 1989 Act.

THE PROBATION SERVICE

Established in the late nineteenth century,[35] the Probation of First Time Offenders Act 1886 saw a nationwide service initiated under the control of local magistrates, but not until 1928 did it extend its remit from adults to include children discharged from borstal and reformatory institutions. Thereafter the service acquired independence from direct court management and extended its reach by developing welfare-oriented preventative modes of intervention with children at risk of becoming offenders.[36]

Care and protection

The law governing cruelty to animals preceded and provided the stimulus for the civil law relating to the care and protection of children. It emerged in the latter half of the nineteenth century following a number of reported cases where the Society for the Prevention of Cruelty to Animals had turned its attention to the rescue of children from abusing adults. This was a period of well-publicised philanthropic 'child rescue' initiatives which saw orphanages and special schools established.[37] The views of writers such as Macpherson[38] proved very influential. In 1884, the London Society for the Prevention of Cruelty to Children was formed. The introduction of the Prevention of Cruelty to Children Act 1889 was largely due to effective lobbying by this precursor of the NSPCC. It defined 'cruelty' as wilful ill-treatment, neglect or abandonment in a manner likely to cause unnecessary suffering or injury to health, and, if proven, the court could commit the child to the care of a 'fit

35 In 1876, the Church of England Temperance Society assigned 'missionaries', tasked with reforming drunkards, to certain London courts.

36 The Criminal Justice and Court Services Act 2000 consolidated the probation service and its management.

37 See Bean, P. and Melville, J., *Lost Children of the Empire*, London, Unwin Hyman, 1989; and Platt, A., *The Child Savers*, Chicago, University of Chicago Press, 1969.

38 See Macpherson, W., *A Treatise on the Law Relating to Infants*, London, Maxwell & Son, 1842.

person', which could be a relative or an institution. The current law may be traced through s 1 of the Prevention of Cruelty and Protection of Children Act 1889, s 1 of the Prevention of Cruelty to Children Act 1894, s 1 of the Prevention of Cruelty to Children Act 1904 and s 12 of the Children Act 1908.[39] The legislative intent was considered in a number of important cases at the turn of the century. For example, in *R v. Senior*[40] the father of a child who died was charged with wilful neglect on account of his failure to provide medical aid and medicine for the child, contrary to the 1894 Act. Russell LJ then considered the effect of s 1(2)(a) of that Act:

> a parent or other person legally liable to maintain a child or young person shall be deemed to have neglected him in a manner likely to cause injury to his health if he has failed to provide adequate food, clothing, medical aid or lodging for him, or if, having been otherwise unable to provide such food, clothing, medical aid or lodging, he has failed to take steps to procure it to be provided under the enactments applicable in that behalf.

In a comment that presaged the approach adopted a century later, he held that the offence of neglect was committed by 'the omission of such steps as a reasonable parent would take'. In *R v. Connor*[41] the judiciary had the opportunity to examine the statutory paternal duty to provide care and protection. This case concerned an allegation that the father had departed, leaving the mother with insufficient money to feed the children. The evidence was that the children were clean but poorly clad and fed. The father was found guilty of wilful neglect under s 1(1) of the Prevention of Cruelty to Children Act 1904. In this case Lord Alverstone CJ referred to 'the intention of the legislature as early as 1868 [Poor Law Amendment Act 1868] to make a parent who neglected to provide adequate food for his children in his custody amenable to the criminal law' as an aid to interpreting s 1 of the Prevention of Cruelty to Children Act 1904.

CARERS

The child-care responsibilities assumed by third parties, with or without parental consent, was a defining issue for family law at least a century ago. English cities in the throes of the Industrial Revolution, particularly in Dickensian London, harboured many homeless and begging children abandoned by parents when they were young and needing care and maintenance but reclaimed when they were old enough to earn a wage. Charitable organisations, which had been providing care, sought to retain the children within a rehabilitative environment

39 See *R v. Connor* [1908] 2 KB 26, where Lord Alverstone notes the history of this legislation.
40 [1899] 1 QB 283.
41 [1908] 2 KB 26, per Lord Alverstone CJ at p 30.

despite the proprietary demands of parents. The Custody of Children Act 1891 was introduced to provide a remedy for third party carers where their provision for destitute children was opposed by fathers demanding restitution of their custody rights. The rationale for the 1891 Act was explained in the course of the preceding House of Commons debates: 'the Bill is intended to deal with … children who have been thrown helpless on the streets, and wickedly deserted by their parents, and who are taken by the hand by benevolent persons or by charitable institutions'. Its purpose was to provide a civil remedy to protect abandoned children from their neglectful parents by not enforcing parental rights. As such it was the first piece of legislation to offer protection for children from their parents and to others acting in *loco parentis.* A third party (e.g. a foster-parent, voluntary agency or whoever had care of the child) could thereafter rely on a statutory 'right' created by the legislation to resist a parental claim to custody. A parent could recover their right only by proving 'fitness'. The Act provided an important benchmark for the respective rights of parents and third parties in relation to the welfare interests of children, anticipating both the rationale for compulsory care orders, for 'fit person orders' and for the concept of 'custodianship' in the Children Act 1975.[42]

This was also the era of 'baby farming'. The Infant Life Protection Act 1872 had sought to extend legal protection not only to the vulnerable young residents of workhouses but also to all those whose care was entrusted by their unmarried mothers to child-minders who would then often arrange for their informal adoption. This statute, the precursor of contemporary child-minding legislation, required all such care arrangements to be registered with the local authorities, and inspected by them, and all deaths to be reported to the coroner. It was deficient in that its protective provisions applied only to care arrangements in respect of children aged less than one year. This was remedied by the Children Act 1908, which raised the age to seven years and introduced the concept of state responsibility for supervising the arrangements made for all children, from poor or wealthy parents, who were placed in the care of third parties.

Not until the introduction of the Children and Young Persons Act 1963, however, did the law relating to the welfare of children develop a preventative function. Section 1(i) of that Act required local authorities 'to make available such advice, guidance and assistance as may promote the welfare of children by diminishing the need to receive children into or keep them in care … or to bring children before a Juvenile Court'.

THE CHILDREN AND YOUNG PERSONS ACT 1969

The 1969 Act, as a matter of policy, sought to assimilate court disposal options in respect of children guilty of an offence[43] and children who were

42 See also the Houghton Report, op cit, para 116.
43 The Reformatory Schools Act 1866, s 14.

victims of parental inadequacy.[44] The statute owed a good deal to the recommendations of the Departmental Committee on Young Offenders,[45] which advised that there was 'little or no difference in character or needs between the neglected and the delinquent child. It is often a mere accident whether he is brought before the court because he has committed some offence.' This extension of the welfare principle to bridge the care and justice jurisdictions was to prove highly controversial until the separation of the two categories was formally restored at the end of the twentieth century when the former was reassigned to the Children Act legislation and the latter to criminal justice. The vulnerability of the welfare principle to manipulation by ideology-based policy developments was to attract comment in other contexts in the late twentieth century.

THE CHILDREN ACT 1975

This trend towards increased coercive intervention culminated in the years following the introduction of the Children Act 1975. The period between the Children Acts 1975 and 1989 was one in which the coercive intervention powers of local authorities were maximised. Their unilateral use of discretionary powers was boosted by the ruling in *A v. Liverpool City Council*[46] which thereafter prevented the court from reviewing any local authority exercise of power vested in it. Most notably, this was a period when very many children, placed in local authority care by their parents on a voluntary basis, found their status changed to compulsory care as resolutions were passed vesting full parental rights in the local authorities. It was also an era when adoption agencies refined their suitability criteria to exclude adoption applicants who did not conform to a preferred model of parenthood (married, heterosexual, etc.) and when the Houghton Report[47] recommended making the welfare of the child the paramount consideration and suggested introducing 'custodianship'. Again, local authorities were escalating their recourse to the wardship jurisdiction (an option that was unavailable to parental applicants) in order to supplement their statutory powers in relation to children. New surveillance systems were introduced, such as the 'at risk register' and the multidisciplinary case conference.

THE CHILDREN ACT 1989

In a reversal of the ideology embodied in the 1969 Act, the Children Act 1989 was an entirely civil piece of legislation, combining the private law relating to

44 The Industrial Schools Act 1857, s 14.
45 See *Report of the Departmental Committee on the Treatment of Young Offenders* (Cmnd 2831), London, HMSO, 1927, np.
46 [1982] AC 363, [1981] 2 All ER 3 85, [1981] 2 WLR 948, 79 LGR 621, 2 FLR 222, 145 JP 318, 125 Sol Jo 396, HL.
47 Op cit.

matrimonial and separation proceedings with the public law relating to care and protection, but excluding any overlap with the criminal jurisdiction. This formative child welfare statute established basic principles that were to govern court and local authority decisions in relation to the needs of children – at risk as a consequence of parental separation, neglect or abuse – for several decades. The strategic role played by the paramountcy principle, the welfare 'checklist', a menu of court orders, together with the parental responsibility concept did much to bind together the public and private sectors of family law and facilitate a more coherent and integrated approach to issues affecting the welfare interests of children in a civil law context.

General public welfare and social care legislation

Parliament, from at least the time of the Poor Law 1601, had made a distinction between public and private responsibilities in relation to children and sought to ensure that the onus to safeguard the latter's welfare rested on parents rather than the state. Where family care was not possible – in circumstances of parental death, absence or criminal abuse – then Parliament had used the Poor Laws to place responsibility on public authorities for the provision of residential child-care facilities. This responsibility can be seen as derived from the feudal concept of *parens patriae* (see Chapter 1). The duties of the person or body 'standing in the shoes of the parent' included responsibilities for the nurture, safety and education of the child. In legal terms this simply amounted to the state assuming all first-party parental responsibilities for the child concerned.

By the nineteenth century, Parliament had begun to extend the principle of public responsibility in circumstances of family failure to include a level of responsibility in circumstances where family care remained intact. The duties of public authorities in respect of children, whether in the nature of direct service provision or the setting and monitoring of standards, were no longer assumed by the state acting solely *in absentia* of the parents. The nurture, safety and education of children were not to be left exclusively to first-party parental discretion. The state would also assume some third-party responsibilities in respect of all children in relation to such matters. This application of the *parens patriae* concept, to vest a level of responsibility for aspects of child development in the state, laid the foundations for the evolution of the modern comprehensive public welfare and social care legislative framework. This evolutionary process may be traced in relation to three distinct areas of general public welfare and social care as they affect the welfare interests of children: working conditions; education; and health and social care.

Employment

From at least the times of the Roman Empire, through the Middle Ages and the Industrial Revolution, until the beginning of this century, children of six to eight years of age worked on farms and in shops, factories and professions; girls of eight to ten were servants in the households of other families; boys were apprenticed. The dangerous and arduous working conditions suffered by young children in the factories, mines and mills during the early years of the Industrial Revolution in Britain are well documented. By 1830, an estimated 26,000 children under the age of 14 were working in factories.[48]

But this new machine age was also an era of opportunity for the many families which benefited from the labour of their children. Sending children out to work for long hours in dangerous environments was, for some, no more than a natural extension of the paternal rights doctrine. The prevailing attitude towards paternal authority and the autonomous marital family unit was reflected in the opinion of a late nineteenth-century writer who stated:[49]

> I would far rather see even a higher rate of infant mortality than has ever yet been proved against the factory district or elsewhere ... than intrude one iota further on the sanctity of the domestic hearth and the decent seclusion of private life.

Fox Harding suggests that there was considerable opposition to laws restricting child labour and introducing compulsory education because these were seen as constituting unwarranted state interference with parental authority.[50] Parliament, however, viewed the private exploitation of small children as a matter of public concern, and reformers, such as Lord Shaftesbury, worked to safeguard children from exploitation by factory owners. In a series of paternalistic statutes Parliament prohibited the employment of children as chimney sweeps and set standards for publicly acceptable working conditions for all children.[51] Eventually, the Education Act 1918 prohibited the employment of children aged 12–14 in factories.

Education

The history of the development of education in England is one in which the separate provision made by the Church and the wealthy initially prevailed at the expense of a national system. Public secular education for young children in England was not universally available until the latter half of the nineteenth century. Private education had been available to those who could afford it at

48 See Thompson, F.M.L., *The Rise of Respectable Society: A Social History of Victorian Britain*, Oxford, Oxford University Press, 1988, p 23.

49 See *Transactions of the National Association for the Promotion of Social Sciences* (1874), quoted in Pinchbeck, I. and Hewitt, M., *Children in English Society*, vol 2, London, Routledge & Kegan Paul, 1973, p 359.

50 See Fox Harding, L., *Perspectives in Child Care Policy*, London, Longman, 1997, p 35.

51 See: the Health and Morals of Apprentices Act 1802; the Factories Acts 1802, 1819, 1833 and 1867; the Workshop Regulation Act 1867; etc.

least a century earlier, and a patchy system of schooling for poor children was provided by the Church and voluntary campaigners such as Mary Carpenter, who, in the 1840s, established the 'Ragged Schools' movement.[52] For most of the nineteenth century, state intervention took the form of providing grants to Church-based and nonconformist schools. The 'public school' system, providing education for the children of a wealthy elite, was established during this period and consolidated in the early decades of the twentieth century.

In 1856 a Department of Education was established and the first legislation was finally introduced when the Education Act 1870 laid the foundations for a system of mandatory primary education which was to be secular and freely available to all children. The Education Act 1902 provided for the abolition of school boards, which had become obstructive in their protection of the Church's vested interest in controlling education, allowed for state assimilation of voluntary schools and required local government funding to be made available for Church-based schooling. The Education Act 1918 raised the school leaving age to 14 and made education freely available for all children. However, not until the Education Act 1944 were the basic components of a modern national education system put in place. This legislation:

- made provision for free secondary education as well as free school meals, milk and transport;
- introduced standard examinations, notably the 11+;
- made grants available to assist entry to university; and
- raised the school leaving age to 15 (increased to 16 in 1972).

The extension of this national approach to higher and further education was undertaken in the 1960s.

Health

Health and social care initiatives, relating to the welfare interests of children, also owed a good deal to the work of voluntary organisations and children's charities, which played a significant role in providing initial care and treatment facilities for poor children in need. The Thomas Coram Hospital for foundling children, for example, was established in 1739. The Infant Life Protection Society, founded in 1870, provided such support as was then available for the protection of newly born babies in workhouses and campaigned for the introduction of the Infant Life Protection Act 1872. But for the most part the health and welfare of poor children depended upon the rudimentary state care system provided by the Poor Laws through the workhouses, which remained in effect until 1929, when the local authorities were established. This limited recognition of a level of state responsibility for children within the Poor Law system was in time extended to an acknowledgment of broad responsibilities towards all

52 See Carpenter op cit.

children within the welfare state. Certain contemporary services, child healthcare practices and welfare benefits originated with the Poor Laws.

During the nineteenth century the Poor Law authorities initiated boarding-out schemes. These enabled children to be placed, where possible and for a fee, with families in country areas. Boarding-out children increased their likelihood of survival as many would otherwise die in the appalling conditions that prevailed in most workhouses. The current practice of giving preference to family-based rather than institutional care, as provided by foster-parents, had its origins in the Poor Law era.

The Poor Law Act of 1834 placed new responsibilities on workhouse inspectors to prevent or control the spread of infectious diseases, but it was not until the Public Health Act 1848 that this approach was extended nationally to become underpinned by specific duties in the Acts of 1871 and 1875 and the Sanitation Act 1866. It was this legislation that gave rise to public healthcare duties and the responsibilities of health visitors, which were to be consolidated within a comprehensive National Health Service in 1948.

Welfare benefits

Arguably, the single most important factor in raising physical standards of child care was the introduction of a scheme of financial benefits payable to mothers and enabling them to buy the essentials necessary to ensure the welfarc of their children. The Royal Commission on the Poor Laws was set up in 1832 and its findings formed the basis for the Poor Law 1834, which made provision for a financial benefit to be paid to an unmarried mother in her own right. This was amended in 1844 to place the responsibility on such a mother to take affiliation proceedings against the putative father and secure maintenance payments from him. The financial difficulties faced by single mothers led to an increase in the rates of infanticide and abandonment. In 1918 the National Council for the Unmarried Mother and her Child was formed and maintenance payments were at first increased and then doubled in 1923, but not until financial support was addressed on a centralised basis, linked to schemes of national insurance, assistance and family allowances, were single mothers placed on a more secure financial footing to provide for the welfare of their children.[53]

Conclusion

The balance between the three legislative strands changed significantly during the period under review in this chapter. Intervention in family affairs, coercive and consensual, on matters relating to the welfare interests of the child

53 See: the National Insurance Acts 1911 and 1946; the Family Allowances Act 1945; and the National Assistance Act 1948.

became increasingly prevalent under the headings of public law and general social welfare. As private family law was legislatively prised open, despite judicial defence of the doctrine of paternal rights, responsibilities in respect of child welfare were steadily extended to other parties. In particular, as the foundations of the welfare state were laid by demarcating those areas of responsibility that should be met by national service provision, such as education, health and benefits, so the parameters were established for private and public family law.

In private family law, paternal rights slowly gave way to parental rights and duties. Custody, which had been viewed as the hallmark of paternal rights, directly and intimately vested in the father as head of his autonomous marital family unit, came to be regarded more as a legally transferable parental function. Guardianship – which, like wardship, had always been concerned with the duties of care, protection and maintenance of children – became the legislative vehicle which first introduced the welfare interests of the child as a criterion for judicial determination of disputed custody arrangements. However, this criterion came into play only after proof of parental death, absence or fault. A judicial finding of fault in matrimonial proceedings, usually on proof of adultery, would result in a ruling that the spouse was thereby unfit to be a parent.

In public law, fault also came to be the central rationale for disentitling a parent, usually on proof of child neglect, ill-treatment or abuse. The indices of parental fault established a century ago – such as failure to provide adequate food, shelter, maintenance, being found 'likely to cause' unnecessary suffering or refusal to consent to an operation – still ground judicial decisions to transfer care responsibility. Extending fault liability from parents to third parties was accelerated through an ever-broadening swathe of statutes proscribing circumstances and conduct identified as detrimental to the welfare of children. Parental decisions to entrust day-care responsibility to third parties were made subject to rules governing the registration and inspection of child-minding arrangements. The legal position of third-party carers such as foster-parents and voluntary child-care organisations was given a degree of statutory protection. Parental relinquishing of children into the long-term care of the state was facilitated, and informal adoptions were left unregulated until 1926.

The three legislative strands set the thresholds for intervention in family affairs on matters relating to the welfare interests of children. However, they and the underpinning indices of welfare, first statutorily identified at least a century ago and largely still in place today, failed to establish any coherence of structure, content and process to the manner in which the law relates to children. From time to time the proposal to establish a family court[54] resurfaced as a means of bringing such coherence and transcending the inbuilt adversarial nature of proceedings. Although this

54 Not until 2014 was the Family Court established, under s 31A of the Matrimonial and Family Proceedings Act 1984 (inserted by the Crime and Courts Act 2013).

movement acquired some traction in the wake of the Cleveland Inquiry,[55] it failed to gain sufficient parliamentary support and the piecemeal approach of incremental adjustments to procedural and administrative law continued for some time after the introduction of the 1989 Act.[56]

55 See *Report of the Inquiry into Child Abuse in Cleveland 1987* (Cmnd 412), London, HMSO, 1988.

56 See, for example: Lord Chancellor's Office, *Improvements in the Arrangements for Care Proceedings*, London, HMSO, 1988; and Murch, M. and Hooper, D., *The Family Justice System*, Bristol, Jordan Publishing, 1992.

Part 2

The content and role of the welfare principle

4 Welfare interests and the child

Introduction

The principle of the welfare of the child is notoriously imprecise. Any elucidation of the principle's content can be sensibly attempted only in relation to the particular needs of the child to whom it is to be applied. Those needs will be defined according to the values of the cultural context to which the child belongs. They will also vary according to the age of the child. It is technically difficult to identify objectively the components of a principle which only acquires a valid meaning when applied subjectively. But three key questions remain:

- What actually constitutes welfare?
- Who decides?
- In what way do welfare considerations affect legal decisions?

This chapter concentrates on examining the substance of welfare, rather than its role or weighting, as interpreted and developed by the judiciary in judgments given on matters concerning a child's upbringing. Its central concern is to identify the main components currently considered by the judiciary to constitute a child's welfare interests. It begins by examining problems of definition and interpretation before considering who has the right to take decisions in respect of a child's welfare interests. It then identifies developments which show how the meaning given to the principle has broadened, noting its susceptibility to judicial rules. This approach reveals that while certain core traditional aspects of welfare continue to be consistently taken into judicial account, some have changed and new dimensions to welfare have been added. It also reveals that perhaps the most significant change to this principle has been in the role played by a child, the subject of proceedings, in assisting the court to define and interpret the meaning of his or her welfare relative to other considerations.

DOI: 10.4324/9781003268512-7

Welfare interests: problems of definition and interpretation

The welfare principle has never been a fixed standard capable of uniform application across diverse circumstances and across the entire age range of childhood. Because it is a value-based standard, its meaning at any point in time derives from the prevailing cultural context of the society applying it. Parenting and child welfare always reflect cultural values. The welfare of a child is currently construed differently in the *favelas* of Rio de Janeiro and the hamlets of Sussex and has been construed quite differently over time in the latter. While readily understood in the context of children who are victims, welfare is construed with more difficulty in the context of children who kill and children who are themselves parents.

Welfare: an indeterminate social construct

The fact that it is such an indeterminate concept has allowed 'welfare' to be used creatively and flexibly by the judiciary of this jurisdiction in many different circumstances for several centuries. Its meaning has had to be derived from its immediate context. This has most usually been a legislative context, where it has been defined by the legislative intent. Where the provisions specified particular aspects of welfare interests, such as health or education, then the courts have been required to interpret a child's welfare in accordance with that specific definition. Other statutes have referred broadly to 'welfare' or 'best interests', etc. This has given the courts great discretion to determine a child's welfare in accordance with the full range of options available. The former objectifies welfare and requires judicial decisions to be tied to the specific legal context. The latter employs welfare as a subjective standard and allows judicial decisions to explore the family context and tailor the legal solution to the needs of a particular child. It is this subjective approach which has permitted the judiciary to extend the interpretation of welfare to include not only the traditional elements of physical well-being and maintenance but also religious and moral upbringing and psychological needs, such as emotional attachments, enduring relationships and notions of risk and security. The judgments contain many illustrations of the judiciary taking into account such subjective aspects of welfare as the stigma attached to illegitimacy, the impact of parental adultery on the child and the desirability of parental access. Increasingly the courts have come to interpret welfare in terms of a child's relationships; establishing those relationships, their viability and quality, and the likelihood of their interruption or termination are all aspects of welfare of growing importance. While the subjective approach allows judicial discretion to interpret welfare relative to the needs of a particular child, the objective approach requires the judiciary to apply the welfare specification to the needs of all children appearing before the court; but the latter rule will often also contain subjective elements[1] and the children involved will each have their own very individual set of needs.

1 For example, the rule regarding the reasonableness of a parental withholding of consent for adoption carries the caveat that a reasonable parent would take into account the welfare of the child.

There has never been any uniformity of policy in relation to the role of welfare in legislation.[2] In many instances the legislative intent of a statute is to pursue objectives other than securing or promoting welfare but in fact it may be highly relevant, albeit indirectly, as in attempts to reduce poverty, improve sewage treatment, ban smoking in public places, etc. Alternatively, the legislative intent may be to safeguard welfare by placing duties on others. Legislation may deal with welfare in the present tense. Reference will then tend to be made to it in relatively objective and precise terms: abandonment, parental unfitness, danger to health and detrimental environment or premises, for example. Legislation may also deal with welfare in the future tense. Where it does so, the references lack comparable precision. Legislation may or may not require the judiciary to have regard for welfare at the threshold or adjudicative stages of proceedings, but this will always be a factor at the disposal stage.

Welfare interests: the child and the decision-makers

Traditionally, a decision affecting the welfare interests of a child could be made only by the mother of an illegitimate child, by either or both parents of a marital child, by the court or by a guardian or person acting in *loco parentis* with authority from one of the aforementioned. The child and his or her welfare were the subject of decisions taken by others. The consent of the child was not required. The law confined itself to licensing the decision-makers and establishing the terms for the legitimate exercise of their authority. This has changed over the past few decades.

THE CHILD

Under the common law a child was defined as such until he or she attained the age of 21. Since the introduction of the Family Law Reform Act 1969, the operative age has been 18. A valid consent for a third party to undertake a course of action affecting the welfare interests of a child could be obtained only from a parent, guardian or court, not from the child. A child was held to be legally incapable of determining his or her own welfare interests and of binding others to respect them. Two cases radically altered the legal standing of a child's welfare interests relative to

2 Until the Children Act 1989, with its checklist of considerations to provide for more judicial consistency in the interpretation and application of welfare indicators. This has diluted the strength of Maidment's observation that:

> The 'welfare of the child' principle is therefore now a deliberately indeterminate standard incorporated into the law in order to allow current social and cultural views about the needs of children, and also, it must be said, of their parents to be embodied in the legal decision-making process.
>
> (Maidment, S., *Child Custody and Divorce*, London, Routledge, 1985, p 3)

all other parties: *J v. C*[3] and *Gillick v. West Norfolk and Wisbech Area Health Authority.*[4]

The first case concerned foster-parents in England who had cared for the ten-year-old son of a Spanish couple for all but 18 months of his life. In the House of Lords, on appeal from wardship proceedings, their lordships held that even if the parents were 'unimpeachable', the welfare interests of the child were of paramount importance, outweighing all other considerations. In the frequently quoted words of Lord MacDermott in this leading case:[5]

> the words 'shall regard the welfare of the infant as the first and paramount consideration' in their ordinary significance ... must mean more than that the child's welfare is to be treated as the top item in a list of items relevant to the matter in question, I think they connote a process whereby, when all the relevant facts, relationships, claims and wishes of parents, risks, choices and other circumstances are taken into account and weighed, the course to be followed will be that which is most in the interests of the child's welfare as that term has now to be understood. That is the first consideration because it is of first importance and the paramount consideration because it rules on or determines the course to be followed.

Thereafter, this principle was embodied in legislation and it has grown to become a benchmark standard for the law relating to the welfare interests of children.

In the second case it was the law relating to the consent of an adolescent that was radically changed; indeed, the position of a consenting minor was altered more radically by the decision in *Gillick*[6] than by the provisions of the 1969 Act. In this case, the House of Lords ruled that in some circumstances a doctor could prescribe contraceptives for a child under the age of 16 without consulting the child's parents. Since then the legal standing of a child in any decision-making process affecting his or her interests has depended on their age and their understanding of the issues involved. As Lord Scarman explained: 'a minor's capacity to make his or her decision depends upon the minor having sufficient understanding and intelligence to make the decision and is not to be determined by reference to any judicially fixed age limit'.

The *prima facie* presumption that a child below the age of 16 is non-competent may be rebutted by evidence based on age and understanding, as was demonstrated, for example, in the Bulger case, when two ten-year-old boys were found to have had the necessary competence – as illustrated by their cunning and methods – and were convicted of murdering two-year-old James

3 [1970] AC 668.
4 [1986] AC 112, [1985] 3 All ER 402, HL.
5 *J v. C*, op cit at pp 710–711.
6 Op cit.

Bulger in 1993.[7] Where a child is aged 16 or is deemed to be '*Gillick* competent', then the law requires that his or her consent be sought in relation to the matter at issue (see, further, Chapter 8).

In legal terms, the distance between these two cases is enormous. *J v. C* marks, perhaps, the apotheosis of a welfare jurisprudence in which the child is objectified to become merely the recipient of a welfare allocation calibrated in accordance with a standardised judicial formula. The *Gillick* ruling may be seen as the first step away from the objectification of the child, within a paternalistic welfare philosophy, towards welfare as a matter capable of subjective interpretation and of justifying action as a right, by the child concerned.

Distinguishing a child's legal interests from those of his or her parents, particularly in private proceedings, has always been a fraught and complicated area of family law. This is less so where the distinction to be made is between a child's interests and those of a third party. In the context of proceedings where an offence involving a child is known or alleged to have been committed, the legal issues at least are usually relatively uncomplicated and will dictate the separation of a child's interests from those of any first or third parties. Where the child is of an age and understanding to express views[8] on the issues raised, these will have a bearing on the judicial task of separating the different sets of legal interests.[9]

The courts usually have cause to adjudicate on the separateness of the interests of parents and children where the latter are either too young to express any views or are mature enough to have their legal competence recognised when doing so. They are occasionally also called upon to do so in circumstances where both parent/s and child are children, which, of course, can give rise to complex difficulties in terms of disentangling and prioritising their respective welfare interests.

7 Confirmed on appeal to the House of Lords: *Regina v. Secretary of State for the Home Department, Ex parte Venables, Regina v. Same, Ex parte Thompson* [1998] AC 407.

8 This has not always been the case: see *R v. Howes* (1860) CA, when Cockburn LCJ, in deciding whether a father should recover custody of a teenage daughter, thought the views of the 15-year-old to be dangerously precocious and might lead to 'irreparable injury'.

9 See *Hewer v. Bryant* [1970] 1 QB 357 at p 369, where the court recognised a gradual displacement of parental rights by an adolescent's right of self-determination. See also: *M v. M (Child: Access)* [1973] 2 All ER 81, where the court established that a right of access between parent and child attached more to the latter than the former; *Re H (Minors) (Access)* [1992] 1 FLR 148, where the court held that the test was not 'What positive advantages would the child gain by a resumption of contact?' but rather 'Did any cogent reason exist for denying a child the opportunity to have contact with a parent?'; and *Re R (A Minor) (Contact)* [1993] 2 FLR 762, where Butler-Sloss LJ emphasised that the companionship of a parent is so important for a child that it gives rise to a basic right in a child to such companionship.

When determining the welfare interests of a baby, the courts have always held pretty much to the view[10] that the younger the child, the greater the weight to be attached to preserving the 'psychological bond' between mother and child. The inference is that the welfare of a very young child is not readily separable from the legal interests of the mother. In the words of Romilly MR in *Austin v. Austin:*[11]

> The welfare of the child is so intimately connected with its being under the care of the mother that no extent of kindness on the part of any other person can supply that place. It is the notorious observation of mankind that the loss of a mother is irreparable to her children and particularly so if young.

This approach has had – and continues to have – a virtually determining effect on contested private family law proceedings, though it offered little resistance to the 'protectionist' ethos which characterised child-care proceedings under the 1969 Act. In relation to a foetus, the courts recognised[12] that a mother owes a duty of care to her unborn child, albeit one that is not actionable until after birth. The significance of this landmark decision, in terms of the light it sheds on the judicial rationale for distinguishing between the welfare of the child and the legal interests of the mother, is difficult to judge. It may, perhaps, be seen as a logical extension of the judicial view that the younger the child, the more fused are the interests of mother and child and, therefore, the greater is the maternal obligation to safeguard her own well-being as only by doing so will her child's interests be protected.

THE PARENTS

'Parent' has been defined in law as meaning both the mother and father of a legitimate child as well as the unmarried mother of an illegitimate child.[13] This definition excludes such others as a stepfather[14] and an unmarried father. The latter may, however, acquire 'parent' status. Traditionally, in law, the welfare interests of a child were to be identified and determined by the parent

10 See Holmes, J., *John Bowlby and Attachment Theory*, London, Taylor and Francis, 1993.

11 (1865) 34 Beavan 257 at p 263. The enduring consistency of the judicial view on this matter can be gauged by the following pronouncement by Lord Jauncey for the House of Lords in *Brixey v. Lynas* [1996] 2 FLR 499, HL at pp 504C–505C: 'Nature has endowed men and women with very different attributes and it so happens that mothers are generally better fitted than fathers to provide for the needs of very young children.'

12 See *D (A Minor) v. Berkshire County Council* (1987) 1 All ER 33.

13 See *Re M* [1955] 2 QB 479. Note also that after some uncertainty as to whether the 1886 and 1925 Acts applied to illegitimate children, the positions of legitimate and illegitimate children were equated for the purposes of parental custody applications in 1959 (Legitimacy Act, s 14(1); also 1971 Act, s 14(1)).

14 See *Re N* [1974] 1 All ER 126.

as so defined, not the child. This usually occurred when the proposals of a third party, such as those of a medical practitioner who wished to conduct an intimate physical examination or administer anaesthetic, could lead to a possible charge of trespass to the person of the child unless properly authorised. However, in the 100 years between the decisions taken in *In re Agar-Ellis*[15] and *Gillick v. West Norfolk and Wisbech Area Health Authority*[16] there was a quiet revolution in the relative legal standing of parents and their children in proceedings concerning the latter's welfare. The former case is a reference point for the law's recognition of a father's exclusive rights to determine matters affecting his children within an autonomous marital family unit (see, further, Chapter 2). The latter provides a marker of equal significance for the law's recognition of the emerging right of a 'mature minor' to take unilateral decisions on such matters either within or without a marital unit and in relation to matters defined as falling within public or private family law. Now, judicial acknowledgment is readily given to the fact that there will be some circumstances where parental consent will be displaced by a child's wishes and feelings. As was stated in the *Gillick* case:[17]

> An underlying principle of the law … is that parental right yields to the child's right to make his own decisions when he reaches a sufficient understanding and intelligence to be capable of making up his own mind on the matter requiring decision.

It is axiomatic that to some extent the law relating to children creates a delicate balance between the interests of the child and those of other persons, particularly the child's parents. It is probably a matter of debate whether the conferring of rights upon parents and other persons is intended to benefit the recipient of the right or the child. Most instances probably benefit the parent by complementing parental common law rights, while the others may no doubt be justified as beneficial on the ground that, for example, parental care is *prima facie* preferable to institutional or similar upbringing. Some measures which provide for a child's welfare interests are statutorily made subject to the rights of a parent. So, for example, advance parental consent is required before a child can be ordered to attend a special school or before a child can be operated upon.

THIRD PARTIES

Prior to the decision in *Gillick*, a valid consent for a third party to undertake a course of action affecting the welfare interests of a child could be obtained only from a parent, guardian or court, not from the child. The main statutory exception to this rule was provided by s 8(1) of the Family Law Act 1969:

15 [1883] 24 CH D 317.
16 Op cit.
17 Ibid at p 251B.

> The consent of a minor who has attained the age of sixteen years to any surgical, medical or dental treatment which, in the absence of consent, would constitute a trespass to his person, shall be as effective as it would be if he were of full age; and where a minor has by virtue of this section given an effective consent to any treatment it shall not be necessary to obtain any consent for it from his parent or guardian.

Since then the courts can be seen looking to this decision as a reference point for determining the consent capacity of an older child in relation to third parties on issues affecting his or her welfare.

Distinguishing a child's legal interests from those of a third party has tended to be a fairly straightforward matter.

Welfare: refining the common law legacy

The common law judiciary regarded certain aspects of a child's upbringing as constituting the core elements of welfare. These were: care and maintenance; education; religious upbringing; and, arguably, control. They were of such importance that the safeguarding of each constituted both a right and a duty vested in parent or guardian in respect of a child in their care. In due course they each came to be the subject of a considerable body of legislation and caselaw.

The substance of welfare

As the jurisprudence developed many other components of welfare were identified, differentiated and regulated by statute. Together they may be grouped under the headings of physical welfare, moral welfare and psychological welfare.

PHYSICAL WELFARE

The composite duty to safeguard a child's welfare by providing appropriate care and maintenance consists of satisfying his or her needs in relation to physical integrity, health, medical and dental care, accommodation, environment, hygiene, food and sanitation. From common law origins, through the period of legislative endorsement in the Poor Laws and the subsequent reforms of the mid-nineteenth century, to the welfare state in the late twentieth century, the law relating to a child's physical and material well-being has remained fundamentally the same. Statute law has steadily raised the required standards for meeting such needs and has increased the range and sophistication of related duties. The law dealing with some of the more traditional aspects of physical well-being, most notably in regard to protection and medical treatment, has burgeoned in volume and complexity. Entirely new branches of law have evolved around such modern determinants of physical well-being as genetics, pre-natal healthcare and abortion. But the basic duty owed to children by their parents – or, failing them, by the state – to provide for their physical needs and safeguard them from any foreseeable harm has not changed.

The law has always been most clear and objective in its specification of duties in relation to a child's care and maintenance. This has usually been achieved by statutorily proscribing the exposure of children to conduct or circumstances held to harm or threaten their physical well-being (see, further, Chapter 2). A child has long been held to have an entitlement to an adequate standard of physical care and to protection from an abusive, exploitive or neglectful parent, an entitlement which warrants enforcement – or coercive removal of care responsibility – by the state. Provision of physical care is the primary responsibility of those with parental responsibility; providing a safe home for the child in question, or determining where he or she shall live, is the most basic duty.[18] The ancillary duty – to provide maintenance adequate to meet the care needs of the child – has also long been recognised by the courts and in a body of legislation of increasing complexity.[19]

MORAL WELFARE

For at least the past century the courts have acknowledged that while nurture needs were fundamental to a child's welfare interests, meeting such needs was in itself insufficient to discharge the duty in respect of the welfare principle in full. The quotient of welfare implied more than a requirement to fulfil a child's minimal needs for physical and material well-being. Lindly LJ drew attention to this in *Re McGrath*:[20]

> The dominant matter for the consideration of the Court is the welfare of the child. But the welfare of a child is not to be measured by money only, nor by physical comfort only. The word welfare must be taken in its widest sense. The moral and religious welfare of the child must be considered as well as its physical wellbeing. Nor can the ties of affection be disregarded.

The law recognised the moral and religious components of child welfare by enforcing a parental duty to provide education in relation to the former while also acknowledging a parental right to provide religious training. Both came to be addressed, in effect, by the state through mandatory education programmes. Initially an objective within such programmes was to protect or enforce the parent's interest in the child's religion; this has largely given way

18 See, for example, *Hitchcock v. WB* [1952] 2 QB 561, where the duty was restricted to 'the provision of a home'.

19 The statutory duty requiring a parent to maintain his or her child is now to be found mainly in the Child Support Act 1991 and also in the provisions of the Social Security Act 1986 and those of the Children Act 1989.

20 (1893) 1 Ch 143.

to provisions which enforce the child's own interest in his or her religious education. The education of children became an integral aspect of their welfare enforceable in law. Statute law provided for this welfare component by conferring and imposing powers and duties upon parents, education authorities and other educational administrative bodies. A duty was placed upon parents to cause every child of school age to receive efficient and suitable education. A corresponding duty was placed upon an education authority to ensure adequate educational provision. A lack of education became a sufficient ground for care proceedings.

The moral welfare of a child cannot be fully assured solely by statutory provision relating to education and religious upbringing. The common law basis for protecting such welfare has been extended by a raft of statutes continuously added to as developments in society's values indicate new areas for protective intervention. Most obviously these have sought to preserve the moral integrity of children in relation to sex and violence by setting threshold criteria of age and consent for access to a range of audio/visual material and involvement in sexual relations, particularly homosexual relationships. Many statutes prohibit specific conduct or circumstances considered likely to undermine moral welfare, such as indulgence in or access to alcohol, cigarettes, solvents, betting, gaming and pornography. While the legal function of prohibition was directed towards the activities of adults and commercial bodies, the function of enforcement was often also directed towards control of the children concerned. A child, the subject of conduct or circumstances statutorily proscribed on moral welfare grounds, could as a result find himself or herself also becoming the subject of a court order made to control future behaviour.

PSYCHOLOGICAL WELFARE

As society has developed a more sophisticated awareness of children's needs and an understanding of the developmental stages of childhood so the law has refined its recognition and protection of welfare interests. Although, traditionally, there were never any statutory references to emotional or psychological welfare,[21] the judiciary have in recent years demonstrated a willingness to view these as inherent components of welfare. Since the mid-1960s, judicial notice has increasingly been taken of the work of leading child psychiatrists and psychologists[22] and decisions grounded on evidence of the child's emotional and psychological welfare, as distinct from material welfare.[23] The case of *In re L*

21 The first statutory reference to such matters came with the inclusion of 'wishes and feelings' as welfare considerations in the Children Act 1989.

22 See, for example, Bettelheim, B., *Love is Not Enough*, Glencoe, IL, Free Press, 1950.

23 See evidence of such a trend beginning with the judgment in *Re C(L) (an infant)* [1965] 2 QB 449 and culminating in the HL judgment in *Re W (an infant)* [1971] AC 682.

(An Infant)[24] provided a not untypical example. When the mother was unable to decide whether to give her consent to the adoption of her child, some considerable time after the child had been placed for that purpose, the court took into consideration the psychological and physical harm which could follow if the child were removed from the adoptive home – a *ratio decidendi* to be followed in many cases. Where attachment existed between the adopters and the child, a reasonable parent might be expected to consider whether a refusal to consent would disrupt that attachment with consequent implications for welfare. The concept of a 'psychological parent' emerged from such cases to gain widespread judicial approval. This is defined as follows:[25]

> whether any adult becomes the psychological parent of a child is based on day-to-day interaction, companionship, and shared experiences. The role can be filled by a biological parent or by an adoptive parent or by any other caring adult … but never by an absent, inactive adult, whatever his biological or legal relationship to the child may be.

The courts have been reluctant to look at the psychological aspects of welfare in isolation.

Presumptive judicial rules relating to welfare

The role of the welfare principle, ascribed or permitted by the law, has always been conditioned by its context. This is most explicit in a legislative context, particularly in the distinctions between public and private or civil and criminal proceedings (see Chapter 3). It is also evident in a procedural context, where it is governed by the relative legal standing of the parties engaged in the proceedings: the role is quite different where the dispute lies between first parties, between third parties or between first and third parties.

Judicial discretion

Most obviously, because of its intrinsically subjective nature, the principle has lent itself to a range of interpretations in the context of the discretionary use of judicial powers. In this context the formulation of certain judicial rules at first inhibited then positively advanced the role, functions and understanding of the welfare principle. In some instances the rules attained the status of legal presumptions. In other cases they offered little more than optional guidance in certain circumstances. Some were explicitly directed towards the needs of children, others affected their needs implicitly. The judiciary employed such

24 (1962) 106 Sol Jo 611.
25 See Goldstein, J., Freud, A. and Solnit, A., *Beyond the Best Interests of the Child*, New York, Free Press, 1974, np.

rules and guidelines to remedy actual legislative deficiencies and to counter what they viewed as conservative legislative principles.

NEGATIVE JUDICIAL RULES

The legal standing of the marital family has always had a decisive influence on the potential for the welfare principle to influence judicial determination of issues affecting the upbringing of children. From the era when the law was resolved to uphold the twin principles of patriarchy and matrimony, three areas of parental relationships gave rise to enduring judicial rules which initially inhibited the potential for a more positive application of the welfare principle. These concerned paternal rights, the conduct of the parties and legal status.

The first of these was the rule that a father had a *prima facie* right to the custody of his legitimate child. This common law presumption – that custody vests in the father unless and until a court orders otherwise – found statutory endorsement in s 5 of the Guardianship of Infants Act 1886. It survived the legislative intent that it should provide a counterbalance to paternal rights in judicial considerations of custody issues (see, also, Chapter 2). Until the mid-twentieth century, court judgments frequently demonstrated that this presumption had sufficient residual viability to persuade the judiciary to make awards of custody to divorced or separated fathers in the absence of evidence that this would be harmful to the child concerned. Even where a father candidly disclosed an intention to delegate total care responsibility to his mother, the courts would defer to his right to do so rather than give preference to the custody claims of the child's caring mother. Not until Parliament introduced further guardianship legislation nearly a century later was judicial defence of this rule finally quashed and the welfare interests of the child legislatively asserted as the paramount judicial consideration.

The second judicial rule concerned the conduct of the parties. The so-called 'doctrine of the unimpeachable parent', which required that custody be awarded to a parent only if he or she was without fault in relation to the marital breakdown, once played a determining role in custody disputes[26] (see Chapter 3). So if, for example, a wife had been found to be adulterous[27] or

26 During the late nineteenth and early twentieth centuries the guilt of a party provided the grounds for both the spouse's divorce action and the rejection of claims for custody. The waning of judicial weight given to this factor began with the judgment in *Stark v. Stark and Hitchins* [1910] P 190. The demise of the presumption in favour of an innocent parent in custody disputes was confirmed by Ormrod LJ in *S v. S* [1977] Fam 109 at p 115, and by Stamp LJ in *Re K* [1977] Fam 179 at p 183. In the former case it was noted that although no longer applicable in such issues between parents, this doctrine may still apply where the issue lies between a parent and a third party, per Ormrod LJ at p 116. See also MacDermott LJ in *J v. C* [1970] AC 668 at p 715.

27 See, for example, *Clout v. Clout* (1861) 2 Sw & Tr 391.

either parent had 'abducted'[28] their child, then that parent would not be awarded custody. The judicial approach to the latter offence may also be seen as an aspect of the more general rule that no guilty party should be permitted to benefit from wrongdoing.[29] The eventual neutralising of the doctrine and with it that whole judicial approach, thereafter enabling preference to be given to the parent who was most effective in safeguarding their child's welfare interests, even if proven to be a culpable spouse, was due in large part to the role played by the judiciary in the wardship jurisdiction. However, where culpability directly affects parental fitness, as when the conduct in question is incest, then the right to custody may still be lost.

The third area in which judicial rules inhibited the development of the welfare principle concerned the legal status of the parties. In the case of a non-marital child, or *filius nullius*, the judiciary were free to focus wholly on the child's welfare interests as there were no legal interests to impede judicial discretion:[30] neither child nor father, nor any third party, could have an inherent legal right that had to be taken into account; the presumptive rule was that full care responsibility vested in the birth mother. Where a third party, such as a foster-parent or birth father, had acquired sufficient legal interests to challenge a mother's right to possession, then the court was nonetheless able to give a determining role to the welfare principle when deciding future custody rights. In the case of a marital child, however (which initially constituted the bulk of custody disputes), the court has always had difficulty in accommodating the welfare principle. When faced with a supervening legal right, such as the traditional paternal right to custody, or with the competing legal rights of more contemporary marital parents, the court has had to place welfare considerations in abeyance while adjudicating the dispute in terms of the rights of the parties, with the presumptive rule being that the welfare principle was at best a secondary consideration in first-party marital disputes.

POSITIVE JUDICIAL RULES

An important element in the development of the law relating to the welfare interests of children has been the influence of judicial notice given to certain factors held to be significant and positive determinants of welfare. By reaching behind such statutory synonyms for child welfare as 'best interests', 'well-being',

28 This judicial approach to 'kidnapping parents' was reviewed by Buckley LJ in *Re L (Minors)* [1974] 1 WLR 250 at p 265, where he concluded that 'the weight to be attributed to it must depend upon the circumstances of the particular case'. He formed the view that the court could deduce that, notwithstanding the conduct of the 'kidnapper', the child should remain in his or her care. See also: *McKee v. McKee* [1951] AC 352; *In re E (D) (An Infant)* [1967] Ch 287; *In re TA (Infants)* [1972] 116 SJ78; and *R v. D* [1984] AC 778, [1984] 2 All ER 449, HL.

29 See, for example, *Re L (Minors)* [1973] 3 All ER 743.

30 Not until the Family Law Reform Acts 1969 and 1987, together with the Legitimacy Act 1976, did their legal interests acquire statutory recognition.

'for the good of', 'to the advantage of', etc., and using their discretionary powers to inject some specific indicators of what in particular may be held to constitute the substance of 'welfare', the judiciary were able to advance the role of the principle relative to other considerations. This occurred most frequently in wardship and in cases which most often concerned children and/or adults whose *locus standi* was compromised by non-marital status or care orders.

Firstly, the age and gender of children had a consistent bearing on judicial decisions regarding custody arrangements. Until the 1989 Act, there had never been a legislative requirement that a child's age or gender should play any part in the determination of custody proceedings in respect of that child. The judiciary, however, developed certain rules of thumb to guide decision-making on such matters. Although first applied in wardship cases, these rules prevailed to gain a more generalised judicial credence in cases of custody contests. One such rule was that the younger the child, the stronger the judicial presumption that maternal rather than paternal care was to be preferred;[31] maternal care for such a child was also preferred to third-party care.[32] In due course maternal preference would mutate to become the 'blood-tie' rule.[33] This was offset by another such rule to the effect that the older the child, the stronger the presumption that he or she should be cared for by the parent of corresponding gender.[34] The extent to which these rules of thumb may be compatible with the dictates of the paramountcy principle has, over time, become steadily more contentious.

Secondly, the judiciary have consistently emphasised the importance of keeping siblings together.[35] The rationale for this approach has been

31 See, for example, *Re K (Minors) (Children: Care and Control)* [1977] Fam 179, CA. This approach owed a good deal to the Bowlby dictum as to the importance of preserving the bonding relationship between mother and baby; see Bowlby, J., *Attachment*, London, Penguin, 1969. Subsequent research has seriously challenged Bowlby's thesis: see, for example, Rutter, M., *Maternal Deprivation Reassessed*, London, Penguin, 1972.

32 As Hanna LJ noted in *Re B* (1962) 1 AER 872 at p 873:

> True it is that the Chancery Judges, and I think those in the Divorce Division also, have in the past years rather taken the view that as long as the child is young enough to need the day to day care of his or her mother, it is better to leave the child with the mother unless the mother is an entirely unsuitable person.

See also *Re W (A Minor) (Custody)* (1982) 4 FLR 492, CA.

33 An early example of the 'blood-tie' presumption can be seen in *Ord v. Blackett* (1724) Modern 116 at p 117, where a putative father succeeded against the executrix and guardian of a child's dead mother 'since he owned her to be his child'. Questioning the validity of this presumption, Dr Kellmer Pringle once said: 'A misplaced faith in blood-tie, and unjustified optimism about the chances of successfully treating the battering parent by casework or psychiatric methods, has placed many a child at risk of repeated injury' (*The Times*, 26 November 1973).

34 See, for example, *May v. May* [1986] 1 FLR 325, CA.

35 See, for example, *Re Besant* (1879) 11 Ch D 508, 512 CA. More recently, see: *Re C (A Minor) (Custody of Child)* (1980) 2 FLR 163, CA; *B v. B (Custody of Children)* [1985] FLR 166, CA; and *C v. C (Minors: Custody)* [1988] 2 FLR 291, 302 CA.

succinctly expressed as follows:[36] 'brothers and sisters should, wherever possible, be brought up together, so that they are an emotional support to each other in the stormy waters of the destruction of their family'.

Thirdly, the judiciary have stressed the importance of keeping children in a familiar environment, albeit tempered by the view that the younger the child, the more this factor diminishes in importance. That said, a seven-year-old has been considered capable of forming an attachment to his or her surroundings.[37] This approach, which is sometimes been referred to as 'maintaining the *status quo*', is very evident in a long line of judgments, most often concerning guardianship, going back to at least the late nineteenth century. As Lindley LJ once explained:[38] 'The duty of the court is, in our judgment, to leave the child alone, unless the court is satisfied that it is for the welfare of the child that some other course should be taken.'

Fourthly, judicial weight has long been given to the opinion of the child.[39] Caselaw, particularly from the wardship jurisdiction, reveals a consistent judicial concern to establish a direct relationship with the children who come before the court, accompanied by a willingness to solicit, and take into account, their views on matters affecting their welfare.

Fifthly, when making determinations, the judiciary will have regard for the children's future welfare. It is a characteristic of the wardship jurisdiction that, unlike statutory law, it has not been tied to past or present circumstances but has had the capacity also to consider the likely bearing of future probabilities. Throughout the judgments, decisions were clearly taken with reference to such projected welfare considerations as the ages, career potential and domestic relationship of the prospective custodians.

Conclusion

From humble beginnings as an inert threshold existing only in statutorily prescribed circumstances, acting no more than as a brake on the enjoyment of the rights of others, to be activated only in retrospect, following its breach, the welfare principle evolved to become a powerful weapon for assertively protecting the welfare of a child. This has largely been achieved by the judiciary utilising the principle's inherent flexibility to extend its interpretation and role in the law relating to children, mainly in a private family law context.

36 See *C v. C (Minors: Custody)* op cit, per Purchas LJ.

37 See *Re Thain* [1926] Ch 676.

38 See *In re McGrath (infants)* [1893] 1 Ch 143 at p 148. See also *In re X, X v. Y* [1899] 1 Ch 526.

39 See *R v. Smith* (1734) 2 Strange 982 for an example of a case where the common law considered the child's wishes.

5 Identifying welfare interests

Introduction

The Children Act 1989 introduced the requirement to ascertain the wishes and feelings of the child as the first item on a 'welfare checklist'[1] to be judicially applied in all public and some private proceedings instigated under this legislation. It also made some decisions by judiciary and local authority conditional upon their acceptance by the child concerned and required the local authority to involve a child in other areas of decision-making. This chapter considers these and other ways in which the law now identifies the welfare interests of a child. It examines when and to what effect the views of a child may contribute to a decision taken by the judiciary, local authority or others in relation to that child's legal interests. It assesses the interrelationship between a child's views, welfare and legal interests, as provided for within this legislation.

Welfare interests: as identified by the child

The Children Act 1989, in particular s 1(3)(a), is now the primary source of legal authority for the principle that a child's views should be ascertained and taken into account when decisions are to be taken on matters concerning that child's welfare. This important, comprehensive and relatively recent legislative recognition of the changed *locus standi* of a child in family proceedings has been brought about by a gradual convergence of pressures emanating from international sources as well as from local judicial practice.

Indeed, there is considerable evidence to suggest that legislative recognition of the importance of a child's views on matters concerning his or her welfare was a response to pressure from outside the UK. For example, in 1984 the Parliamentary Assembly made a recommendation to the Ministers of the

1 See Article 3:

In the circumstances referred to in paragraph (4), a court shall have regard in particular to –

(a) the ascertainable wishes and feelings of the child concerned (considered in the light of his age and understanding).

DOI: 10.4324/9781003268512-8

Council of Europe on the subject of 'parental responsibilities' and incorporated advice in relation to the views of children. It then argued that when decisions are to be taken affecting the legal interests of children, the latter 'should be consulted if their degree of maturity with regard to the decision so permits'. Moreover, the United Nations Convention on the Rights of the Child,[2] which was adopted by the UN General Assembly in November 1989 and ratified by the UK in December 1991, probably influenced the contemporaneous shaping of some of the more formative principles governing the 1989 Act.[3] It may be that the assimilation (though not the formulation and development) of the paramountcy principle within the Children Act 1989 owes at least as much to the Strasbourg initiative as it does to domestic caselaw. The significance of the latter was particularly apparent with the ruling in *Gillick* (see Chapter 4), which was a landmark decision for recognition of the separate legal interests of children.[4] Arguably, however, with hindsight, it may be seen as forming a watershed in UK jurisprudence in the area of 'children's rights', as subsequent caselaw reveals, if anything, a steady constriction of the *Gillick* principle. The judicial approach to the views of children, and the weighting accorded to such views, has since remained essentially paternalistic.

Child's views to be sought and taken into account

The guiding principle, now firmly established by the 1989 Act, is that when, in certain circumstances, decisions are taken by the state on matters affecting the welfare of a child, those taking such decisions should do so only after having fully assessed the legal interests of the child concerned. The views of the child on the presenting issue should also be sought and taken into account. However, such views are not determinative, and may not even be particularly relevant; they are merely an ingredient in the totality of factors which constitute an overall assessment of the child's legal interests. As the Court of Appeal pointed out in *Re P (Minors) (Wardship)*,[5] although there is a duty to seek out and take into account the views of a child, the court could disregard those views where they were deemed to be in conflict with the child's welfare interests.

2 See, in particular, Article 12(1).
3 Article 5 of the Convention, for example, recognises the inherent mutuality between the rights of parents and the welfare of their children in its declaration:

> States Parties shall respect the responsibilities, rights and duties of parents ... to provide, in a manner consistent with the evolving capacities of the child, appropriate direction and guidance in the exercise by the child of the rights recognised in the present Convention.

See also Article 12, which deals with the right of a child to express his or her opinion freely, and have that opinion taken into account, in any matter or procedure affecting him or her.
4 *Gillick v. West Norfolk and Wisbech Area Health Authority* [1986] AC 112, HL.
5 [1992] FCR 261.

The statutory duty placed on the courts is to apply the paramountcy principle in certain proceedings when determining matters affecting the welfare interests of a child. This is stated in s 1 of the 1989 Act as follows:

> (3) In the circumstances mentioned in paragraph (4), a court shall have regard in particular to –
> (a) the ascertainable wishes and feelings of the child concerned (considered in the light of his age and understanding).

There are many issues on which the court will seek the views of a child of sufficient age and understanding. There are also some few issues where consent rather than views will be sought. This is an important statement of principle but it has some limitations as a legal duty. Although binding on the courts, it has no application to others; in particular, this provision does not apply to decisions taken by local authorities. The duty does not come into play until after problems have arisen and decisions then need to be taken in the particular circumstances allowed for under the 1989 Act. There is no general principle in UK legislation that a child has a right to participate in decisions affecting his or her welfare.

The limits to the application of this provision can be appreciated from a brief examination of its key clauses. Firstly, 'the circumstances' are those where contested proceedings are commenced to make, vary or discharge a s 8 order and proceedings to make, vary or discharge an order under Part IV. The mandatory application of this duty in all public but only in contested private family law proceedings reflects the legislation's underpinning philosophy of minimal judicial intervention in consensual family law matters, but comprehensive and consistent judicial scrutiny of public law matters, where the welfare interests of children are involved.

Secondly, 'shall have regard' gives statutory effect to a trenchant observation made by Butler-Sloss LJ:[6]

> The child is a person and not an object of concern … Children are entitled to a proper explanation appropriate to their age … The views and wishes of the child, particularly as to what is to happen to him/her, should be taken into consideration by the professionals involved … and should be placed before whichever court deals with the case.

However, this requirement stops well short of importing any suggestion that a child's consent should be sought. Indeed, the court may overrule a *Gillick* competent minor[7] and the parents or any professional.

6 See *Report of the Inquiry into Child Abuse in Cleveland 1987* (Cmnd 412), London, HMSO, 1988 at p 245.
7 See *Re R* [1991] 4 All ER 177.

Finally, 'ascertainable wishes and feelings' clearly implies that while the judiciary should be guided by this provision when applying the paramountcy principle, its discretion is not to be fettered in the interpretation and relative weighting it gives to the different factors which will constitute the welfare of the child in each case. The wishes and feelings of the child are not synonymous with his or her legal interests. The first may inform judicial appreciation of the latter but they may also be biased, wrong and obscure the legal issues.

This composite duty heads the checklist of factors to be considered by the court when giving effect to the paramountcy principle. But it remains only one of seven such factors, all of which require judicial consideration and none of which will necessarily weigh more than any other in the circumstances of a particular case. The judicial checklist is clearly not a definitive slide rule to be uniformly applied in all cases.

Welfare interests: the parties

In addition to the child concerned, the 1989 Act makes provision for other parties to identify that child's welfare interests and contribute to related decision-making processes.

The child

In the Children Act 1989 the law explicitly and systematically addresses the circumstances in which the child's views should be sought and taken into account on matters affecting his or her welfare interests. But the effect of the ruling in *Gillick* has also become very apparent. For example, the court has indicated that it would respect the wishes of a 14-year-old regarding his education but also commented that, had he been 11, it would not have hesitated to 'pack him off to boarding school'.[8] The critical factor in this and many similar cases is the age and understanding of the child concerned. As Sir Thomas Bingham MR has observed:[9] 'Children have different levels of understanding at the same age. And understanding is not absolute. It has to be assessed relative to the issues in the case.' The child's 'wishes' and 'feelings' are not seen as the sole indicators of his or her appreciation of the matters at issue; nor are these necessarily accorded the same weighting in each case. The subjects on which a child refuses to communicate, or refers to obliquely, may be of greater importance. An assessment of a child's wishes and feelings is acknowledged to be a difficult task. It can be sensibly achieved only by taking into account factors such as: particular attributes and/or needs; personality and character development; attachments; and each child's understanding of where he or she fits into the family dynamics. In court proceedings, intermediaries such as the guardian *ad litem* and local authority social workers,

8 See *Re P (A Minor) (Education)* [1992] 1 FLR 316 CA.
9 See *In re S (A Minor) (Independent Representation)* [1993] 2 FLR at p 444H.

the Official Solicitor and/or expert witnesses, such as psychologists and child psychiatrists, may be available to assist the court to ascertain a child's wishes and feelings. It should be noted, however, that the court has held[10] that evidence, in the form of such views and wishes, could be withheld from a party to proceedings (the mother) only in the most exceptional circumstances: disclosure to all parties is the normal rule.

Wishes and age of a child

The importance to be attached to hearing the views of a child was the subject of judicial comment in *Re W (A Minor) (Contact)*,[11] where the children – aged 10 and 12 – expressed a wish to see the judge to explain why they wanted to live with their father. Butler-Sloss, in the course of her judgment, stated:

> If children of 10 and 12 express the view that they wish to see the judge, that is in line with Section 1(3)(a) of the 1989 Act … If children have views which they wish the court to hear that is entirely in accordance with Parliament's requirement for the first time that courts should ascertain the wishes and understanding of children who are of an age and maturity to give them.

Where the child is aged at least 16 – or, if younger, is deemed to be of an age and understanding to give an informed consent – then parents, the court and other third parties will be legally obliged to do more than ascertain and have regard for his or her views. If the child satisfies the 'competence test' then he or she may assert his or her views by instigating proceedings (though sometimes leave of the court is required), instructing a solicitor and/or participating as a full party in proceedings (see, also, Chapter 7). Such a child may also give or withhold consent in relation to the proposals of such others as parents and local authority. There are circumstances in which others may have to defer to the views of a child; some of these circumstances are stated in or arise from the Children Act 1989.

The parents

The position of parents or those with parental responsibility, in relation to the authority necessary for a valid consent to be given on matters affecting their child's welfare, is not as clear and simple as formerly. It can at least be stated with some certainty that where a child is aged 16 or satisfies the competence test then the courts will be extremely reluctant to impose a parental decision against the wishes of that child. Further, where parental consent is unavailable, for whatever reason, then a third party would be entitled to rely on the

10 See *Re M (Minors) (Disclosure of Evidence)* [1994] 1 FLR No 6.
11 [1994] 2 FLR 441.

authorisation of such a child. However, when a third party is faced with a clear contradiction between the wishes of a parent and such a child legal certainties become harder to find. The decision in *Re W (A Minor) (Medical Treatment: Court's Jurisdiction)*[12] provides authority for the limited proposition that if a child aged 16 or *Gillick* competent has given a valid consent then this cannot be subsequently overridden by the parent. Indeed, s 8 of the Family Law Reform Act 1969 had long provided children aged at least 16 with the right to give an independent consent to surgical, medical or dental treatment.

The judiciary also acknowledge that in some circumstances parental consent will be congruent with a child's wishes and feelings. In keeping with the spirit of the Children Act 1989, particularly the approach which has substituted for the previous exclusivity of parental rights a new concept of shared parental responsibility, the courts have since been interpreting consent in relation to welfare-related decisions as a power which may be vested jointly in a number of office-holders. Therefore, either parent, or a competent child, could unilaterally exercise authority to give a valid consent. It would then be open to a third party to choose the office-holder from whom they would seek authorisation; a refusal by one would not debar the other from granting authorisation.[13]

Other third parties

Consent for a course of action relating to the welfare interests of a child can be given only by a parent, the court, someone or some body with parental responsibility or the child concerned, if he or she is of an age and understanding to do so. Among the third parties who would be recognised as having capacity to give consent are: any local authority vested with a care order; a putative father, if he has legally acquired parental responsibility; a guardian; or any person in whose favour the court has made a residence order.

Public family law: the duty to identify welfare wishes

The Children Act 1989 gives more prominence to the views of the child in public family law proceedings than in private. Whereas the application of s 1(1) is selective in relation to the latter, it is universal to all public proceedings.

Duty to identify

Section 1(3) of the 1989 Act places a dual duty on the court when hearing public law proceedings commenced under the 1989 Act. Firstly, the court has

12 [1992] 3 WLR 785, [1992] 4 All ER 627.

13 This approach can be seen in *Re R (A Minor) (Wardship: Medical Treatment)* [1992] 1 FLR 190, where Donaldson LJ held that a parent retained the right to consent to treatment on behalf of a child, even though the child was of age and understanding and had refused her consent.

a duty to ascertain a child's wishes and feelings. How these are to be ascertained will vary to some extent in accordance with the age and assertiveness of the child concerned. Where a guardian *ad litem* is appointed – which will be in virtually all public law cases – that person will ascertain and present such wishes and feelings to the court. In a minority of cases the child will be the applicant and proceedings will in effect be driven by their views. In many their views will be represented by a solicitor engaged by a guardian *ad litem* and/or be the subject of assessment by expert witnesses (see, further, Chapter 7). Whether elicited by intermediaries, sought by judicial interview or directly expressed at the insistence of the child, the 1989 Act requires the latter's wishes and feelings to be ascertained by the court.

Secondly, the court has a duty to have regard for wishes and feelings. This requirement clearly leaves to judicial discretion the crucial issue of how much weight is to be attached, in any particular instance, to the views of a child when determining a matter affecting his or her welfare. The fact that such a consideration will seldom be the deciding factor was apparent in a 1992 ruling of the Court of Appeal.[14] In considering the equivalent provision of the 1989 Act, it was held that the court should always elicit and respect the views of a child which it may not be able to act upon but which may tip the balance in a difficult case.

Local authorities also incur duties in relation to the identification of welfare wishes. Once a local authority incurs responsibilities in respect of a child it will now, thereby, incur an obligation to ascertain the wishes and feelings of that child. This may arise by implication in the context of service provision for children with special needs. It may arise by explicit statutory directive in relation to children being either accommodated or 'looked after' by a local authority. It may also arise from the considerable body of regulations which detail a local authority's implementation of its various statutory duties towards children, including those who are going through the adoption process.

Duty to ascertain a child's wishes

There are several different and specific sets of circumstances in which such duties may arise.

Firstly, the duty to identify a child's welfare wishes will arise in relation to children being accommodated by a local authority. As is stated in s 20 of the 1989 Act:

> (6) Before providing accommodation under this section, a local authority shall, so far as is reasonably practicable and consistent with the child's welfare –
>
> (a) ascertain the child's wishes and feelings regarding the provision of accommodation; and

14 See *Re P (A Minor) (Education)* [1992] 1 FLR 316 CA.

> (b) give due consideration (having regard to his age and understanding) to such wishes and feelings of the child as they have been able to ascertain.

The form of words employed in this and the following provisions to delineate the duty of a local authority differs slightly from that used earlier in respect of the equivalent judicial duty. It may be that the change from 'have regard' to 'give due consideration', and the occasional absence of a local authority's duty to do so in relation to 'feelings', is intended to imply a subtle distinction in the extent and weighting to be attached to the views of a child by local authority and judiciary. The regulations governing the agreements made between a local authority and parents, in respect of arrangements for a child being accommodated, provide for the views of the child concerned to be ascertained. The requirement is that every local authority shall record the arrangements it makes for ascertaining the views of the child in relation to the matters dealt with in the accommodation agreement.

Secondly, the duty will arise in relation to children being 'looked after' by a local authority. Under s 22 of the 1989 Act:

> (4) Before making any decision with respect to a child whom they are looking after, or proposing to look after, a local authority shall, so far as is reasonably practicable, ascertain the wishes and feelings of –
> (a) the child ...
> [and]
> (5) In making any such decision a local authority shall give due consideration –
> (a) having regard to his age and understanding, to such wishes and feelings of the child as they have been able to ascertain.

When so considering a child's views, in the context of such decision-making, a local authority is also directed to consider the child's religious persuasion, racial origin and cultural and linguistic background. This requirement – that a local authority consult, where practicable, with a child before making decisions affecting that child and before making arrangements regarding his or her future home – ensures that the child is at least briefed and at best given a chance to participate in the choices to be made as to the manner in which he or she is 'looked after' by the local authority.

Thirdly, the duty will also arise in relation to the reviews of children being 'looked after' by a local authority. Under s 26 of the 1989 Act:

> (1) The Secretary of State may make regulations requiring the case of each child who is being looked after by a local authority to be reviewed in accordance with the provisions of the regulations.
> (2) The regulations may, in particular, make provision –
> ...

> (d) requiring the authority, before conducting any review, to seek the views of –
> (i) the child …

The regulations emanating from this provision provide comprehensively for the responsibility of local authorities to ascertain and take into account the wishes and feelings of children across the full range of settings in which they may be met, including those of children in secure accommodation. How this is achieved – so as to ensure that the child is therapeutically engaged and that his or her legal interests are effectively and assertively represented while welfare interests are not compromised – remains a challenge for the practice of a local authority as much as for the court.

Finally, the duty will also arise when a local authority receives representations (including complaints) from children. The duty of a local authority to establish a complaints procedure in relation to children whom it is 'looking after' is addressed in regulations which derive from the authority of s 26:

> (3) Every local authority shall establish a procedure for considering any representations (including any complaint) made to them by –
> (a) any child who is being looked after by them or who is not being looked after by them but is in need.

In addition to the above duties of court and local authority, the duty to identify the welfare wishes of a child may fall on other bodies and persons. For example, s 61 of the 1989 Act places such a duty on voluntary organisations:

> (1) Where a child is accommodated by or on behalf of a voluntary organisation, it shall be the duty of the organisation –
> …
> (c) to advise, assist and befriend him with a view to promoting his welfare when he ceases to be so accommodated.
> (2) Before making any decision with respect to any such child the organisation shall, so far as is reasonably practicable, ascertain the wishes and feelings of –
> (a) the child … regarding the matter to be decided.
> (3) In making any such decision the organisation shall give due consideration –
> (a) having regard to the child's age and understanding, to such wishes and feelings of his as they have been able to ascertain …

This provision extends to voluntary organisations the duty to identify and take into account a child's views regarding his or her welfare. Under s 64(1)(c), (2)(a) and (3)(a) of the 1989 Act, the stated duties of any person carrying on a private children's home replicate those outlined in the corresponding provisions of s 61. The inclusion of private children's homes within the scope of this mandatory duty thereby ensures its uniform legal application across both the statutory and voluntary sectors of child care. Under s 46, a constable has the power to remove, and provide accommodation for, a child in an emergency. The exercise of this power is subject to a requirement in (3) of the same section that, as soon as is reasonably practicable after the child has been taken into police protection, the designated officer shall '(d) take such steps as are reasonably practicable to discover the wishes and feelings of the child'. However, under s 46 (10), the issue of whether the child is then to have contact with parents or any other stated persons is a matter to be determined by the designated officer in light of his assessment of the child's best interests; there is no requirement that he or she should seek the views of the child on this matter.

Under Part III, Schedule 3 of the 1989 Act, the duties of a supervisor in respect of a child the subject of an education supervision order include, under s 12, the power to give such directions to the child as may be necessary to ensure that he or she is properly educated. This power is subject to the instruction that the supervisor, 'so far as is reasonably practicable, ascertain the wishes and feelings of … the child'. Sub-para (3) adds: 'when settling the terms of any such directions, the supervisor shall give due consideration[,] having regard to the child's age and understanding, to such wishes and feelings of his as the supervisor has been able to ascertain'. These instructions do not lie solely in relation to the child; they are exactly replicated in respect of the child's parents. Not only are the views of the child thus accorded no greater weight than those of the parents, there is no suggestion in this provision that the supervisor should comply with the views of either party.

Duty to defer to child's wishes

There is no such thing as a sweeping statutory duty directing that a child's views, as opposed to his or her legal interests, must prevail over all other considerations in the determining of issues affecting the welfare of that child. The essential point of the paramountcy principle, after all, is a recognition that the responsibility for decision-making is to be placed not in the hands of a child but in the hands of certain authorised others. Additionally, the party primarily bound by the outcome of any decision to which the principle applies is the child concerned.

However, there are now some areas of decision-making governed by the 1989 Act where such authority has been extended to enforce the views of a child that, in effect, responsibility for a decision rests with that child. There are also other areas which, because decisions turn on the consent rather than the views of a *Gillick* competent child, the outcome will be the same.

THE COURT

The judiciary have certain duties in regard to the non-consensual medical treatment of a child in care. The circumstances in which the wishes and feelings of a child may, in public family proceedings, be permitted to override a refusal of parental consent is an area of law which seems set to experience an exponential increase in litigation. The issues arise most commonly, and most urgently, in relation to medical treatment, where consent of parent or child is an essential precondition for doctors to commence treatment, except in an emergency. Such cases usually appear before the courts in private family proceedings where the criteria to be applied and the appropriate forum for hearing them have greatly exercised the judiciary in recent years. In public family proceedings, where the child is in care, it is evident[15] that the appropriate forum is the inherent jurisdiction of the High Court. Occasionally, circumstances arise in which the person whose consent is required to authorise treatment lacks the capacity to do so, usually due to mental illness. This was the situation in a case[16] where a local authority sought permission to disconnect a life-support system which was sustaining the life of a severely brain-damaged child. The High Court, exercising its inherent jurisdiction, provided the necessary authority (see, also, Chapter 7). Where the child is a mature minor and parental consent is, for whatever reason, unavailable, there is authority under the ruling in *Gillick* for the courts to endorse the consent of the child, though it would very seldom do so.

The local authority

Local authorities are frequently faced with problems in relation to older adolescents in care who make reasoned decisions which are not in keeping with their welfare interests. An adolescent will often hold strong views as to what he or she believes constitutes their welfare interests and what should be done to further those interests. The question then arises as to what power a local authority might have to override the decision of a *Gillick* competent minor. In *Re W (A Minor) (Medical Treatment: Court's Jurisdiction)*[17] the court considered an application made in respect of a 16-year-old anorexic girl in care for permission to arrange medical treatment, and for this to be provided without her consent, if necessary. The Court of Appeal unanimously gave its consent. It held that: it had authority to do so under the court's unlimited inherent *parens patriae* jurisdiction; the authority of those holding parental responsibility for a child would be insufficient to override the decision of a *Gillick* competent child; its authority when exercising this jurisdiction exceeded that which came within the definition of 'parental responsibility'; and the High Court's inherent jurisdiction may apply regardless of whether or not the child in question was a ward.

Where the views of a mature minor in care are being unreasonably opposed by a parent the court will not hesitate to give precedence to the views of the

15 See *Re R (A Minor) (Blood Transfusion)* [1993] 2 FLR 757.
16 See *Re TC (A Minor)* [1994] 4 BNIL.
17 Op cit.

child if the evidence shows that to do so would be compatible with their welfare interests. This approach is very much in keeping with the decision in *Re O (A Minor) (Medical Treatment)*[18] which provides authority for the view that the inherent jurisdiction is the most appropriate forum to authorise a blood transfusion for a child against the wishes of the child's parents, who, in the latter case, were Jehovah's Witnesses.

Paramountcy

The fact that a court is bound by the paramountcy principle in its determination of most proceedings arising under the 1989 Act does not of itself give rise to any presumption that other factors must give way to the views of a child. Indeed, quite the opposite is the case. However, in certain circumstances the courts have little or no option when faced with a resolute child.

Firstly, this can occur in relation to child assessment orders. Under s 43 of the 1989 Act, the court is empowered, on the application of a local authority or authorised person, to make a child assessment order if satisfied that the requirements stated in that provision have been met. However, under para (8), 'if the child is of sufficient understanding to make an informed decision he may refuse to submit to a medical or psychiatric examination or other assessment'. This effectively gives the child a power to determine his or her welfare interests and to veto an entire court order.

Secondly, it may occur in relation to assessment conditions attached to other court orders. Under s 44(1) of the 1989 Act, the court may make an emergency protection order which can be subject to a direction made under para (6)(b) requiring a medical, psychiatric or other form of assessment for the child. However, para (7) adds that the child concerned may, 'if he is of sufficient understanding to make an informed decision, refuse to submit to the examination or other assessment'. The child is thus given a power of veto, restricted to an ancillary aspect of the order, and to that extent may determine his or her welfare interests. Also, under Sched 3, the power of a court to attach a direction to a supervision order made under s 31(1), requiring the child to attend for psychiatric or medical examination, is subject to s 4:

> (4) No court shall include a requirement under this paragraph in a supervision order unless it is satisfied –
> (a) where the child has sufficient understanding to make an informed decision, that he
> consents to its inclusion …

The case of *Leeds City Council v. C*[19] demonstrated the difficulties presented by this provision.

18 [1993] 2 FLR 149.
19 [1993] 1 FLR 269.

Finally, it can occur in relation to applications for the discharge and variation etc. of certain orders. Under s 39(1) and (2), the court may discharge a care order or a supervision order, respectively, on the application of the child concerned; and under s 45(8)(a), the court may do the same where the child's application is in respect of an emergency protection order. Similarly, under Sched 3, the court may do so where the child's application is in relation to an education supervision order. These provisions require the court to treat an application from a child as it would an application from a local authority, parent or a person with parental responsibility: if the applicant satisfies the conditions then the court must defer and discharge the order.

In certain circumstances the duties of a local authority leave it with little or no option other than to defer to the wishes of a child. Under the 1989 Act and other legislation, a local authority may find that its obligation to so defer is such that, in effect, it is recognising and conceding a right held by that child. This may occur, for example, in relation to the provision of accommodation. Section 20(11) of the 1989 Act eliminates both a local authority's right not to provide accommodation and the right of any person with parental responsibility to remove a child from local authority accommodation 'where a child who has reached the age of sixteen agrees to being provided with accommodation under this section'. Effectively, this provision would seem to place a duty on the local authority to provide accommodation to such a child or allow him or her to remain in local authority accommodation if that child has determined that this is in accordance with his or her welfare interests. The independent legal status of such a child is further recognised by s 29(4)(b), under which a local authority is authorised to recover from that child contributions towards the maintenance costs incurred in looking after him or her.

Private family law: the duty to identify welfare interests

The requirement to ascertain the wishes and feelings of a child has a restricted application to private family proceedings.

Duty to identify

This statutory duty falls on the judiciary only in respect of contested proceedings, and its bearing on local authority procedures is virtually limited to forming an item in the court reports of social workers and guardians *ad litem* in adoption and some wardship and matrimonial proceedings.

The judiciary have virtually no obligation to identify welfare interests in the context of uncontested private family law proceedings. The welfare 'checklist' has no application and therefore there is no statutory requirement that the wishes and feelings of the child concerned be ascertained. This non-interventionist stance is well illustrated by the two provisions in the 1989 Act relating to the intention to change a child's surname. Section 13 states that:

(1) Where a child arrangements order is in force with respect to a child, no person may –
    (a) cause the child to be known by a new surname; without either the written consent of every person with parental responsibility or the leave of the court.

Under s 33(7)(a), 'no person shall cause the child to be known by a new surname', except in the same circumstances. In neither instance is there a requirement to seek the child's views. Indeed, the child's views may be discounted where they are brought before the court.[20] This was precisely what occurred in *Re B (Change of Surname)*.[21] The unequivocal wishes of three children (aged 12, 14 and 16), supported by mother and social worker, proved insufficient to convince the court that a change of surname to that of their stepfather would be justified. This approach contrasts with that advocated in Articles 2 and 9 of the UN Convention on the Rights of the Child.

In adoption, wardship and matrimonial proceedings where an application is being contested the judiciary have a well-established practice of seeking the views of the children concerned. Information on their views will also be made available to the court in the form of reports from local authority social workers in respect of all such proceedings, augmented by reports from guardians *ad litem* in adoption applications and in all cases by occasional evidence from expert witnesses.

In adoption proceedings, the statutory requirement in s 6 of the Adoption Act 1976 to 'ascertain the wishes and feelings of the child … and give due consideration to them, having regard to his age and understanding' is binding on both court and local authority in relation to any decision. The significance attached to this requirement was apparent in *In Re B (Minor) (Adoption: Parental Agreement)*,[22] where the court's decision to dispense with the need for parental agreement was significantly influenced by the wishes of the 11-year-old subject.

In matrimonial proceedings, the checklist considerations, as stated in s 1(3) of the 1989 Act, now apply to any disputes concerning the parties' proposed care arrangements for their children. Such is the significance attached to the requirement to seek the views of the children concerned that it has been held[23] that a failure to do so ought to be a ground of appeal. It is, however, a matter of some concern that this requirement applies only when such proceedings are contested. By far the majority of judicial determinations affecting the future upbringing of children occur in the context of matrimonial proceedings. Most of these are undisputed. In the majority of cases affecting child welfare, therefore, the law does not require the views of the children

20 See *W v. A (Child: Surname)* [1981] 1 All ER 100.
21 [1996] 1 FLR 791.
22 [1990] 2 FLR 383.
23 See *M v. M (Minor: Custody Appeal)* [1987] 1 WLR 404.

involved to be heard in settling the arrangements for their future upbringing. This is a significant constraint on the application of the welfare principle. The Family Law Act 1996 requires the welfare interests of the child concerned to be identified in divorce proceedings: s 8(9)(b) states that information must be given to parents about 'the importance to be attached to the welfare, wishes and feelings of the child'; s 11(4)(a) obliges the court to have particular regard to the wishes and feelings of the child. However, these provisions have not altered the established practice of leaving the ascertainment of a child's wishes and feelings to the routine enquiries of solicitors and/or court welfare officers (and, in future, 'mediators'), usually directed towards parents rather than the child concerned, and discouraging the participation of children in court proceedings.

In the wardship jurisdiction, the caselaw reveals a consistent judicial concern to establish a direct relationship with the children who come before the court. In recent years this has been accompanied by a judicial willingness to solicit, and give more weight to, their opinions.

Duty to defer

The duty upon others in relation to the views of a child is at its weakest in private family proceedings but this is balanced by the powerful right of a child in such proceedings to assert his or her views at the expense of others. After all, the decision in *Gillick* resulted from private family proceedings and remains the leading case and reference point for a developing body of jurisprudence on the autonomous legal interests of children and the weighting of such interests relative to those of parents and others. It is private family proceedings which have since witnessed the emergence of such children's 'rights' as: to sue for damage caused while a foetus; to 'divorce' parents; to have access to parents; and to have access to information on pre-adoption family background. This is in keeping with the general philosophy underpinning the 1989 Act that state intrusion in family matters should be minimised while the capacity of family members to assert their autonomous legal interests should be facilitated. However, the decision in *Re B*[24] was indicative of a firming up of the judicial approach towards children's 'rights': a child's wishes may not prevail where they are in conflict with rights traditionally regarded as hallmarks of parental status (e.g. the right to determine religious upbringing, surname, etc.).

The duties of the court in relation to leave to apply for s 8 orders are outlined in s 10:

> (8) Where the person applying for leave to make an application for a section 8 order is the child concerned, the court may only grant leave if it is satisfied that he has sufficient understanding to make the proposed application for the section 8 order.

24 Op cit.

This would seem to imply that where the condition is satisfied the court is then virtually required to grant the leave sought.

Court duties in relation to contact arrangements have been established since the decision in *M v. M (Child: Access)*.[25] It is clear that they will defer to the views of a child, where these are judged to be compatible with his or her welfare interests, when faced with a conflict between such views and those of a parent in respect of contact arrangements. In relation to applications for the termination of guardianship appointments, the court may, under s 6(7)(b) of the 1989 Act, at any time order the termination of an appointment of a guardian made under s 5 'on the application of the child concerned, with leave of the court'. Again, the court is required to treat the application on its merits and will be obliged to accede to the child's wishes if satisfied that to do so would be in keeping with his or her welfare interests.

Finally, in private law cases, the assessment of a *Gillick* competent child is dependent upon the prior consent of that child. However, his or her right to refuse might depend upon mental competence.[26] This may also be overridden by the court if the latter should be of the opinion that an examination is in his or her best interests.[27]

Conclusion

It is paradoxical that although the legal changes inaugurated by the 1989 Act specified an increased range of welfare indicators to be taken into account when determining matters affecting a child's upbringing, it also drastically reduced the opportunities for applying them. The removal of the mandatory welfare test as a condition for a judicial order terminating a marriage has removed professional scrutiny from the largest category of proceedings in which the future welfare of children needs to be safeguarded. The retreat of state intervention across the range of private family legal proceedings marked a significant milestone in family law: it transferred from public to private law the decision-making process regarding the future welfare of the large majority of children affected by family breakdown, and in effect abandoned decision-making on welfare issues to the families concerned.

25 [1973] 2 All ER 81.
26 See *R v. Waltham Forest London Borough ex parte G* [1989] 2 FLR 138.
27 See *Re W (A Minor) (Consent to Medical Treatment)* [1993] 1 FLR 1.

6 Representing welfare interests

Introduction

Audi alteram partem – the right of a person likely to be directly affected by the outcome of proceedings to put their case to the court – is a right of natural justice and one long denied to children in the essentially adversarial proceedings of the common law courts. Indeed, a person below the age of 18 had for centuries been construed as non-*sui juris* (without legal capacity), their legal interests subsumed within those of a parent or guardian. Children were therefore regarded as not legally competent – in their own right – to take decisions, contract, give testimony as witnesses, nor to manage or even participate in the management of their affairs. The transformation of the legal position of a child – from being the subject of decision-making processes regarding their welfare to having a right to participate and at least influence the outcome – has been a relatively recent development (evolving over the latter part of the twentieth century) that remains incomplete.

This chapter builds on its two immediate predecessors: while making room for welfare interests in legislation and court proceedings is clearly crucial, as is the judicial capacity to identify what constitutes the 'welfare interests' of a particular child in particular circumstances, these count for little unless those interests can also be firmly championed by appropriate representatives in any and all proceedings where they conflict with the interests of others.

Background

Until the mid-twentieth century, children's legal and welfare interests were not regarded as requiring representation – separate and distinct from that of their parents – in court proceedings. Traditionally the law held the latter responsible for safeguarding those interests, which were treated as lying within the umbrella of parental rights, and they would have been permitted and expected to represent such interests in court on behalf of the child (see, also, Chapter 7).

DOI: 10.4324/9781003268512-9

Competence

Not until certain age-specified levels of competence were met could a child be held to satisfy the legal definition of 'person', as understood by Salmond.[1] The dismissive judicial approach to the *locus standi* of young children was exemplified by Lord Goddard when he rejected the witness statement of a five-year-old girl, remarking 'the jury could not attach any value to the evidence of a child of five: it is ridiculous to suppose they could'.[2]

Under the common law, competence had been determined by applying the construct 'age of discretion', as exemplified in the criminal law by rules of *doli incapax* in relation to children under the age of ten,[3] the rebuttable presumption of incapacity for those aged ten to fourteen and the presumption of full adult capacity thereafter (see, further, Chapter 8). Under statute law, the stipulated age of majority[4] marked the point at which a 'child' acquired a fully developed legal personality, although the body of statute law relating to children contained an assorted spread of age criteria for participation in different proceedings. Attaining the age of majority brought with it the right to initiate and/or appear as a party in court proceedings. Until then, the law stated that a child:[5]

> may not bring, or make a claim, in any proceedings except by his next friend and may not acknowledge service, defend, make a counterclaim or intervene in any proceedings, or appear in any proceedings under a judgment or order notice of which has been served on him, except by his guardian *ad litem*.

The status of legal 'person' was not so much denied a child as held to be absorbed within the personality of an adult recognised by the legal system as entitled – and obliged – to speak for the child's interests. Inherently, this responsibility was held to vest in the child's parent, usually the father,[6] or a guardian appointed to act in their place (see, further, Chapters 1, 2 and 7). Where the parent was unavailable, unable or disqualified from acting on behalf of the child then the court would appoint a 'next friend' to do so.

Towards separate representation for children

In the wake of changes wrought within the body of substantive law relating to children (see, further, Chapter 3), there eventually followed some related

1 See Salmond, J., *Jurisprudence*, London, Sweet & Maxwell, 1947.
2 *R v. Wallwork* [1958] 42 CAR 153.
3 Children under the age of ten are in law held to be incapable of committing a crime. See the Children and Young Persons Act 1933, s 50.
4 Altered from 21 years to 18 by the Family Law Reform Act 1969 in response to recommendations made in the *Report of the Committee on the Age of Majority* (Latey Report) (Cmnd 3342), London, HMSO, 1967.
5 See Rules of the Supreme Court 1965, Ord 80, r 2(1).
6 See *Woolf v. Pemberton* (1877) 6 Ch D 19.

procedural adjustments. The welfare interests of a child began to be brought before the court by persons other than parents, parent substitutes or 'next friends' as recognition was given to the need for independent representation of a child's interests (see, further, Chapter 7). Mandatory welfare reports were required in an increasing range of public and private family law proceedings for the purpose of providing the court with information relating to the home surroundings, school record, health and character of the child appearing before it. Rules were introduced to disentitle parents from appearing as representatives on behalf of their children in circumstances where there was a clear conflict of interest.

However, the history of judicial efforts to 'hear the voice of the child' (and those of others representing the interests of a child) in proceedings that affected their welfare long preceded the substantive changes to child-related law.

GUARDIAN

This court-appointed official is one with a long history of representing the welfare interests of children. The origins of guardianship probably lie in the jurisdiction of wardship, and can be dated to the Court of Chancery and the Tenures Abolition Act 1660, when those courts, exercising their inherent *parens patriae* powers, conferred the protection of wardship on its young charges and appointed a guardian to bear day-to-day care and protection responsibilities (see, further, Chapter 1). The person so appointed was required to have no interest in the proceedings that could be adverse to those of the minor.[7]

THE OFFICIAL SOLICITOR

The origins of this office can also be traced back through the centuries to the Court of Chancery. In the late nineteenth century, the office was transferred and reconstituted as part of the High Court jurisdiction. While traditionally responsible for the welfare and property of wards, by the twentieth century the Official Solicitor's remit had been broadened as *amicus curiae* to include responsibility for the welfare and legal interests of any child the subject of proceedings in the Family Division of the High Court – usually adoptions but also issues arising as a consequence of family breakdown – that might be judicially referred as in need of the specialist expertise of that office.

Primarily, the role of this official is to determine the child's best interests and wishes, represent his or her views, instruct specialist consultants or negotiate with overseas officials and generally, by acting as a solicitor on his or her behalf, ensure that he or she 'has a voice' in proceedings and make such recommendations to the court as are compatible with his or her best interests. Moreover, and significantly, the role is ongoing: unlike other forms of issue-based professional involvement, which end with relevant decisions,

7 *Smith v. Palmer* (1840) 3 Beav 10.

the engagement of the Official Solicitor can be maintained as long as necessary. In practice, the functions of this office are now the responsibility of a large Official Solicitor's Department.

'NEXT FRIEND'

A 'next friend', subsequently known as a 'McKenzie man',[8] has long been held entitled to seek permission of the court to be appointed to represent the interests of a minor,[9] with responsibility for participation in while not being a party to proceedings.[10] Any person being within the jurisdiction,[11] with capacity,[12] being neither the defendant[13] nor a friend of the defendant,[14] nor in anyway connected with the defendant, nor otherwise having an interest in the proceedings adverse to the minor's interests[15] may so act as the 'next friend' of an infant plaintiff or applicant.[16]

THE COURT WELFARE OFFICER

This is a probation officer who reports to the court in family breakdown circumstances – largely matrimonial and custody disputes, wardship matters – with profile information on the family and their problems. The role may date back to legislation such as the Divorce and Matrimonial Causes Act 1857 and the Married Women's Property Act 1870, with the attendant need to advise the court on the circumstances of mothers separating from their husbands. In cases of parental separation, where there is a dispute about where and with whom the child should live and/or contact arrangements with the other parent, the court welfare officer will investigate the circumstances and report to the court with the aim of assisting it to reach a decision about the child's best interests. The role is generally understood as being one of investigation and information gathering, to 'act as the eyes and ears of the court': to serve as a neutral court officer without any responsibility to make assessments or recommendations; and without any mandate to represent, or act as advocate for, the welfare interests of a child. However, this may well include the provision of mediatory or conciliation services and result in an assessment as

8 See *McKenzie v. McKenzie* [1971] P 33; [1970] 3 WLR 472, where the plaintiff was accompanied by a 'learned friend' who assisted in presenting the case by taking notes and giving advice.
9 *Morgan v. Thorne* (1841) 7 M&W 400.
10 *Sinclair v. Sinclair* (1845) 13 M&W 640.
11 *Jones v. Lloyd* (1874) LR 18 Eq 265.
12 *Re Duke of Somerset, Thynne v. St Maur* (1877) 34 Ch D 465.
13 *Lewis v. Nobbs* (1878) 8 Ch D 591, 593.
14 *Re Burgess, Burgess v. Bottomley* (1883) 25 Ch D 243 CA.
15 *Jack v. Lucas* (1839) 1 Beav 436.
16 *Whitaker v. Marlar* (1786) 1 Cox EEq Cas 285 at 286; *Harrison v. Harrison* (1842) 5 Beav 130.

to the relative capacity of the parties to further the welfare of the child concerned.

THE REPORTING OFFICER

The role of reporting officer was introduced by the Children Act 1975 to provide the court with information on family circumstances, protect the interests of the birth parent/s in adoption cases and advise the court in contested cases where matters concerning the welfare of a child were being considered. This role would be allocated to a probation officer rather than a local authority social worker.

LOCAL AUTHORITY SOCIAL WORKER

In addition, the local authority social worker engaged in provision of social services, or in monitoring a child placed for adoption, or in a child-protection role with the family would generally be required at least to submit a family background report to the court.

Public and private law

The welfare interests of children arose for consideration in quite different sets of proceedings: traditionally this was the case in the private law jurisdictions of wardship, guardianship, adoption and in matrimonial disputes; later in relation to public law and in the ever-expanding, if fragmentary, field of child protection; as a factor in criminal proceedings; and, later still, in relation to general health, safety and education matters (see, further, Chapter 3). This disparate range of proceedings brought with it a matching complexity of organisational context, heavily influenced by factors such as the availability of legal aid, and generated an equally broad range of professionals with a varying brief to protect, represent or assert a child's welfare interests.

Private family law

The legal differentiation between the interests of child and parent probably commenced in the later years of the nineteenth century in the context of civil proceedings.[17] Parental disputes and disputes between parents and third parties regarding a child's property or arrangements for their custody forced the courts to recognise that the interests of a parent and those of their child could be in conflict and require separate representation.

17 See: legislation such as the Judicature Act 1873, the Custody of Infants Act 1873 and the Guardianship of Infants Acts 1886 and 1925; and cases such as *R v. Senior* [1899] 1 QB 283 and *In Re O'Hara* [1900] 2 IR 232.

Wardship

In this, the oldest private family law jurisdiction, the child was never automatically a party to proceedings, but could be made a party in his or her own right, and the Official Solicitor appointed to represent his or her interests.

In circumstances of parental death, absence or default, almost always where property was involved, the court would refer to the wardship jurisdiction of the High Court where the Official Solicitor, acting as guardian, would make arrangements for the management of a child's affairs (see, further, Chapter 2). As has been explained, when appointed to act as guardian *ad litem* the Official Solicitor is 'not only an officer of the court and the ward's guardian, but he is a solicitor and the ward is his client'.[18] As responsibilities for wards and guardians devolved to the Official Solicitor, and as this official became available to accept judicial referrals from any Family Division proceedings involving children, he or she had discretion to assume a representational role in relation to a child's interests as and when the necessity to do so arose.

Matrimonial proceedings

Children involved in matrimonial proceedings did not have party status and were not generally granted legal representation unless the proceedings were contested, when a court welfare officer would be appointed. In 1956 the Morton Commission[19] reported that, in marital proceedings,[20] the most suitable arrangements were not always made for children due to the fact that no one was 'specifically charged to look after the child's interests'[21] and recommended changes to the law to allow such representation (see, further, Chapter 3). In 1968, the Hall Report,[22] reviewing provision for the mandatory assessment of child welfare interests in the context of establishing the rate of child maintenance payments following marriage breakdown, found the arrangements for assessing those interests to be to some extent unsatisfactory.

Adoption

Following the introduction of adoption as a statutory process in 1926, the child subject of such proceedings did not have party status and was not entitled to legal representation. Guardians *ad litem* were appointed to serve as their independent representatives – that is, independent of parents and the local authority, accountable only to the court – and protect their interests in adoption proceedings.

18 *Re R (PM) (an infant)* 1 All ER (1968), per Goff J at p 692.
19 *Report of the Royal Commission on Marriage and Divorce – Report 1951–1955* (Morton Report) (Cmnd 9678), London, HMSO, 1956.
20 Ibid at para 366.
21 Ibid at para 367.
22 See, further, at: https://hansard.parliament.uk/Commons/1968-06-21/debates/e47af258-3dcd-4b8e-adaf-2d944cb9997d/Clause1.

Public family law

Provisions of the Protection of Children and the Prevention of Cruelty Act 1889 separated the welfare interests of a wilfully ill-treated or neglected child from the criminal liability of an abusive or neglectful parent, allowing such a child to be placed with a 'fit person'. However, court removal of a child from their parent remained conditional upon that parent having first been convicted of a criminal offence against the child: parental disqualification came before child welfare; civil law considerations regarding the welfare interests of an abused or neglected child were an adjunct to prior criminal proceedings. This continued until the Children and Young Persons (Amendment) Act 1952 dispensed with the need for a prior parental criminal conviction.

Care and protection

The ideology underpinning the Children and Young Persons Act 1969 maintained the approach which had launched the Juvenile Courts (see, further, Chapter 3) and rested on an assumption that a child – whether engaged in criminal behaviour or the subject of neglect or abuse – was the victim of family dysfunction and required the law to focus on their welfare interests: that is, on needs rather than deeds. However, although both deprived and depraved children were to be the subject of civil proceedings, this approach failed to deal with the necessity for such children to have separate representation from their parents.

SEPARATE REPRESENTATION FOR CHILDREN

The likelihood of a conflict of interest between parent and child became apparent in the increasing volume of care and protection proceedings, particularly as illustrated in the death of Maria Colwell[23] in 1973 at the hands of her stepfather and the representation of the child's interests by the parent's solicitor. Subsequently, ss 64 and 65 of the Children Act 1975 provided for separate representation for parent/s and child in cases of child abuse by directing that a guardian *ad litem* be appointed to provide representation for any child the subject of care proceedings in the Juvenile Court. This in turn led to the establishment of the guardian *ad litem* (GAL) service to report to the court in both adoption and care-and-protection proceedings – on child welfare rather than on legal matters – and in respect of proceedings relating to parental rights and contact arrangements.[24]

23 See Department of Social Security, *Report of the Committee of Inquiry into the Care and Supervision Provided for Maria Colwell*, London, HMSO, 1974.

24 The Children's Act 1975, s 103, empowered the Secretary of State to establish GAL panels from which GALs could be appointed to represent children in adoption, care and protection proceedings, and in proceedings relating to parental rights resolutions.

The GALs were social workers, acting as officers of the court, employed by either local authorities or by the NSPCC, with a duty to investigate, report and recommend on all matters relating to the welfare of the child. Testimony to the value of their contribution in such proceedings was provided in the report of the Committee of Inquiry into the death of Jasmine Beckford, who died from parental abuse in 1984:[25]

> The essential feature of the role is that for the first time there is someone, other than a legal representative, whose concern is exclusively the welfare of the child, independent of both the child's parents and the local authority which has the duty to protect the child.

Criminal offences

The legislation governing criminal activity by children and youths remains largely as iterated in the Children and Young Persons Act 1933. This provides for representation by a solicitor – legal aid permitting – but not by a GAL.

Developments leading to the Children Act 1989

An increased rate of family breakdown in the 1970s and 1980s generated such a volume of public and private family law cases that the conflicting tensions in the 1969 Act became very apparent and rapidly led to lobbying for legislative change.[26]

International developments

It would be difficult to overstate the importance of the UN Convention on the Rights of the Child (UN CRC) and the persuasive leverage of rulings of the European Court of Human Rights (ECtHR) on the timing and content of the Children Act 1989. In particular, as a signatory nation to the 1989 UN CRC, the United Kingdom was under a strong obligation to amend its laws so as to ensure compliance with Article 12:[27]

1 States parties shall assure to the child who is capable of forming his or her own views the right to express those views freely in all matters affecting the child, the views of the child being given due weight in accordance with the age and maturity of the child.

25 See *A Child in Trust: The Report of the Panel of Inquiry into the Circumstances Surrounding the Death of Jasmine Beckford*, London, London Borough of Brent, 1985 at p 253.

26 See, for example, DHSS, *Review of Child Care Law*, London, HMSO, 1985.

27 Subsequently endorsed in more emphatic terms by Article 24 of the Charter of Fundamental Rights of the European Union, which states: '1. Children ... may express their views freely. Such views shall be taken into consideration on matters which concern them in accordance with their age and maturity.'

2 For this purpose, the child shall in particular be provided the opportunity to be heard in any judicial and administrative proceedings affecting the child, either directly, or through a representative or an appropriate body, in a manner consistent with the procedural rules of national law.

Articles 13 and 14 add that a state should ensure a child has the right to freedom of expression and the right to express his or her own views. Moreover, all of this is given additional weight by the Article 3 requirement that in all actions concerning children the best interests of the child must be the primary consideration.

ECtHR rulings

The European Convention on Human Rights (ECHR), particularly the Article 8 requirement of respect for family life and related rulings of the ECtHR, was also influential in the years leading up to the 1989 Act. For example, in *W v. UK*[28] the court had emphasised the importance of timely professional representation for the parties concerned in decision-making processes regarding the care arrangements for children.

National developments

The ground for some of the changes introduced by the 1989 Act had been prepared by domestic judicial rulings giving recognition to the legal capacity of discerning children.

Gillick *competent child*

The judgment delivered by Lord Scarman in *Gillick v. West Norfolk and Wisbech Area Health Authority*[29] had established the decision-making rights of children of 'intelligence and understanding'. This sentiment was reinforced some years later in *R v. CAZ*,[30] when Lord Lane CJ acknowledged

> a change of attitude by parliament reflecting in its turn a change of attitude of public in general to the acceptability of evidence by young children and of increasing belief that the testimony of young children, when all precautions have been taken, may be just as reliable as that of their elders.

At much the same time, the Pigot Committee recommended that judges should, in exceptional cases, permit 'the relaying of questions from counsel through a paediatrician, child psychiatrist, social worker or person who

28 (1988) 10 EHRR 29.
29 [1986] AC 112; [1986] 1 FLR 224.
30 (1990) 91 Cr App R2O3 (CA).

enjoys the child's confidence'.[31] Subsequently, the Criminal Justice Act 1991 introduced the video-recording of child testimonies.

CHILD ADVOCACY ORGANISATIONS

In addition, the UN CRC and the Council of Europe were strong advocates of Children's Ombudsmen: the first was founded in Norway in 1981, while England's Office of the Children's Commissioner was finally established in 2004. All of this was indicative of growing pressure to establish children's rights and improve the capacity of the court to 'hear the voice of the child'.[32]

THE CLEVELAND CHILD ABUSE SCANDAL

Of the many high-profile child abuse scandals in the 1970s and 1980s, the removal of some 121 children from their homes in the Cleveland area by local authority social workers in 1987 following (subsequently largely dismissed) accusations of sexual abuse probably focused most public and professional attention on the need to provide effective representation and protection for children.[33]

THE CHILDREN AND YOUNG PERSONS (AMENDMENT) ACT 1986

This was an important milestone in the lead-up to the 1989 Act as it confirmed the right of a child to party status in public law proceedings as well as his or her right to legal representation.

Representation and the Children Act 1989

The Children Act 1989 came into effect in October 1991, accompanied by the Family Proceedings Rules 1991.

Representation: public law

Of all the changes introduced by the 1989 Act, the most notable has been the change to the *locus standi* of the child in public proceedings. Granting a child party status together with rights of representation by a solicitor, working in tandem with a guardian *ad litem*, together with input from a local authority

31 Home Office, *Report of the Advisory Group on Video Evidence* (Pigot Report), London, HMSO, 1989.

32 See, also, Murch, M., Hunt, J. and Macleod A., *Representation of the Child in the Civil Courts: Research Report for the Department of Health, Summary of Conclusions and Recommendations*, Bristol, Socio-legal Centre for Family Studies, University of Bristol, 1990.

33 See *Report of the Inquiry into Child Abuse in Cleveland 1987* (Cmnd 412), London, HMSO, 1988.

social worker, transformed the capacity of the court to be informed on matters relating to the welfare interests of a child. In some proceedings all three will appear, and in some only the social worker, but almost always there will be a role for at least the GAL, who will usually then appoint a solicitor.

Guardian ad litem

One of the more powerful changes brought about by the 1989 Act has been the introduction of a guardian *ad litem* (GAL) in public family proceedings to safeguard the legal interests of the child concerned. The need for that development emerged – as mentioned above – as a consequence of the inquiry into the death of Maria Colwell. A GAL is appointed by the court in public law proceedings in order, as stated in s 41(2)(b) of the 1989 Act, 'to safeguard the interests of the child', though the previous additional requirement that they do so 'until he achieves adulthood' has been omitted. A GAL is the only party in such proceedings who has this duty.

APPOINTMENT

Under s 41(6) of the 1989 Act, such an appointment must be made, regardless of the level of court (unless the court is satisfied that it is unnecessary) in all applications to make, vary, extend and discharge a care or supervision order; all proceedings relating to emergency protection orders, child assessment orders and secure accommodation; and in all appeal proceedings regarding these matters. The GAL is no longer confined to advising the court whether the local authority's application should succeed, but can also advise on possible alternatives to care, such as residence with a member of the extended family, or contact. The procedure for appointment is governed by the Rules but may be made by the court of its own motion at any stage in specified proceedings.[34]

GAL RESPONSIBILITIES

A GAL's duty 'to safeguard the interests of the child' is achieved by conducting an investigation on such interests and compiling a report to the court, which the latter 'may take account of'; copies of the report are served on the other parties. The GAL is obliged to represent the best interests of the child even if the latter holds contrary views as to what constitutes those best interests[35] and may be represented by a GAL despite his or her wishes to the contrary.[36] In so doing he or she must have regard to the paramountcy

34 The Family Proceedings Courts (Matrimonial Proceedings etc.) Rules 1991.
35 See *Oxfordshire County Council v. P* [1995] 1 FLR 552.
36 See *Re S (A Minor) (Independent Representation)* [1993] 2 FLR 437, where the Court of Appeal upheld the earlier judicial decision to overrule the wishes of an 11-year-old boy who sought to dismiss his GAL in what was a complex case.

principle and to the welfare checklist. The powers and duties of a GAL are further specified in the Rules, which require that official to:

- appoint a solicitor, if one has not already been appointed;
- give such advice to the child as is appropriate having regard to his age and understanding;
- instruct the solicitor, as appropriate;
- attend all directions appointments and hearings in relation to the proceedings;
- advise the court on certain matters;
- notify certain parties;
- serve and accept service of documents on behalf of the child; and
- carry out such investigations as may be necessary.

When conducting investigations, the GAL must, in particular:

- contact or seek to interview such persons as they think appropriate or as the court directs;
- bring to the attention of the court and of any persons the court may direct all records and documents which may in the opinion of the GAL assist in the proper determination of the proceedings; and
- obtain such professional assistance as the GAL thinks appropriate or the court directs.

The GAL is empowered to have access, at all reasonable times, to records and may seek expert advice. He or she may examine and take copies of any records held by a local authority which are relevant to the welfare of the child concerned, including adoption records, and may seek expert advice, coordinate the pooling of information from experts, and analyse the issues for the court.

A GAL remains accountable to the court, which must be appraised and its permission sought, prior to the divulging of *sub judice* matters to a third party. Their appointment is at the commencement of proceedings but involvement with the child should cease at the close of proceedings[37] or at the close of that part designated as 'specified proceedings'.[38] There can be no ongoing monitoring role. The court will not routinely make such an appointment in all cases.[39]

37 As was demonstrated in *Kent County Council v. C and Another* [1993] Fam 57.

38 See *Re S (Contact: Grandparents)* [1996] 1 FLR 158.

39 As is illustrated by the decision not to do so in *Re J (A Minor) (Change of Name)* [1993] 1 FLR 699, where it was held that a GAL could do no more than others had already done.

Solicitor

Representation, properly understood, can only be provided by a solicitor, acting on and abiding by instructions from their client, even if not agreeing with those instructions. Recognition that a GAL was not the right person to provide legal representation had been established at the time of the 1975 Act but not until 1984, following amendments to the Magistrates' Courts Rules, was provision made for the appointment of solicitors to act in tandem with GALs. Rule 14A of these Rules was amended to allow the court, when exercising its power to order separate representation, to appoint a guardian *ad litem*, and 'on the same occasion consider whether the infant should be legally represented and may direct that the guardian *ad litem* so appointed is to instruct a solicitor to represent the infant'. Alternatively, the Rules permitted the guardian to ask the court whether there should be legal representation if a solicitor for the child had not already been appointed, and then 'unless the court otherwise directs, appoint a solicitor to represent the infant'.

APPOINTMENT

Normally, a solicitor will be both appointed by the GAL and take instructions from them, unless the child is directly instructing the solicitor. Should the further appointment of counsel be necessary, it will be made by the solicitor. In certain circumstances the court is prohibited from making orders unless the child is legally represented.

A child with 'sufficient understanding' is entitled to instruct a solicitor. This is determined on the basis of whether the child fully comprehends the nature of the proceedings and appreciates their likely long- and short-term consequences. Where a child instructs a solicitor (which may occur either in specified proceedings when the wishes of a mature child conflict with those of the GAL or in private proceedings, where no GAL involvement is necessary), then such instructions must be followed even if they conflict with the solicitor's views. The solicitor must ensure that proceedings are at the child's pace and must give the child space and permission to express their views. The responsibility to equip the child with sufficient information to make an informed decision falls on the solicitor. As with any other client, the solicitor is under a general duty of disclosure to a child in respect of documentary evidence held by the solicitor in preparation for the case; but discretion is called for in the manner in which this is done.

Local authority social worker

In any public or private family proceedings, s 37 of the 1989 Act provides a broad judicial discretion for the appointment of a local authority social worker to report to the court on matters affecting the welfare of a child; where the court considers that grounds may exist for a care or supervision order, it is empowered to direct such an appointment. In public cases the local authority would almost always have initiated the court proceedings and its social worker could expect to be examined and cross-examined to justify the local authority's application for a care or supervision order. Like the court welfare officer, he or she would have no legal responsibility to represent, or act as advocate for, the welfare interests of a child.

Once appointed, the social worker then acts as the court's officer by making enquiries, compiling a report on all matters affecting the welfare of the child concerned and attending the hearing to provide such evidence as the court may require. The social worker does not act as advocate for that child; the submission made to the court in report form and/or in person is not required to represent the child's views or legal interests on the matters at issue. Where a GAL informs a local authority social worker of information regarding child abuse, given to the GAL in confidence, the social worker may disclose such information to the police.[40]

Having investigated the circumstances of the family concerned, the social worker then provides the court with background factual information on the family, its individual members, its history and present difficulties; he or she coordinates the provision of information from other disciplines and agencies and assesses the proposed future care arrangements for the child.

Representation: private law

The 1989 Act continued the traditional approach of denying a child full party status in private law proceedings, though he or she may, with leave of the court, acquire such status. In cases arising from parental separation, a court welfare officer or local authority social worker, rather than a GAL, will conduct enquiries on family circumstances and report to the court. Otherwise, the child is dependent upon the court inviting the Official Solicitor to act on his or her behalf. However, in recognition of the right to parental contact, a child with sufficient understanding of the issues involved can initiate proceedings with the court's leave for a s 8 order, and apply to make or terminate a parental responsibility order.[41]

Guardian ad litem

The role of the GAL in adoption proceedings long preceded the 1989 Act. It was probably first examined by the Hurst Committee[42] and came to be stated in Rule 14A of the Magistrates' Courts (Children and Young Persons) Rules 1970, which required the guardian to

40 See *Oxfordshire County Council v. P* [1995] 1 FLR 552.
41 See, for example, *Re CT (A Minor) (Wardship: Representation)* [1993] 2 FLR 278; [1994] Fam 49, CA.
42 See *Report of the Departmental Committee on the Adoption of Children* (Cmnd 9248), London, HMSO, 1954.

> decide how the case should be conducted on behalf of the child, and where appropriate, instruct a solicitor to represent the child; where the child is not legally represented, conduct the case on behalf of the child, unless he otherwise requests.

The Houghton Report subsequently led to a separation of the investigatory, support and supervisory role of the placing agency from the welfare assessment role of the GAL. This role was extended to care proceedings by the 1975 Act, to take effect in respect of proceedings instigated under the Children and Young Persons Act 1969,[43] but was not implemented until 1984.

Under the 1989 Act, a GAL must be appointed:

- in all private family proceedings where the court is considering making a care order;
- in any case where the court is considering making a residence or contact order for a child subject to a care order;
- in all cases concerning a possible change of name, contact, emigration or removal from the jurisdiction; and
- in all appeal proceedings regarding these matters.

If appointed, their role and responsibilities are as specified in the Rules and, in practice, much as outlined above in respect of care and protection, as are those of the solicitor and local authority social worker.

Solicitor

The appointment of a solicitor, governed by s 41 of the 1989 Act, is required to represent the child, in furtherance of the latter's best interests, or in accordance with instructions received from either child or guardian *ad litem* (see, also, Chapter 7).

Local authority social worker

In contested private proceedings, where the interests of a child are among the matters being disputed, the 1989 Act requires the court to arrange for the appointment of a local authority social worker to report to the court on all matters affecting the welfare of that child.

Conclusion

By the last decades of the twentieth century, the legal system was under serious pressure to recognise and provide effective representation for the welfare interests

43 The role and responsibilities of the GAL being outlined in s 14A of the Magistrates Courts (Children and Young Persons) Rules 1970.

of the rising numbers of children placed at risk due to family breakdown. The increased volume of cases coming before the courts was flowing from both the private sector (rates of divorce and separation were escalating) and the public sector (there had been a succession of inquiries into instances of child abuse), which together focused attention on the adequacy of state protection afforded to children following its consensual or coercive intervention into family life. Simultaneously, all involved professionals and prominent child-care organisations – such as the NSPCC, the Children's Society and Barnardo's – were aware of international initiatives and judicial rulings requiring states to provide advocacy services that would enable children to make more assertive contributions to the decision-making processes affecting their future upbringing when parental arrangements collapsed. As a consequence of these and other pressures, the preparations for the Children Act 1989 – which had been under way for many years – adopted a tougher approach towards children's rights and gave representation of their interests through the duality of the GAL/solicitor partnership – a priority which it might not otherwise have had.

7 The legal system and welfare interests

Introduction

The principle of the welfare of the child is no longer confined to the role and functions assigned to it in substantive law. It now also has a significant part to play in the legal system as it relates to matters affecting the upbringing of a child. However, identifying with any precision the nature and effect of the part it plays is problematic.

This chapter examines the modern structural role of the welfare principle as a determinant of how the legal system relates to children. It sets out to establish, as a baseline, a picture of this legal system as it stood at the close of the twentieth century, formed by a cluster of laws – primarily the Children Act 1989, the Family Law Act 1996 and the Human Rights Act 1998 – from which the twenty-first-century developments can later be measured. It primarily considers the impact made by the 1989 Act in terms of organisational change to the legal system and concentrates on outlining and examining the changes made to the consequential interpretation and application of the welfare principle. In so doing, it introduces the post-1989 era and the subject matter of subsequent chapters, but it leaves consideration of the court orders now available in public and contested private family proceedings to Chapters 8 and 9, respectively, and study of further twenty-first-century developments to the jurisdiction-specific study in the second book in the series.

The role of welfare in the legal system

The role played by the welfare principle has evolved to the point where it is fundamentally changing the way in which the legal system accommodates the law relating to children. The principle is infused throughout the system, which itself has been restructured in order to give better effect to it. Matters of substantive law, procedure and administration have, to a greater or lesser extent, been adjusted to respond to welfare indicators. It is no longer confined simply to a role in the threshold requirements for commencing proceedings and as a discretionary component in judicial disposal of such proceedings. From being previously restricted to the fabric of legislation, as a factor in or

DOI: 10.4324/9781003268512-10

the objective of a statute, the principle has now grown to assume a role that affects the organisation of courts and puts in place new court processes, new officials and new rules of evidence.

Court structure, access, proceedings and principles

The 1989 Act provided for the introduction of a concurrent system of jurisdiction covering Magistrates' Courts, County Courts and the High Court, until that jurisdiction was consolidated into the present system of Family Courts. This arrangement allowed all civil proceedings relating to a child to be consolidated and heard together, and cases to be allocated to courts on the basis of case complexity or gravity. It put in place the infrastructure necessary to facilitate ease of access to the appropriate court, greater uniformity in the use of orders and increased flexibility and consistency in court procedures, and generally to systematise the application of the civil law to the welfare needs of children. Such organisational changes were accompanied by welfare-oriented adjustments to the administration of court business. Public and private proceedings, for example, commenced in any court under the 1989 Act are to be preceded by directions hearings which, in theory, promote greater consistency and efficiency in the overall management of the means whereby the courts respond to issues affecting the welfare of children. These provide for findings of fact to be made in order to establish whether the threshold criteria, under s 31 of the Children Act 1989, have been met to justify state intervention into family life. The decisions of all courts, and the accompanying rationale, were required to be recorded, which placed a new obligation on all Magistrates' Courts to summarise the grounds for decisions reached. Similarly, the introduction of 'Family Care Centres' provided a new mechanism for reviewing efficiency and effectiveness in the conduct of court business and an appropriate forum for highlighting problems in inter-agency coordination. However, the findings from subsequent socio-legal research projects indicated that the manner and processes, the pace, the multiplicity of officials and the formality of court language and surroundings were combining to obstruct the influence of the welfare principle.[1] Although the 1989 Act gave a new priority to this principle, there remained a significant gap between its role in substantive law and in the procedures and administration established to give effect to it.

Court structure

Section 92 of the 1989 Act introduced the concept of 'family proceedings', separated such proceedings from those allocated to the Youth Court, and

1 See, for example, Booth, Dame M., *Avoiding Delay in Children Act Cases*, London, Lord Chancellor's Department, 1996. See also Plotnikoff, J. and Woolfson, R., *The Pace of Child Abuse Prosecutions*, London, DoH, 1995; Lord Chancellor's Office, *Children Act Advisory Committee Final Report*, London, HMSO, 1997.

provided for the allocation of family proceedings between the High Court (FD), County Courts and Magistrates' Courts. Much later, in 2014, the Family Court was established under s 31A of the Matrimonial and Family Proceedings Act 1984 (inserted by the Crime and Courts Act 2013), vesting a concurrent system of jurisdiction in those courts for hearing family proceedings. Ancillary legislation gave effect to this by:

- specifying those proceedings which must commence in the Family Court;
- specifying at which level proceedings must commence;
- providing for the transfer, upward or downward, of proceedings between courts; and
- establishing the Family Courts and the Family Care Centres.

THE YOUTH COURT

The jurisdiction of this court is restricted to children and youths between ten and seventeen years of age, inclusive, against whom allegations of an offence have been lodged.[2] Those within that age group alleged to have committed serious offences – murder, or charged jointly with an adult on an indictable offence – are referred to the Crown Court. The Youth Court deals with a range of cases, including antisocial behaviour, drug offences, knife crimes, theft and burglary. While the court is required to have regard to the welfare of the child or young person,[3] this is secondary to its principal aim of preventing offending.[4]

THE FAMILY COURT

A Family Court is a court of summary jurisdiction. It is a particular form of Magistrates' Court constituted by a magistrate and two members of the lay panel. These courts sit to hear proceedings brought under the Children Act 1989.

THE FAMILY CARE CENTRES

A Family Care Centre is a particular form of County Court. They hear cases on transfer from other courts and on appeal from the Family Court.

THE HIGH COURT

The Family Division of the High Court is constituted by a judge, with specialist knowledge and experience of family law, sitting alone.

2 See, further, *Re TB (Care Proceedings: Criminal Trial)* [1995] 2 FLR 801.
3 Children and Young Persons Act 1933, s 44(1).
4 Crime and Disorder Act 1998, s 7(1).

THE COURT OF APPEAL

The Court of Appeal hears appeals on issues affecting the welfare of children. Appeals on decisions of lower courts on such issues are not governed by any special rules; the appeal procedure is the same for all types of cases. As has been said:[5] 'Even if the appellate court would itself have preferred a different conclusion, it must leave the decision of first instance undisturbed unless it could say that decision was wrong.'

THE SUPREME COURT

Cases giving rise to complex issues, particularly of principle or involving international law, may occasionally be heard by the Supreme Court.

Court administration

The 1989 Act brought together for civil purposes most provisions of public and private civil law affecting the welfare and upbringing of children. Partly this was achieved by introducing certain organisational and administrative changes to the legal system, but also by relying on the integrating effect of certain unifying principles such as 'parental responsibility' and the 'paramount welfare interests of the child'. These, together with a range of new legal rules and presumptions (see below), were the most obvious of the elements used to bind together public and private dimensions of child-care law. The fact that s 8 orders were available to the court in both public and private family law proceedings commenced or continued under the 1989 Act was a useful technical device for promoting greater coherence in judicial application of the welfare principle. In the same way, the involvement of guardians *ad litem* (subsequently Cafcass) in identifying, safeguarding and representing the welfare interests of children in public proceedings, as in adoption, assisted the legislative intent to introduce greater consistency in court management of welfare-related issues (see, further, Chapter 6).

SEPARATION OF CRIMINAL AND CIVIL PROCEEDINGS

The introduction of the Children Act 1989 marked an ideological sea change in legislative intent. Whereas the Children and Young Persons Act 1969 had deliberately provided for the possibility of welfare-oriented disposal options being available to the court in respect of child perpetrators as well as child victims of criminal behaviour, where the needs of the former justified such a liberal approach, this overlap ended with the implementation of the 1989 Act. In effect, the result, as far as children were concerned, was that two legal

5 See *Bellenden (formerly Satterthwaite) v. Satterthwaite* [1948] 1 All ER 343, per Asquith LJ at p 345.

systems were established: family proceedings, in which their welfare would be accorded a paramount weighting; and criminal proceedings, where the welfare principle would be balanced against considerations of justice and public policy.

By removing all residual traces of the criminal jurisdiction from the definition of family proceedings – consigning the alleged offences of those aged between ten and seventeen years old to be addressed in separate legislation and processed through the Youth Courts – this legislation permitted the welfare principle to govern a restricted range of proceedings more fully. The legislative intent to break the ideological commitment to treating children similarly, whether appearing before the courts on proceedings grounded on their needs or deeds, where justified by their welfare interests, had been achieved: thereafter the court system had a binary structure, providing separately for children as offenders and for children in need of care and protection.

CHILDREN AND CRIMINAL PROCEEDINGS

While the welfare interests of children less than ten years of age are recognised and protected by their exemption from criminal proceedings,[6] there are continuing protests that this threshold of criminal responsibility – the lowest in Europe – is too low and should be raised, perhaps to fourteen. The Children's Commissioner and others have expressed strong reservations about the capacity of the Youth Court to respect the welfare interests of children.[7]

Welfare considerations in respect of children subject to criminal proceedings may be brought to bear at a preliminary stage – at the directions hearing, perhaps – when the criminal/family proceedings interface may be navigated and result in a child being rerouted from one set of proceedings to the other. Factors relevant in justifying such a switch would include the gravity of the alleged offence, the degree of genuine remorse expressed and the prospect of the child's rehabilitation to parental care. Welfare considerations are also evident in such provisions as:

- the prohibition on revealing the child's identity and other reporting restrictions;
- the proceedings are less formal, the public are not permitted to enter the court and defendants are addressed by their first names; and
- special measures, including ensuring that support services are available.[8]

CHILDREN AND FAMILY COURT ADVISORY AND SUPPORT SERVICE (CAFCASS)

This organisation amalgamated the services previously provided by the Family Court Welfare Service, the Guardian *ad Litem* Services and the

6 Children and Young Persons Act 1933, s 50.
7 See, for example, the 'Children in the Dock' investigative series (2019) at: www.theguardian.com/society/series/children-in-the-dock.
8 Youth Justice and Criminal Evidence Act 1999.

Children's Divisions of the Official Solicitor's Office. Established under the Criminal Justice and Court Services Act 2000, and functioning from 2001 in accordance with ancillary rules and directions of the Family Courts,[9] Cafcass is an independent, non-departmental body that is statutorily required to safeguard and promote the welfare of children in certain family proceedings. Essentially, this entails ascertaining and ensuring representation for the best interests of the children involved in proceedings for contested divorce or separation, care and protection and adoption (see, further, Chapter 6).

CHILDREN AND CARE PROCEEDINGS

A signature hallmark of the 1989 Act was its introduction of 'family proceedings', which, for most purposes, combined the public and private sectors in order to promote a consistent approach to welfare issues. Family proceedings also accommodated domestic violence proceedings commenced under the Family Law Act 1996.

Whether public or private in nature, following introduction of the 1989 Act, family proceedings are now preceded by a preliminary court hearing when the following matters are determined:

- the appropriate court;
- the timetable for the ensuing proceedings and its individual stages;
- the appointment of a guardian *ad litem* (where necessary in specified public law proceedings) or solicitor;
- the preparation and submission of any reports;
- the service of documents;
- the necessity for the attendance of the child concerned;
- the presentation of evidence, particularly that of expert witnesses; and
- the involvement of witnesses in contested proceedings.

All parties are served with notice and must attend a directions appointment or hearing unless the court directs otherwise.

All proceedings relating to a child may be consolidated and heard together in the same court. Cases may be allocated to or transferred between courts on the basis of their complexity or gravity. The wardship jurisdiction of the High Court has ceased, for most purposes, to be available for determining issues relating to the welfare of children. Private law proceedings, concerning arrangements for children following the divorce or separation of their parents, can be heard in any of the three courts. Public law proceedings will usually be heard in the Magistrates' Courts except where the gravity or complexity of the case requires a transfer to a higher court, other proceedings concerning the child are already under way in another court, or a transfer to a higher court is necessary to avoid delay.

9 See, for example, Family Proceedings Rules 2010.

Family proceedings are no longer conducted on the basis that the specific order sought in the appropriate public or private set of designated proceedings must be granted, adjourned or refused. That simplistic dynamic left an applicant in a win/lose situation and the court facing a sought order/no order choice. Now the court has a breadth of discretion in the responses available to it in any family proceedings brought before it, whether public or private and regardless of the order sought. It may either direct a local authority to conduct an investigation into a child's circumstances or make an s 8 order, instead of or in addition to the order sought, where it has concerns regarding the welfare of a child. This pick-'n'-mix approach to the making of orders concerning children has placed a broad discretionary power, reminiscent of that employed for centuries in wardship, in the hands of magistrates in all family proceedings.

At the conclusion of such proceedings the court must state its findings of fact and give the reasons for the decision it has reached, and records must be kept of findings and of decisions reached.

ADDITIONAL PROTECTION FOR WELFARE INTERESTS IN CIVIL AND CRIMINAL PROCEEDINGS

In civil proceedings, particular arrangements were made to safeguard the welfare interests of children. These included, for example:

- the separation of children from adults in police stations and courts;
- hearings could be held in camera;
- the court could be cleared;
- in care proceedings whole or part of evidence could be heard in the absence of the child concerned;
- identity could be hidden by use of serial numbers; and
- restrictions could be imposed on publishing accounts of proceedings.

However, the powers of the court in care proceedings were limited to making either a care order or a supervision order.

In criminal proceedings, restrictions were introduced to the fingerprinting of suspected children and young persons; after a finding of guilt, the court could take note of any particular welfare circumstances and use its discretion to direct a treatment rather than a punishment disposal option. Duties were placed on the court to explain the nature of care proceedings and the grounds on which they were being brought or to explain the substance of a charge to child or young person in offence proceedings and to allow representation in the case of juvenile offenders. In addition to procedural changes, adjustments were made to the rules of evidence. The rules were made more flexible to assist in promoting the objective of positively advancing the child's welfare by, for example, rendering admissible the depositions of children and increased reliance on expert witnesses.

Court access

The Legal Aid and Advice Act 1949 established the United Kingdom's first state-funded legal aid system. Although this statute was principally directed towards making divorce more accessible, its scope was almost unlimited. The introduction of legal aid to defray the expenses of representation for indigent parties in court proceedings may have generated debate on the general issue of grounds of entitlement – who should be assisted and in respect of what proceedings – and led to consideration of the merits of providing separate recognition for the needs of children, particularly where their interests conflicted with those of an abusing parent.

Access to the courts was also eased by the 1989 Act. Legal aid was thereafter granted in many family proceedings, such as applications for injunctions, ancillary relief on divorce and orders relating to the upbringing of children, subject to means and merits tests. The 1989 Act directed that legal aid be made available to the child concerned in any application for a care or supervision order, a child assessment order, an emergency protection order or for an extension or discharge of an emergency protection order.[10]

Family proceedings

Civil proceedings for determining issues relating to the welfare interests of children have traditionally been treated as those of either private law (where the matter in dispute lay between private individuals, usually family members, most often in the context of family breakdown) or public law (where the dispute lay between family and state, usually between parents and a local authority, most often in the context of a breakdown in parental responsibility). In both, the law sought to identify and be guided by the welfare interests of the children concerned and settle arrangements for their future care.

Party status

An important limitation of the 1989 Act, with direct relevance for all parties, and for the welfare of all children involved, was the denial of party status to children – accompanied by no GAL representation – in uncontested matrimonial proceedings. Otherwise, the main changes were those giving effect to the legislative intent that welfare interests be prioritised.

The child

The 1989 Act brought changes to the *locus standi* of a child in proceedings affecting his or her welfare. Thereafter the only form of civil proceedings

10 See the Legal Aid Act 1988, s 15 and the Civil Legal Aid (General) Regs 1989 as amended by the Children Act 1989, s 99.

heard in a Magistrates' Court in which a child may be made a party were 'family proceedings'. In 'specified' proceedings this was automatic and mandatory but otherwise it was to be permissible only in circumstances where the child is the applicant with leave of the court. Under the Family Proceedings Rules, in any public law proceedings, the child concerned (in addition to the local authority, parents, any other person with parental responsibility and such other persons as may be granted leave by the court to be joined) was to be automatically conferred full party status. Entitlement to full party status brought with it a right to attend court, to be represented in court and to appeal from the decision of the court.[11] It also entitled the court to compel the attendance of a child where necessary. In public proceedings the court has discretion, under the 1989 Act,[12] to waive the necessity for a child's attendance, even where the child is a party (see, further, Chapter 6).

The position of a child relative to other parties was strengthened by a number of other adjustments. The rule against admitting the hearsay of children was generally disapplied.[13] Removed also, at least in public proceedings, was the rule permitting a married person to claim a privilege exempting himself or herself from the normal obligation to make a full disclosure of information on the grounds that to do so would be self-incriminating or would incriminate the spouse.[14] Further, the welfare interests of a child acquired more protection by a new rule prohibiting any medical examination or assessment of a child without prior court approval.[15]

The Children Act 1989 imposed a duty on the court to appoint a guardian *ad litem* to represent a child in specified family proceedings[16] (see, further, Chapter 6). Where, in such proceedings, a solicitor was not retained to represent a child and the court considered such an appointment to be necessary then, subject to certain specified conditions, it could make the appointment.[17] Where a guardian *ad litem* had already been appointed it then fell to the latter to make such an appointment (under the Rules).

Arguably, the net effect of the change to the role of the child in family proceedings has been to consolidate the adversarial nature of the framework within which the welfare principle must operate. In particular the measures conferring full party status on a child, giving him or her a right to be heard by the court and providing for more assertive advocacy on his or her behalf, have served to reposition the child in the legal system as another combatant. No longer merely the subject and recipient of measures judicially determined to be in keeping with his or her welfare interests, the child – by proxy of his or

11 Children Act 1989, s 94.
12 Children Act 1989, s 95(1).
13 Children Act 1989, s 96.
14 Children Act 1989, s 98(1).
15 See Family Proceedings Rules 1991, r 18(1); Family Proceedings Courts (Children Act 1989) Rules 1991, r 18(10).
16 Children Act 1989, s 41.
17 Children Act 1989, s 41(3).

her legal representative – may now have to compete with other parties in defining the nature of such interests and in claiming an entitlement to an appropriate disposal option (see, further, Chapter 6).

Principles

The Children Act 1989 laid down a new synthesis of principles, procedures, court orders and court administration in the civil law relating to children. For most purposes, it consolidated the public and private sectors of family law insofar as these affect the care and upbringing of children.

In all family proceedings – though not in criminal proceedings – whether initiated in a public or private family law context, the same rules now broadly apply to define most aspects of the welfare principle in any judicial determination of issues relating to the upbringing of a child. These are:

- the concept of parental responsibilities;
- the new weighting given to the principle of the welfare of the child;
- other related principles; and
- the checklist criteria.

While the welfare principle provided the main tool for shaping this legislation, the concept of parental responsibilities functioned as a natural counter-balance. Other principles were also at work, and important new structures and processes were developed, but primarily the 1989 Act can be seen as being built on a foundation created by a radical juxtaposition of child welfare and parental responsibilities.

Balancing responsibilities: parents, court and local authority

In marked contrast to previous legislation, the 1989 Act specifies, partialises and differentiates the use of authority in relation to decisions affecting the welfare of children. The legislative intent behind this firm regulatory approach is that by prescribing the indicators for interpreting the welfare principle, and identifying how and when the court and a local authority should apply the principle, some parameters would then be placed on discretionary exercises of authority by both decision-making bodies.

PARENTAL RESPONSIBILITIES AND THE WELFARE PRINCIPLE

The 1989 Act, which more than three decades later continues to provide the governing legal framework for applying the welfare principle, replaced the concepts of 'parental rights' and 'parental duties', which for centuries formed the basic constructs of family law in this jurisdiction, with the composite term 'parental responsibilities'. This change signalled a profound difference of approach from a proprietorial frame of reference to one implying that parental use of authority is valid only if employed for the benefit of the child. It also suggests that such responsibilities are exclusively an attribute of parenthood which may be temporarily met by other persons or bodies but can never be wholly shed by a 'parent' to whom, by definition, they must continue to attach. Only those attributes with a functional bearing upon the nurture needs of the child, rather than those traditionally associated with the status of parent, are now held to comprise such responsibilities. The reframing of this concept allows it to play a more consistent role across both public and private family law.

The exact nature of parental responsibilities will clearly depend on the age and circumstances of the child concerned. Broadly speaking, however, 'the effect of having parental responsibility is to empower a person to take most decisions in the child's life'.[18] Bromley, more specifically, suggests that this composite term comprises at least 16 separate areas of responsibility, including those relating to:

- providing a home;
- having contact;
- determining and providing for education;
- determining religion;
- discipline;
- consent to treatment, marriage, adoption, emigration and change of surname;
- vetoing the issuing of a passport;
- taking the child outside the jurisdiction;
- administering property;
- protection and maintenance;
- representing the child in legal proceedings;
- burial or cremation; and
- appointing a guardian for the child.[19]

More than one person may bear such responsibility in respect of the same child at the same time. Having parental responsibility does not entitle the bearer to act in any way that is incompatible with a court order made under the 1989 Act in respect of the child. The mother does not lose parental responsibility merely because the father has it or because he later acquires it. Nor do either or both parents lose it when the court grants a care order to a local authority.

18 See: https://assets.publishing.service.gov.uk/government/uploads/system/uploads/attachment_data/file/1000549/The_Children_Act_1989_guidance_and_regulations_Volume_2_care_planning__placement_and_case_review.pdf at para 2.4.

19 See Bromley, P.M., *Bromley's Family Law*, 8th ed., London, Butterworths, 1992, p 301. See Chapter 1 for judicial interpretation of the role and responsibility of a parent.

THE PARAMOUNTCY PRINCIPLE

Parental responsibility is juxtaposed in the 1989 Act with the paramountcy principle. The weight and bearing of the latter is declared in s 1 as follows:

> (1) Where a court determines any question with respect to –
> (a) the upbringing of the child; or
> (b) the administration of the child's property or the application of any income arising from it, the child's welfare shall be the court's paramount consideration.

This principle, drawn initially from caselaw[20] and first statutorily stated[21] in s 1 of the Guardianship of Minors Act 1971, now governs judicial determination of all issues affecting a child's upbringing and administration of his or her property in any court where related issues arise; the principle is not restricted to proceedings commenced under the 1989 Act. It ends the uncertainty associated with the fine distinctions previously made between different statutory definitions of the welfare test. From being one among many factors to be judicially considered in family proceedings, 'welfare' was elevated by the 1989 Act to become the primary objective of such proceedings. The approach pioneered by the wardship jurisdiction has now been comprehensively endorsed. As Sir Stephen Brown P has said:[22]

> the proceedings under the Children Act are not adversarial, although an adversarial approach is frequently adopted by various of the parties. However, as far as the court is concerned, its duty is to investigate and seek to achieve a result which is in the interests of the welfare of the child … Children's cases … fall into a special category where the court is bound to undertake all necessary steps to arrive at an appropriate result in the paramount interests of the welfare of the child.

However, in addition to matters statutorily excluded as not constituting 'upbringing' or administration of property, caselaw has established some further limitations to the principle's applicability. It has been held[23] that it does not apply to the issue of whether leave should be granted to allow application to be made for a 'section 8' order under s 10 of the 1989 Act. The principle is expressly excluded from having any bearing on certain statutory procedures

20 See *J v. C* [1970] AC 668.
21 Although it had previously appeared in the UN Declaration of the Rights of the Child (1959).
22 See *Oxfordshire County Council v. M* [1994] 1 FLR 175.
23 See *Re A & W (Minors) (Residence Order: leave to apply)* [1992] 2 FLR 154. See also *Re SC (A Minor) (Leave to Seek Residence Order)* [1995] 1 FLR 96 and *Re C (Residence: Child's Application for Leave)* [1995] 1 FLR 927, both of which concerned adolescent girls.

where the main issues affect adult interests: on applications for secure accommodation orders, for child maintenance or for ouster orders; and on matters falling within the scope of Part III of the 1989 Act, s 6 of the Adoption Act 1976 or s 25(1) of the Matrimonial Causes Act 1973.

THE NO-DELAY PRINCIPLE

The 1989 Act introduced other welfare-related principles. One of these is the no-delay principle, given effect by s 1(2), as follows:

> In any proceedings in which any question with respect to the upbringing of a child arises, the court shall have regard to the general principle that any delay in determining the question is likely to prejudice the welfare of the child.

This is the first legislative statement of a principle which addresses a matter that, for some years, had been the focus of growing concern to the judiciary and child-care practitioners both within and without the United Kingdom.[24] In a number of UK cases judicial dismay had been expressed at some inordinate – and perhaps deliberately orchestrated – delays that had prejudiced the outcome of proceedings.[25] A child's 'sense of time' is not the same as that of adults and psychological damage may be caused to a child by the anxiety of protracted proceedings. Indeed, it has been claimed[26] that a child's welfare interests are better served by a wrong decision taken swiftly than the right one taken after a lengthy delay. The courts, however, do recognise that there are some circumstances in which delay may be in a child's best interests.[27]

THE NO-ORDER PRESUMPTION

Another welfare-related principle introduced by the 1989 Act was the no-order presumption, given effect by s 1(5), as follows:

> Where a court is considering whether or not to make one or more orders under this Act with respect to a child, it shall not make the order or any of the orders unless it considers that doing so would be better for the child than making no order at all.

24 See, for example, *H and O v. UK* Series A, No 120, where the ECHR ruled that by the undue delay in its litigation process, the UK was in breach of Articles 6 and 8 of the Human Rights Convention.

25 As documented in *Law Commission Report No. 172 Family Law Review of Child Law, Guardianship and Custody*, London, HMSO, 1988, para 4.55.

26 See *Re P (Minor) (Education)* [1992] 1 FLR 316, CA.

27 See, for example, *S v. S (Minors) (Custody)* [1992] Fam Law 148, where, despite the equivalent directive under the 1989 Act, it was nonetheless decided to defer making a permanent order until such time as the children concerned had time to adjust and settle down in their 'volatile family situation'.

This statement is an important declaration of principle which crystallises the minimal intervention ethic underpinning the 1989 Act. It applies equally to public and to private family law proceedings brought under that statute. The legislative intent was to replace the 'winners and losers' approach with one which instead presumes that the parties should be able to make their own arrangements outside the court. Once the matter comes before the court, the presumption will necessitate judicial scrutiny of any proposed arrangements for children to establish whether authority should be exercised by court rather than family. Only if decision-making by others is not possible, and/or it is necessary to use authority to secure a child's welfare interests, will the court intervene by issuing an order. The onus is then on the judiciary to show clearly why it would not be best for the child if no order were made.

THE LIMITING OF LITIGATION PRINCIPLE

This principle, which is also clearly welfare related, is stated in s 91(14) of the 1989 Act, as follows:

> On disposing of any application for an order under this Act, the court may (whether or not it makes any other order in response to the application) order that no application for an order under this Act of any specified kind may be made with respect to the child concerned by any person named in the order without leave of the court.

This enables the court to prevent further and unnecessary litigation on a matter upon which it has made a ruling, and so avoid exposing a child to further uncertainty and anxiety.

THE WELFARE CHECKLIST

The introduction of the checklist of considerations, in s 1(3) of the 1989 Act, all clearly welfare related, was perhaps the most emphatic and specific demonstration of legislative intent to ensure that the 1989 Act effected change in the judicial approach to child welfare. It is not a definitive list; other criteria may be added to suit particular cases. Also, individual criteria will have different weightings depending on the circumstances of each case. But it has a mandatory application not only in proceedings brought by a local authority but also in contested parental proceedings. As well as indicating the sort of outcomes the orders should strive to achieve, the legislative intent was that the checklist would promote greater consistency in judicial decisions, practitioner assessments and the overall coherence of family law. It requires the judiciary to have regard in particular to:

a The ascertainable wishes and feelings of the child concerned (considered in the light of his age and understanding);

b His physical, emotional and educational needs;
c The likely effect on him of any change in his circumstances;
d His age, sex, background and any characteristics of his which the court considers relevant;
e Any harm which he has suffered or is at risk of suffering;
f How capable of meeting his needs is each of his parents and any other person in relation to whom the court considers the question to be relevant;
g The range of powers available to the court under this Order in the proceedings in question.

The judicial importance attached to the first consideration was made clear when it was held that the court should always elicit and respect the views of a child which it may not be able to act on but which may tip the balance in a difficult case.[28] However, following the *Gillick* decision, much will depend on the maturity of the child concerned and on the possible bearing of rulings of the ECtHR. This provision gives the child the right to be heard by the court – a right which the latter may direct should be exercised by granting the child full party status with the commensurate freedom to represent his or her own interests.

The second consideration continues the law's concern that these basic common law duties of a guardian must be attended to. The judiciary have consistently singled out these attributes of good guardianship as constituting criteria for granting or removing custody. The similar requirement in respect of emotional needs merely endorses well-established judicial practice and lends statutory weight to the approach developed in this jurisdiction in wardship cases which tended to favour maternal care for very young children and paternal care for older boys. This approach has received further endorsement in subsequent rulings,[29] such as those made by Butler-Sloss LJ where she acknowledged the importance of maternal care for very small children, and particularly the importance of maintaining the bonding relationship. However, this does not amount to a legal presumption favouring such care arrangements. When considering a child's emotional needs, judicial weight will be given to the significance of sibling as well as parental relationships. Again, judicial practice in wardship cases has traditionally recognised the importance of preserving sibling relationships when determining future care arrangements for a child. Its importance was underlined in a case where Purchas LJ commented 'brothers and sisters should wherever possible be brought up together'.[30]

28 See *Re P (A Minor) (Education)* [1992] 1 FLR 316, CA.
29 See *Re S (A Minor) (Custody)* [1991] 2 FLR 388, 390, CA and *Re A (A Minor) (Custody)* [1991] 2 FLR 394, 400, CA.
30 See *C v. C (Minors: Custody)* [1988] 2 FLR 291, 302, CA.

The third consideration affecting the welfare of a child directs that judicial attention be given to the strength of a child's attachment to persons, places and things. This had only relatively recently become judicially recognised as crucial in contributing to any child's psychological development. The early acknowledgment of trauma caused by disrupting the ties between a young child and a caring parent has now been extended to include an awareness that a risk of similar trauma exists where the ties are to siblings, grandparents or other relatives and perhaps friends. The dilemma this poses for the court is apparent in the observation made many years ago by Black J,[31] who advised that when considering a minor's welfare the court 'must not only address itself to the child's present comfort and happiness but must also look forward and try to consider what is ultimately in the best interests of the child'. The tendency of the courts to favour the parent best positioned to maintain the *status quo* was evident in Ormrod LJ's observation that:[32]

> it is generally accepted by those who are professionally concerned with children that, particularly in the early years, continuity of care is a most important part of a child's sense of security and that disruption of established bonds is to be avoided whenever it is possible to do so.

This principle received further endorsement in a subsequent Court of Appeal decision[33] and now ensures that the mother retains care responsibility in the large majority of contested parenting arrangements. Again, however, it cannot be regarded as amounting to a legal presumption. The courts have occasionally granted an order to a 'snatching' parent despite the entailed trauma to the child resulting from being abruptly uprooted from a familiar environment.

The fourth consideration requires and/or permits judicial attention to be given to age and gender considerations, which have long been evident in caselaw[34] and are now given explicit statutory approval. Their significance has undoubtedly been given considerable weight by the judgment in the *Gillick* case and by the influence of the European Convention. However, it has to be said that this provision is likely to be judicially regarded as representing tacit legislative support for the established practice of awarding primary care responsibility for very young children and older girls to their mothers, where feasible, and for older boys to their fathers. Cumming Bruce LJ, for example, was acknowledging the judicial weight given to these considerations when he commented 'if all … factors are nicely balanced, then probably it is right for a child of tender years to be brought up by his or her natural mother'.[35] The

31 See *Re B (An Infant)* [1946] NI 1 at p 4.
32 See *Dicocco v. Milne* (1983) 4 FLR 247, 259, CA.
33 See *Re B (Minors) (Residence Order)* [1992] Fam 157, CA.
34 See, for example, *B v. B (Custody of Children)* [1985] FLR 166, CA.
35 See *Re W (A Minor) (Custody)* (1982) 4 FLR, 492, 504, CA.

reference to 'background' acknowledges the contention that has accompanied some 'mixed-race' placements made by statutory and voluntary agencies for fostering and adoption purposes.[36] By also including a reference to any other characteristics considered relevant the legislators have again sought to build in some of the discretionary flexibility which has characterised judicial use of wardship and enabled creative decisions to be taken in respect of children's welfare interests.

The fifth consideration imposes a requirement that the judiciary address a child's need for protection by taking into account 'any harm which he has suffered or is at risk of suffering'. Section 31(9) of the 1989 Act defines 'harm' as: 'ill-treatment or the impairment of health or development'. On the question of whether harm is significant, s 31(10) not very helpfully suggests: 'Where the question of whether harm suffered by a child is significant turns on the child's health or development, his health or development shall be compared with that which could reasonably be expected of a similar child.' Section 31(9) offers further definitions: 'ill-treatment is held to include 'sexual abuse and forms of ill-treatment which are not physical', while 'development' is 'physical, intellectual, emotional, social or behavioural development'. In addition to its application in a public family law context, 'harm' clearly has a bearing on private issues where there is evidence to show that a child has suffered or may be at risk of suffering undue emotional stress or an impairment of his or her physical, intellectual, social or behavioural development. In the past the courts have had opportunities to consider the significance of 'harm' in relation to children if custody is granted to a parent who, being a Jehovah's Witness, might refuse consent for a blood transfusion.[37] Such evidence will now play a critical role in determining an application for a residence order.

The court may consider that the harm, or the risk of it, could be alleviated by means of a family assistance order. Alternatively, where that 'harm' appears to be 'significant' then the court might well choose to direct the relevant local authority to undertake an investigation of the child's circumstances, which in turn could lead to the issue of a care order or a supervision order.

Previously, wardship was the only satisfactory means of securing the welfare of an unharmed but potentially vulnerable child but now the court may be asked to make a statutory order on the basis of an assessment of predicted risk. This type of situation has in the past often appeared before the courts in cases where immature, inexperienced and perhaps unsupported mothers have been in contest with local authorities in relation to arrangements for the future of their children. Now, this statutory measure rather than wardship is available to a court, enabling it to make an early decision before predictable harm to a child demonstrates parental incapacity and rehabilitation is proven to be unrealistic.

36 See, for example, *Re JK (Adoption: Transracial Placement)* [1991] 2 FLR 340.
37 See *Jane v. Jane* (1984) 4 FLR 712.

The sixth consideration requires the judiciary, when assessing proposed future care arrangements for a child, to pose the question: 'How capable of meeting his needs is each of his parents and any other person in relation to whom the court considers the question to be relevant?' It is probable that in framing this provision the legislators had in mind the contention generated by the influence of the principle of non-discrimination on judicial and social work practice in relation to arrangements for the custody and placement of children. The extent to which ideology may obscure an objective assessment of the parenting abilities of, for example, a very young mother, a lesbian or homosexual person, an older or disabled person, a couple of mixed race, or perhaps a member of a minority religious group has caused considerable professional and political debate and resulting media interest.

However, prior to the Same Sex Marriage Act 2014, it was in relation to the sexual orientation of a parent that this consideration had most notably exercised the judiciary. Two cases, both involving lesbian mothers, had fallen to be determined in light of the equivalent provision under the 1989 Act. In *C v. C (A Minor) (Custody: Appeal)*[38] the Court of Appeal overturned the decision of a County Court to grant custody to a lesbian mother because it considered that the judge at first instance had not taken fully into account the significance of the mother's lesbianism: that is, it was a real factor with a bearing on the welfare of the child concerned; it could not be simply discounted. However, on being remitted for a re-hearing to the High Court, the lesbian mother was granted custody. In *B v. B (Minors) (Custody, Care and Control)*[39] the court consulted expert opinion on the issue of whether being reared by a lesbian mother was likely to impair a child's welfare by blurring the latter's sexual identity or by causing the child to be stigmatised. On being advised that neither was necessarily the case and having assessed the mother as loving and mindful of her child's psychological needs, the court granted her custody. This provision also directs the court to assess the parenting abilities of any other person who may have a direct care role in relation to the child. Given the transient relationships which many children are now exposed to, this provision affords important protection in situations where the caring and long-standing relationship of a parent or grandparent may be in danger of being legally displaced by a new cohabitee.

The final consideration allows a flexible response to be made to an application for a specific order by inviting the judiciary to utilise, instead or additionally, 'the range of powers available to the court under this Act in the proceedings in question'. This enables the court to look beyond the wishes of the parties, if necessary, to find the court order – if any – most compatible with the welfare interests of the child concerned. In doing so, it may also look beyond the above checklist of considerations as this is not intended to be a definitive list. The court may, of its own initiative, make any of the following orders which are available under the 1989 Act:

38 [1991] 1 FLR 223.
39 [1991] 1 FLR 402.

- any s 8 order;
- a s 16 family assistance order (in exceptional circumstances and with the consent of every person, other than the child, named in the order);
- a s 5 order, on application, appointing a guardian for the child; or
- under s 37, it may issue a direction to the local authority requiring it to undertake an investigation of the child's circumstances (where a question arises as to the child's welfare and the court believes that a care or supervision order may be necessary).

The court may choose to exercise its authority in a way neither requested nor foreseen by the parties. It is this provision which now provides judicial access to public family law orders in private proceedings, though the responsibility for determining the appropriateness of a care or supervision order is now a matter for local authority assessment, not judicial discretion. Again, this seems to reflect a legislative intent to provide the judiciary with the range of discretionary authority which would previously have been available to them only in wardship proceedings.

Youth Court proceedings

There is a statutory obligation in Youth Court proceedings to have regard to the welfare of a child or young person, though the definition of what constitutes 'welfare' in this context remains largely as framed almost a century ago.[40] It has been held to include obligations to: secure proper provision for education and training;[41] to remove the child or young person from undesirable surroundings, where appropriate;[42] and to choose the best option for the child or young person, taking account of the circumstances of the offence. The fact that the child's parents/guardians are required to attend during all stages of proceedings, unless the court is satisfied that this would be unreasonable having regard to the circumstances of the case,[43] may be perceived as a concession to welfare considerations but is probably more indicative of the law's traditional approach of holding parents/guardians to account for their failure to exercise control over a child's behaviour.

The overriding concern of the court is governed by the public policy obligation to deter further offending. Accordingly, the requirement to have regard to the welfare of a child or young person is subject to the obligation to impose restrictions on liberty that are commensurate with the seriousness of the offence, if only to the minimum extent necessary to satisfy that obligation.

40 See, further, Sentencing Council guidelines at: www.sentencingcouncil.org.uk/wp-content/uploads/Sentencing-Children-and-Young-People-definitive-guideline-Web.pdf.
41 Children and Young Persons Act 1933, s 44.
42 Ibid.
43 Children and Young Persons Act 1933, s 34A.

Conclusion

The 1989 Act changed the role, functions and weighting of the welfare principle in the substantive civil law relating to children radically as well as specifically and comprehensively. It firmly confined its application to civil cases: children alleged to be the perpetrators rather than the victims of criminal offences were diverted away from the welfare-oriented family proceedings court. Within the latter court, unlike the former, the welfare interests of a child are assured of being formally awarded priority over other considerations in public and private family law proceedings. The impact of the principle can also be seen in the restructuring of the courts and in the creation of the many new rules and professional roles which now govern the passage of proceedings.

However, the accompanying procedural and administrative changes have been introduced more to expedite proceedings and coordinate professional input than to further the welfare interests of the children concerned. The structures and processes of the legal system remain essentially adversarial, allowing it to retain its traditional reliance upon precedent, contest and adjudication as the preferred means of conducting business. The continuity of these embedded traditional hallmarks raises the question whether the legal system was appropriately responding to the requirements of the welfare principle.

Part 3

Applying the child welfare principle in the Late 20th century: Public and Private Family Law

8 Public family law

Prevention, protection, care and control

Introduction

Welfare is a relative term. By the end of the twentieth century, however, the Children Act 1989 had brought greater clarity to the legal interpretation of the welfare principle by introducing clear distinctions: firstly, between criminal and civil law; and secondly, as regards the latter, by establishing two strategic thresholds – 'children in need' (a consensual threshold for state intervention in family child-care responsibilities) and 'significant harm' (its coercive counterpart). Both of these thresholds were then clarified by statutorily specified indices of matters constituting 'welfare' in their respective contexts.

This chapter, in the main, examines the developing role of that principle in proceedings for care, protection, supervision and control in the years following the commencement of the 1989 Act. It considers ancillary measures relating to preventative intervention, the promotion of child welfare and local authority responsibilities in respect of children placed for adoption. It also provides an overview of welfare in a criminal context, where it naturally has a much more constrained role. By providing a snapshot of the legal functions of the welfare principle, as defined and deployed mostly under the provisions of the transformative 1989 Act, it establishes the benchmarks against which further developments in the early decades of the twenty-first century – outlined and analysed in the second book in this series[1] – may be measured.

The chapter begins by considering the preventative and promotional functions that give effect to the welfare principle by measures that require the state to boost the coping capacity of parents and families prior to focusing on the main functions of care, protection and control. It takes as its primary themes the prescriptive but negative duties owed by first and third parties to a child in relation to objectively stated circumstances. These circumstances are defined by the fault or default of a person owing a duty of care to a child. State intervention most often occurs after the duty has been breached. The determination of that which is held to constitute a child's welfare is in

1 O'Halloran, K., Children and the Law*: Shaping the Modern Welfare Principle in the British Isles*, Abingdon, Routledge, forthcoming.

DOI: 10.4324/9781003268512-12

accordance with statutorily prescribed indicators together with certain judicial and agency criteria as interpreted and applied by those professionals with a duty to advise the court. A statutory, if uncertain, weighting is given to the wishes of the child in determining his or her welfare. The selection of the most appropriate disposal option is accompanied by a degree of discretion. Finally, the chapter explores the remit of the Youth Court and the extent to which criminal proceedings are impacted by the welfare principle.

Prevention and promotion

Traditionally, when the law had to authorise intervention to safeguard the welfare of a child from circumstances, activities or relationships identified as being prejudicial to his or her interests, it did so by removing or insulating the child from that harmful context. A neglectful parent or an exploitive form of employment, relationships of a contractual or sexual nature, the availability of alcohol, drugs, cars, cigarettes and fireworks and many other sources of harm were (and often still are) legally addressed by removal of the child, either literally or by the use of legal prohibitions.

Concept and function

'Prevention' and the more aspirational 'promotion' are positive legal functions giving effect to a modern interpretation of the welfare principle in a public family law context. The initial iteration of a state preventative duty surfaced in the Children and Young Persons Act 1933, as amended by the 1952 Act, which required the authorities to 'cause enquiries to be made' into any circumstance suggesting that a child was 'in need of care or protection'. This duty was subsequently embodied largely in Part III of the Children Act 1989. The two functions represent the consensual intervention threshold 'children in need', operationalised through the general and specific responsibilities placed on local authorities to provide services for children and their families. They may be viewed as conceptual opposites, both equally removed from the welfare principle's cutting edge of coercive intervention. They are additions, representing legal refinements to the traditional welfare threshold, governed equally by the Children Act 1989.

'Prevention' requires action to avoid any further deterioration in the circumstances of a particular child or children such as might otherwise result in a breach of the welfare threshold. It identifies a form of state intervention that rests in the main on a negative monitoring of child-care standards and on a defensive resource input. As a public law function, it neither authorises nor seeks to achieve anything further than the maintenance of the basic welfare threshold, and it is predicated on a principle that welfare is best assured by parental care. Although a relatively new addition to public law, it has been given a broad and consolidated application under the 1989 Act.

'Promotion' is a function with little application in a public law context. It requires action to create opportunities for enhancing the welfare of a particular child or children whose circumstances are already above the coercive intervention threshold. As such it requires the degree of authority, freedom of choice and command of resources appropriate to a person or body vested with parental responsibility. Precisely because it is a function which comes into play only when the choice to be made is intended to achieve more than the mere maintenance of the welfare threshold, it belongs to private rather than pubic law. While local authorities do have responsibilities to promote the welfare of children in accommodation under a care order and in relation to those placed for adoption, the scattered statutory references in the 1989 Act to promote welfare are otherwise without any specific functional content.

The two functions' joint significance lies in the fact that, following the introduction of the 1989 Act, which built upon foundations laid 30 years earlier,[2] they now ground a legislative intent to require local authorities to provide the support and safeguards necessary to retain and protect the child within a context which carries some risk of harm but is otherwise beneficial to their welfare interests.

Duty of the state to assist children and families

The broad socio-legal context of contemporary paternalistic state assistance for children and their families evolved from the ancient *parens patriae* responsibilities of the Sovereign for the welfare of their more vulnerable subjects (see Chapter 1). It now provides an important backdrop to any view of the particular functions of prevention and promotion. There are several significant features to this backdrop: firstly, the framework of services that constitute the present 'welfare state'; secondly, the influence of the United Nations Convention on the Rights of the Child and the ensuing caselaw precedents established by the European Court of Human Rights; thirdly, the special protection afforded a child in relation to particular circumstances, activities and products; and finally, the legal standing of children in certain areas of civil law.

THE WELFARE STATE

The framework of national services developed after the Second World War under the guidance of Sir William Beveridge continues to make a vital contribution to the preventative and promotional functions of the welfare principle. Without the basic underpinning provided by such services as health, housing, education and child support, the level of poverty and ill-health would be such as to make any discussion regarding the legal role of the welfare principle totally beside the point. The effectiveness of this contribution

2 See the Children and Young Persons Act 1969.

has been made much more focused and potent by the present requirement under the Children Act 1989 that, where possible, the services should be coordinated to address the circumstances of a child in need when so requested by a local authority.

THE UNITED NATIONS CONVENTION ON THE RIGHTS OF THE CHILD 1989

Ratified by the United Kingdom in 1991, the UN CRC is exercising an increasingly important influence on the legal system of this jurisdiction. Primary responsibility for the upbringing and the development of children is ascribed to parents. Article 18 of the UN CRC requires that 'State Parties shall render appropriate assistance to parents and legal guardians in the performance of their child-rearing responsibilities ... [and] ensure that children of working parents have the right to benefit from child care services and facilities for which they are eligible'. Similarly, Article 27 requires State Parties to 'recognise the right of every child to a standard of living adequate for the child's physical, mental, spiritual, moral and social development'. This has become a benchmark document against which present and potential UK family law legislation must be tested.

GENERAL PROTECTION LAW

The law providing protection for children – in relation to specific circumstances, activities and products – is evident across a vast range of disparate statutes, each dealing with a specific product or circumstance known to pose particular dangers. These statutes include: the Protection of Children (Tobacco) Act 1991 and the Licensing Act 1964, which, respectively, prohibit the sale of tobacco and alcohol to children; the Horses (Protective Headgear for Young Riders) Act 1990, which makes it an offence for a child to go horse-riding without head protection; the Tattooing of Minors Act 1969, which makes it an offence to tattoo a person under the age of 18; and the Explosives (Age of Purchase etc.) Act 1976, which seeks to prevent the sale of fireworks to children. These statutes have in common a prescriptive approach to welfare, in which a breach of a particular aspect of the welfare threshold constitutes an offence. The provisions are directed towards the actions of an offender, the related proceedings are concerned with prosecution, and the child is very much the object rather than the subject of legislative intent.

The law imposing a duty on others to respect the welfare interests of children because of their relative lack of competence is to be found in three key areas of civil law: tort, contract and employment.

Tort In tort, the law gives recognition to the vulnerability of children through such means as imposing on others a particular duty of care when dealing with them, by requiring others to be aware of the dangers that an 'allurement' might present to a child and by restricting their use of corporal punishment. The corollary to this legal recognition of third-party duties is that the law also requires parents to protect a child from entering situations where he or she could incur harm and a third party incur a related liability.

Contract In contract, the law is relatively clear. Generally speaking, minors are held not to have contractual capacity. Again, this rests on a child's presumed lack of competence and reflects a concern to protect children from financial harm and third parties from incurring liability. However, in the light of the *Gillick* ruling together with those in the criminal arena – such as in the Bulger case – the presumption of incompetence can be rebutted.

Employment In employment, the general and universalist protective measures designed to regulate the circumstances in which young persons, as opposed to children, could be employed remain as articulated in ss 18–21 of the Children and Young Persons Act 1933.[3] These provide that no child shall be employed:

a so long as he is under the age of 13 years; or
b before the close of school hours on any day on which he is required to attend school; or
c before seven o'clock in the morning or after seven o'clock in the evening on any day; or
d for more than two hours on any day on which he is required to attend school; or
e for more than two hours on a Sunday; or
f to lift, carry or move anything so heavy as to be likely to cause injury to the child.

Other legislation prohibits the employment of children in a range of specific settings, such as shops, mines, factories, ships and quarries. Where children can be employed, their employment is subject to certain conditions. The first of these rests on the definition of 'child' as 'a person who is not over school-leaving age', which in turn means 'the upper limit of school-leaving age'. This implies that it is the actual age at which a particular child is entitled to leave school, rather than a standard application of the 16-year rule, which is all important. In effect, this will vary from 15 years and 8 months to 16 years and 7 months. Restrictions on the employment of children in the performing arts are the subject of detailed provisions in the 1933 Act and the Children

3 See also the Employment Act 1989. Also note Article 7(3) of the European Social Charter, which states that 'persons who are still subject to compulsory education shall not be employed in such work as would deprive them of the full benefit of their education'.

and Young Persons Act 1969. Basically, a licence will have to be obtained from the relevant local authority before children can be so employed.

The Children Act 1989: consensual statutory intervention

The 1989 Act placed a clear but minimalist responsibility on local authorities in respect of the welfare threshold. Central to the Act is the requirement that support be given to vulnerable parenting arrangements and that a child's relationship with the members of his or her family of origin should be safeguarded. This finds expression in three different approaches. Firstly, the legislative intent is to preserve the legal integrity and privacy of the family unit wherever possible. This is to be achieved by restricting coercive intervention to circumstances where a local authority can convince the court that evidence exists to overcome the 'no-order' presumption and to satisfy the 'significant harm' test. Secondly, the legislative thrust was for parents and local authority to work in partnership to secure the welfare interests of children. In furtherance of this aim the local authority is required to make certain support services available to parents. Finally, specific importance is attached to maintaining a child's links with the members of his or her family of origin. To this end, a duty is placed on a local authority to promote the upbringing of children by their families and to promote contact between a child and his or her parents in circumstances where a child is being accommodated by that authority.

Legislative intent is given effect through two different sets of provisions. Those in the first set are 'universalist' in nature in that they have a broad application to all children and essentially continue the established responsibility of local authorities to maintain an overview of service spread and related standards and to ensure the protection of children in certain circumstances. Those in the second set place new specific duties on a local authority in relation to the support requirements of vulnerable family units and thereby positively discriminate in favour of 'children in need'[4] (see below).

Prevention: the broad support responsibilities of a local authority

The Children Act 1989 outlined a local authority's preventative responsibilities in respect of children who, without support, might become 'children in need'. This may be seen as establishing a minimum baseline from which a local authority may ratchet up the deployment of its consensual and coercive intervention resources. They consist of certain powers which are employed at

4 See Utting, D., *Family and Parenthood: Supporting Families, Preventing Breakdown*, York, Rowntree Foundation, 1995. This revealed that preventative services continued to be concentrated on parents whose children are on the child protection registers rather than those identified as vulnerable due, for example, to family pressures or material deprivation. There was little evidence that the anticipated partnership between statutory and voluntary agencies had generated any effective strategies for targeting localised preventative services towards vulnerable families.

local authority discretion to alleviate the difficulties of those whose circumstances are not so extreme as to satisfy the 'children in need' test (see below). They also consist of certain duties which a local authority owes in general to the children resident in its area. These support responsibilities are an important means of giving effect to the preventative function of the welfare principle. However, the requirement imposed on a local authority is not to put in place support services but merely to regulate such provision as may be made by others. The families and children using such services are assured that quality standards will be set, inspected and reviewed but, necessarily, the availability and financial accessibility of such services are also determinants of this function's effectiveness. The fact that regulatory requirements apply only in respect of children aged eight years and under (instead of twelve years, as in Northern Ireland) is also a limiting factor. In effect, the powers and duties of local authorities under the 1989 Act in relation to support services largely take the form of registration and monitoring responsibilities in respect of privately run day-care, child-minding or private fostering facilities for children.

CHILD-MINDING AND DAY CARE

The protection afforded a parent who privately places a child with persons providing child-minding or day-care services is governed by ss 17, 18 and 19 of the 1989 Act and is provided by the system of registration, certification, notification and inspection. These are implemented through duties placed on the local authorities under Part X (ss 71–79) of the 1989 Act and under the Act's Guidance and Regulations.[5] They provide for a duty to register and thereafter inspect any domestic premises used for child-minding purposes within a local authority's area. It is the place as much as the person that must be registered and, therefore, where a person provides day care in more than one place, separate registration is required for each place. There are certain requirements to be met by child-minders if they are to be registered by their local authority. These include provisions relating to the total number of children, the number within each age group, the safety of the premises, the keeping of records and the equipment to be provided. The powers and responsibilities of the local authorities in relation to the inspection of registered premises and the working arrangements within are outlined.

It is the service per se, rather than the service as it affects an individual child, which is the subject of these provisions. As a result, a person providing care for more than two hours in a day, even if no individual child is being looked after for more than one hour and no charge is made, will come within these statutory controls.

5 See Department of Health, *Family Support, Day Care and Educational Provision for Young Children*, vol 2, London, HMSO, 1991.

In determining whether the service meets the criteria for registration, a local authority will assess the fitness of the care provider and the fitness of the premises separately. Whether a person is fit to provide a child-minding or day-care services will be determined according to the advice of the Department of Health in the Guidance and Regulations. In making an assessment, a local authority will have regard to such matters as:

- previous experience;
- qualifications and training;
- ability to provide warm and consistent care;
- multi-cultural awareness;
- capacity to treat each child as an individual;
- physical health;
- attitudes; and
- the existence of any criminal record involving the abuse of children.

These criteria must be applied not only to every applicant seeking registration but also to all persons living or working on the premises to be registered. Whether premises are fit for the purpose of child-minding or day care will also be determined in accordance with the advice provided by the Department of Health within the above-mentioned Guidance and Regulations. In making its assessment, a local authority will have regard to such matters as the suitability of the premises in relation to its situation, construction and size.

Under s 71 of the 1989 Act, certain persons may not be registered as either a child-minder or a day-care provider. The reasons relate to prescribed offences, orders and requirements made under this or other prescribed provisions. An application for registration will be refused if the applicant, or any person living in or employed on the premises to be registered and who may be involved in caring for children, is 'not fit to look after children under the age of eight' or, in certain circumstances, is 'not fit to be in the proximity of children under the age of eight'. Breach of this requirement may ground an action for negligence.[6]For example, registration was refused to a Mrs Davis,[7] a graduate with primary-school teaching and child-minding experience, because she refused to comply with the 'no-smacking' requirement in the Guidance on the Children Act 1989. Yet, the parent had given permission and smacking was then viewed as not constituting a breach of Article 3 ('Inhuman and Degrading Punishment') of the UN CRC.[8] Moreover, as Wilson J observed, in relation to the status of the Guidance, it 'is not intended to be applied so strictly that, if an application for registration is in conflict with part of it, there should automatically be a finding of unfitness'. Clearly, though, neither Mrs Davis nor the parent could now hope to succeed

6 See *T v. Surrey County Council* [1994] 4 All ER 577.
7 See *London Borough of Sutton v. Davis* [1994] 1 FLR 737.
8 See also *Costello-Roberts v. UK* [1994] ECR1 and *R v. Hopley* (1860) 2 F & F 202.

in similar circumstances, which highlights how the indicators for interpreting 'welfare' change over time.[9]

Under s 11, a local authority may also refuse registration if the premises to be used for child-minding or day care are 'not fit to be used for looking after children under the age of eight, whether because of their condition, or the condition of any equipment used on the premises or for any reason connected with their situation, construction or size'.

PRIVATE FOSTER CARE

Part IX (ss 66–70) of the 1989 Act deals with the responsibilities of a local authority in relation to private arrangements for fostering children.[10] Under s 66(1), a 'privately fostered child' means a child who is cared for – and provided with accommodation – by someone other than:

(i) a parent of his;
(ii) a person who is not a parent of his but who has parental responsibility for him; or
(iii) a relative of his.

Section 66(1)(b) defines the term 'foster a child privately' somewhat circuitously as meaning to 'look after the child in circumstances in which he is a privately fostered child'.

For the purposes of this provision, 'a child' means a person under the age of 16 or, if he or she is disabled, under the age of 18. To meet the definition, the child must be cared for and accommodated for a period of at least 28 days. These and the other provisions of Part IX dealing with private arrangements for fostering children are subject to further redefinition under Sched 8, the effect of which is to harden the distinction between domestic and fostering arrangements.

Responsibility for ensuring that the arrangements made do in fact safeguard and promote the welfare of the child concerned rests with the parent. Under s 67, a local authority is responsible for ensuring that the welfare of any child privately fostered in its area is being 'satisfactorily safeguarded and promoted' and that those providing care are appropriately advised. In respect of any proposed private fostering arrangement, the persons making the arrangement, making the placement and receiving the child must all serve advance notice of their intentions on the local authority. The latter must then investigate the suitability of any arrangement prior to placement and is

9 Note also that in England and Northern Ireland the right to physically chastise a child is now prohibited in public facilities (schools, etc.) and relegated to private family law – where it remains a parental right – while it is prohibited in both public and private law in Scotland.

10 Further detail is given in the Children (Private Arrangements for Fostering) Regulations 1991.

required to carry out inspection visits thereafter. A local authority may stipulate requirements in respect of the number, age and sex of the children who may be privately fostered and it may require special equipment and medication to be available. Further, Sched 7 of the 1989 Act includes private foster-parents within its strictures relating to limits on the number of foster-children and related complaints procedures.

Children in need: the threshold for consensual state intervention

The 'children in need' concept is intended to place both an onus on a local authority to be proactive in seeking out such children and a duty to target sufficient resources to maintain them, where practicable, within their families. The legislative intent is that the role of a local authority, in relation to its preventative responsibilities, should be to develop a needs-led rather than a demand-led approach to service provision. This approach is very much in keeping with that advocated in Article 18 of the UN CRC, which emphasises the desirability of state intervention being in the form of partnership with parents so as to enable them to give effect to their parental responsibilities.

This concept sets the threshold for consensual intervention by a local authority in family affairs on child welfare grounds, just as 'significant harm' does in respect of coercive intervention. Eligibility for preventative support services has been tied to the former threshold. Once the threshold criteria are met, the welfare principle comes into play. The statutory requirement that local authorities be proactive in seeking out and offering assistance to those in need, without any inference that the latter are at fault for their circumstances, provides a positive legal reference point for the welfare principle's preventative function. The singular legal characteristic of this threshold is that it mandates state intervention *before* the welfare principle is compromised, rather than retrospectively *after* a child has suffered significant harm.

'Children in need' are defined under s 17(10) of the 1989 Act as follows:

> For the purposes of this Part a child shall be taken to be in need if –
>
> (a) he is unlikely to achieve or maintain, or to have the opportunity of achieving or maintaining, a reasonable standard of health or development without the provision for him of services by a local authority under this Part;
> (b) his health or development is likely to be significantly impaired, or further impaired, without the provision for him of such services; or
> (c) he is disabled, and 'family', in relation to such a child, includes any person who has parental responsibility for the child and any other person with whom he has been living.

This provision reflects a legislative intent to incorporate a number of not wholly compatible objectives. For example, a primary objective would seem to be to place inclusive service responsibilities on a local authority, so certain categories of need are 'defined in'. At the same time, though, it is apparent that there is a wish to avoid granting reciprocal service entitlement rights to those who may meet this definition, so there is a lack of specificity in defining eligibility criteria.

The provision specifies three different categories of 'children in need'. Firstly, there are those children who are 'unlikely to achieve or maintain ... a reasonable standard of health or development', etc. Under s 31 (9) of the 1989 Act, 'health' is to be interpreted as meaning 'physical or mental health' and 'development' as 'physical, intellectual, emotional, social or behavioural development'. The significance of the word 'unlikely' is that it clearly imports a requirement that a local authority acts in a preventative fashion to forestall the prospect of a child becoming a 'child in need'. The legislative intent is to prompt local authorities to correct the approach they had previously adopted towards their preventative and protective duties. In order to redress the balance struck in favour of resource investment for the latter at the expense of the former (on the grounds that this may prove to be a more cost-effective form of intervention in the long run) a firm duty is now placed on local authorities to ensure the early identification of children in need, including the disabled, and, by providing services appropriate to their health and development, promote the upbringing of such children by their families. Experience indicates that this provision is being interpreted as a licence to lower the 'significant harm' threshold, thus allowing agency resources to be targeted at those already within the ambit of coercive intervention, rather than as an obligation to prevent private vulnerable parenting arrangements from becoming matters of public concern.[11] As Eekelaar and Dingwall have observed, there is a tendency towards 'diagnostic inflation' in child protection cases in order to access resources.[12]

Secondly, the provision identifies those children whose 'health or development is likely to be significantly impaired', etc. Again the 'likelihood' factor implies that a duty rests on local authorities to invest resources in a preventative strategy. However, the degree of risk necessary to constitute a likelihood and the extent to which an 'impairment' may need to deteriorate before this becomes 'significant' are both open to question. It may be that a local authority could offer a good defence for not investing preventative resources by claiming that its interpretation of a situation did

11 This is apparent, for example, in Table 3.1 of the annual *Children Act Report* (1992), which shows that, in the first year of the Act, local authorities were directing resources towards families for whom they already had some level of responsibility rather than towards those whose vulnerability was indicated only by difficulties such as rent arrears, disconnected services or school attendance problems.

12 Eekelaar, J. and Dingwall, R., *The Reform of Child Care Law – a Practical Guide to the Children Act 1989*, London, Routledge, 1990.

not lead it to believe that, relative to other situations already within its child protection remit, the level of risk or the significance of probable impairment warranted a diverting of funds.

Finally, the provision classifies 'disabled' children as being 'in need'. Under s 17(11) of the 1989 Act, 'disabled' means 'blind, deaf or dumb or suffering from mental disorder of any kind or is substantially or permanently handicapped by illness, injury or congenital deformity or such other disability as may be prescribed'. The inclusion of children who are disabled within the general definition of children in need is an important landmark in the development of the law relating to children. It reflects an acceptance of the principle that, for children, a recognition of what they share in common by virtue of their childhood is of greater importance than that which may, for whatever reason, separate them.[13] Legislating specifically for the difference between 'normal' and disabled children, and then among disabled children on the basis of disability type, is now seen as stereotyping and constituting a form of discrimination which can be associated with a degree of stigma and is unacceptable in a modern pluralist culture. However, differentiating between children on the basis of the gravity of their needs within the same legislation is seen as acceptable. To that extent, this provision does positively discriminate in favour of children in need.

IDENTIFICATION OF CHILDREN IN NEED

Sched 2 of the 1989 Act requires that every local authority shall take reasonable steps to identify the extent to which there are children in need within its area. A local authority is empowered to assess the needs of any child appearing to be a 'child in need' at the same time as any assessment is being made under any other statutory provision. The 'shall take reasonable steps' requirement emphasises the obligation on local authorities to be proactive rather than reactive in the delivery of their preventative services.

Children in need: the duties of a local authority

The service provision duties of a local authority in respect of vulnerable children are restricted to those whose circumstances bring them within the definition of 'children in need'. Intervention, whether consensual or coercive, is now statutorily authorised only in respect of prescribed welfare thresholds. Once authorised, intervention places both general and particular duties on local authorities.

13 It also reflects the principles embodied in Article 23 of the United Nations Convention on the Rights of the Child 1989.

GENERAL DUTIES

These are stated in s 17(1) of the 1989 Act as follows:

> It shall be the general duty of every local authority (in addition to the other duties placed on them by this Part) –
>
> (a) to safeguard and promote the welfare of children within their area who are in need; and
> (b) so far as is consistent with that duty, to promote the upbringing of such children by their families,
>
> by providing a range and level of services appropriate to those children's needs.

The use of the word 'general' is intended to indicate that the duty on a local authority is to plan and deliver services broadly appropriate to the needs which vulnerable children – as a group – would have in common. Its effect is to statutorily overrule the decision in *AG (ex rel Tiley) v. London Borough of Wandsworth*,[14] which determined that a local authority would be expected to anticipate the consequences of its actions for the welfare of a particular child. In that case the agency was held to be liable to a claimant who, having met the agency-specified eligibility criteria, had nonetheless been denied the corresponding service.

The first such duty is towards children in need, but each individual child may also be a 'child at risk of significant harm'. Such an overlap of thresholds may occur in situations where it comes to the attention of a local authority that a child who is especially susceptible to harm (perhaps due to 'special needs') is exposed to a level of stress which, though insufficient to require protection for an 'average' child, carries a significant level of risk for that particular child. An assessment by a local authority social worker of a breakdown in parenting arrangements occurring in a public or private context may reveal no statutory duty of coercive intervention but may alert the local authority to the presence of a particularly vulnerable child for whom the 'family' requires support services.

The second general duty is to promote upbringing within families. 'Family', as defined in s 17(10), includes any person with whom the child has been living, whether or not a relative. It will not extend to include a person – relative or friend – with whom the child has not been living, no matter how close the relationship. This very wide definition will apply to situations where direct care responsibility for a child has been borne for some time by a carer such as a neighbour, foster-parent or relative, such as a grandparent. Any service that serves to safeguard and promote the welfare of a child may be provided to the 'family' as a whole or to any individual member of it.

14 [1981] 1 All ER 1162.

The third of the general duties is to provide a range and level of appropriate services. It is a duty to which it is the collective responsibility of the constituent parts of a local authority to respond; because any or all of its services may be required, a multidisciplinary team approach is envisaged. This is also likely to have important consequences for entitlement in other areas: that is, success or failure in meeting the terms of the definition will trigger an entitlement to all or none of the spectrum of such related public services as housing and benefits. Under s 27 of the 1989 Act, a number of agencies are directed to cooperate with a local authority requesting assistance for any child in need:

> (2) An authority whose help is so requested shall comply with the request if it is compatible with their own statutory or other duties and obligations and does not unduly prejudice the discharge of any of their functions.
> (3) The authorities are –
> (a) any local authority; ...[15]
> (c) any local housing authority; ...
> (d) any clinical commissioning group, Local Health Board, Special Health Authority, National Health Service trust or NHS foundation trust; and ...
> (e) any person authorised by the Secretary of State for the purposes of this section.

For such reasons, full implementation of the 1989 Act could be successful only if accompanied by a local authority child-care policy and strategy that prioritised the management of integrated teams of health and social service professionals, accompanied by systems for coordinating its service provision with that of other public service agencies, including those listed above.

PARTICULAR DUTIES

The 1989 Act imposed nine separate and specific preventative duties upon a local authority. These were mostly permissive; only a few were mandatory. The prescriptive directives are those with a more marginal bearing on welfare, such as the strict duty to publish information. Of considerable significance to the modern role of the welfare principle is the legislative definition of 'family' and therefore the range of persons whom a local authority should consider when assessing possible service provision to children in need. This public law recognition that persons who bear direct care responsibilities for a child are thereby entitled to local authority assistance, regardless of whether they are related to the child in any way, greatly widens the potential of the welfare principle to consolidate the *status quo* care arrangements of children in

15 (b) was repealed by the Local Education Authorities and Children's Services Authorities (Integration of Functions) Order 2010.

circumstances that may be far removed from the marital nuclear family that traditionally qualified for state protection.

The first preventative duty is to provide assistance. This may be provided as a cash grant, a loan or a grant of 'necessities' and may be subject to such conditions as a local authority shall see fit to impose. Further, as outlined in Sched 2 of the 1989 Act, more specific assistance may be offered.

Secondly, under Sched 2(9), a local authority has a duty to provide such family centres as it considers appropriate within its area for a child, parents of that child, or person with parental responsibilities who may be caring for that child. The facilities offered by such a family centre should include: occupational, social, cultural or recreational activities; advice, guidance or counselling; and accommodation while receiving advice, guidance or counselling. In relation to disabled children, Sched 2(6) requires a local authority to provide services to minimise the effects of their disabilities and opportunities to lead lives that are 'as normal as possible'.

Thirdly, a local authority is statutorily obliged to take steps to avert the necessity for coercive intervention in family care arrangements. The directive in s 17(1)(b) that a local authority should seek to 'promote the upbringing of such children by their families' is an important statement of principle which serves to reinforce the 'no-order' presumption embodied in s 1(5). It is further addressed by a directive in Sched 2(7) requiring every local authority to 'take reasonable steps' to reduce the need to bring proceedings in respect of children, encourage them not to commit criminal offences and avoid the need to place them in secure accommodation.[16]

Fourthly, the preventative duties of a local authority are specifically addressed by Sched 2(4)(1), which requires that: 'Every local authority shall take reasonable steps, through the provision of services under Part III, to prevent children within their area suffering ill-treatment or neglect.' Similarly, Sched 2(4)(2) places a duty on any local authority which believes that a child within its area but living (or proposing to live) elsewhere is likely to suffer harm to notify the relevant local authority accordingly.

Fifthly, a local authority must make certain provisions to enable children to remain at home. Sched 2(8) places a duty on a local authority to provide the following services, as appropriate, in respect of children in need who are living with their families:

(a) advice, guidance and counselling;
(b) occupational, social, cultural or recreational activities;
(c) home help (which may include laundry facilities);
(d) facilities for, or assistance with, travelling to and from home for the purpose of taking advantage of any other service provided under this Order or of any similar service;

16 See also the local authority preventative duties introduced by the Crime and Disorder Act 1998.

(e) assistance to enable the child concerned and his family to have a holiday.

This is the first explicit legislative statement of the services considered appropriate to the role of a local authority in the context of consensual intervention. It indicates the extent of public investment now considered reasonable in order to reinforce the coping capacity of vulnerable families.

Sixthly, where a child in need is not living with his or her family and is being accommodated, but not being looked after by a local authority, then Sched 2(10) requires the latter to take such steps as are reasonably practicable to enable the child to live with that family or promote contact between them if, in the opinion of the local authority, this is necessary to safeguard or promote the child's welfare.

Seventhly, alternative accommodation may be provided for any member of a household posing a risk to a child in that household. Sched 2(5) of the 1989 Act gives a local authority a discretionary power to provide financial assistance to enable a person who may be causing a child to suffer, or who may do so in the future, to find alternative accommodation away from that child. This provision acknowledges the long-standing sense of grievance attached to the practice whereby, in order to afford future protection to a child at risk of abuse from a member of the household, the child was removed from the home. The fact that this is a discretionary responsibility and not linked to a local authority power to apply for an exclusion order in respect of such a suspected abuser has attracted criticism.

Eighthly, under Sched 2(1)(2) of the 1989 Act, every local authority is required to publish information about the support services it has a duty to provide for children in need and their families. It is also permitted to do so in respect of such services provided by other agencies, particularly by voluntary organisations, which it has a power to provide. Every local authority is specifically directed to 'take such steps as are reasonably practicable to ensure that those who might benefit from the services receive the information relevant to them'.

Finally, under Sched 2(11), when making arrangements for day care or for the recruitment of foster-parents, every local authority shall 'have regard to the different racial groups to which children within the local authority's area who are in need belong'.

LIABILITY FOR NON-PROVISION OF SERVICES

A local authority's plea of insufficient finance in *AG (ex rel Tiley) v. London Borough of Wandsworth*[17] was found to be an inadequate defence to the charge that it had failed to meet the claimant's statutory entitlement to support services. However, subsequent caselaw indicates a steady judicial retreat

17 [1981] 1 WLR 854.

from this position.[18] In *R v. Cambridge District Health Authority ex parte B (No 2)*,[19] the Court of Appeal acknowledged that the court was not empowered to review the basis upon which a local authority elected to use its resources; the latter was entitled to prioritise the services it was prepared to fund as it saw fit. Nor does the court have any power to direct a local authority to recognise a child as being 'in need' within the definition of s 17 for the purposes of ensuring a service entitlement.[20]

Children in need: specific support services

The linking of welfare to a range of specified family support services is another indicator of the positive legislative influence on the modern role of the welfare principle. This objectification of incidences of welfare, allowing them to become a listing of duties owed to children, also has a negative history dating back at least to the mid-nineteenth-century criminal law of child cruelty and neglect. In respect of most services listed in the body or schedules of the 1989 Act, a claimant may clear the first hurdle by satisfying the threshold criteria only to fall at the second when their claims are nullified by a local authority's considered decision not to exercise a discretionary duty in favour of that claimant. The two main sets of specific support services relate to day care and accommodation.

DAY CARE

This type of support service is defined by s 18(4) of the 1989 Act as: 'any form of care or supervised activity provided for children during the day (whether or not it is provided on a regular basis)'. In this context 'supervised activity' 'means an activity supervised by a responsible person'. A local authority's basic preventative strategy will rest on the range of services it has available to help and support those children in need who are resident in its area and their families. This usually involves providing direct financial assistance; alternatively, it may involve a local authority paying for places with child-minders, play groups or family centres.

In relation to pre-school children, s 18 places on local authorities a strict duty to provide appropriate day care for children in need within their areas who are under the age of five and not at school but only a power to provide day care for other children of that age who are not in need. In relation to school-aged children, the duty similarly placed is to provide day care outside school hours and during school holidays for those in need and attending

18 See, for example, *Re C (Family Assistance Order)* [1996] 1 FLR 424, where the court was forced to discharge the order on being informed that the local authority lacked the resources to comply with it.

19 [1995] 1 FLR 1055.

20 See *Re J (Specific Issue Order: Leave to Apply)* [1995] 1 FLR 699.

school, while it may also do so for those who are attending school but not in need. A local authority is required to have regard to any local day-care services provided by the appropriate local education authority or other body or person when exercising its functions under this provision. A local authority is empowered to provide such facilities as training, advice, guidance and counselling for persons caring for or accompanying children in day-care settings.

Section 19 makes elaborate provision for reviews and review procedures in relation to day-care services. These must include registered child-minding services and other day-care services provided by registered persons. Every local authority must conduct a comprehensive review of day-care services provided in its area in respect of children under the age of eight. The review should take account of services provided in schools, hospitals and other such establishments which are exempt from the registration requirements; the local authorities are themselves exempted from registration requirements. It should be conducted in conjunction with the appropriate local education authority or other body at three-year intervals. The results of each review, including information about any proposals affecting the day-care services, must then be published as soon as is reasonably practicable.

ACCOMMODATION

The provisions relating to accommodation restore the initial basis of the voluntary admission to care service. They comprise one of the most tangible expressions of the new partnership between parents and a local authority and one with considerable potential for the welfare principle. Section 20(1) of the 1989 Act imposes the following duty:

> Every local authority shall provide accommodation for any child in need within their area who appears to them to require accommodation as a result of –
>
> (a) there being no person who has parental responsibility for him;
> (b) his being lost or having been abandoned; or
> (c) the person who has been caring for him being prevented (whether or not permanently, and for whatever reason) from providing him with suitable accommodation or care.

Furthermore, s 20(3) states:

> Every local authority shall provide accommodation for any child in need within their area who has reached the age of sixteen and whose welfare the authority consider is likely to be seriously prejudiced if they do not provide him with accommodation.

Because this duty rests so unequivocally on the voluntary consent of all parties, an objection from a parent or someone with parental responsibility will relieve a local authority of its obligation to provide accommodation. A discretionary power exists under s 20(5) enabling a local authority to provide accommodation for a person between the ages of 16 and 21 where it considers that to do so would safeguard or promote his or her welfare. The general duty of a local authority to coordinate its activities in respect of children in need with those of other statutory and voluntary agencies finds specific expression in s 27. Among the agencies required to lend their cooperation to a local authority is any local housing authority.

The legislative intent in s 20(1)(c) and (3) is clearly to grant a right to homeless young persons (at least to those aged 16–18) to claim accommodation from their local authority. A corresponding duty is placed jointly on that local authority and the local housing authority to make such provision. The indications (from Shelter, the national charity for the homeless, and New Horizon, the oldest such charity in the UK) are that this provision, which was specifically designed to assist such children in need, is not being fully implemented. This age group is debarred from claiming Universal Credit. The availability of accommodation to destitute and homeless young adolescents who are unable to claim welfare benefits could be of crucial importance. In theory, such persons now have the right to make their claims against the appropriate local authority, which in turn (if convinced that the young person's welfare is likely to be 'seriously prejudiced') will be obliged to act jointly with the local housing authority to meet those claims.[21]

Caselaw[22] has established that a housing authority has no duty to provide accommodation for a homeless family under housing legislation. However, it is clear that such a duty does arise under child-care legislation if the application comes not from a family but from a local authority on behalf of that family. In a case where a local housing authority had refused to consider a local authority's request for accommodation for a family of five children whose parents had rendered them intermittently homeless, the court held that the refusal was wrong. The housing authority must consider the request and must comply with it unless compliance would be incompatible with its own obligations and/or it would unduly prejudice the discharge of any of its functions. It was not enough that the housing body had decided that the request did not meet its own criteria.

21 See *R v. Northavon DC ex parte Smith* [1993] 2 FLR 897, which seemed to continue the rationale of *AG (ex rel Tilley) v. Wandsworth London Borough Council* [1981] 1 WLR 854, where it was held that it was not possible to set aside a duty to provide for a child and family purely on the basis that they had been found to be intermittently homeless.

22 See the House of Lords decision in *R v. Oldham Metropolitan Borough Council ex parte Garlick and Related Appeals* [1993] 2 FLR 194, where the court held that a local housing authority had no duty to a homeless dependent child under Part III of the Housing Act 1985.

Section 21 requires a local authority to receive – and provide accommodation for – children who have been removed or kept away from home under a child assessment order or who have been taken into police protection.

Parents, if they satisfy the aforementioned eligibility criteria, are to be provided with relief as of right without any implication that they have been in any way deficient or at fault (evidenced also by the phrase 'for whatever reason') in the execution of their parental duties. The accommodation must be the subject of a written and signed agreement between the parties. At no time do the parents lose – and nor does the local authority acquire – any parental responsibilities. The child is not 'in care' and may be removed by the parent/s, or by someone with parental responsibility (under s 20(8)), from local authority accommodation at any time. If the child has reached the age of 16 then, under s 20(11), he or she may not be removed from such accommodation without his or her consent.

The 1989 Act transformed the role of a local authority in relation to a claimant and the provision of accommodation services. In theory, there can be no question of a local authority assuming parental responsibilities, and possibly initiating freeing proceedings for adoption, in respect of a child voluntarily admitted to its care. Indeed, technically, a local authority no longer has the right to delay – let alone deny – a parental request for the immediate return of a child for whom it is providing accommodation. However, the requirement in s 22(3)(a) that any authority (e.g. a local authority), when looking after any child (e.g. by the provision of accommodation), should 'safeguard and promote his welfare' may permit a local authority to resist such a parental request until satisfied that compliance would not be in breach of that duty. Alternatively, under s 3(5)(b), the local authority, having care but not parental responsibility for the child, would be entitled to 'do what is reasonable in all the circumstances of the case for the purpose of safeguarding or promoting the child's welfare'. If all else fails, a local authority could always call upon the police to exercise their powers under s 46(1)(b) to prevent the removal of an accommodated child in circumstances where there is reasonable cause for a constable to believe that such a removal would be likely to expose the child to significant harm. In short, a local authority has legal routes for retaining a child in its care and, having done so, may by way of a concurrent placement eventually extend that route towards adoption.

Section 20 also makes some stipulations regarding the position of the child to be accommodated. In particular:

> (4) A local authority may provide accommodation for any child within their area (even though a person who has parental responsibility for him is able to provide him with accommodation) if the authority considers that to do so would safeguard or promote the child's welfare.

A local authority is thereby granted maximum discretion to interpret whether, in relation to any particular child, the proposed accommodation would meet the welfare interests of that child. It may have a particular application to private family law circumstances where, for example, either or both parents are so absorbed in mutual acrimony while pursuing divorce proceedings that neither objects to the child's wish to be accommodated elsewhere. Under s 20 (6) a duty is placed on a local authority, insofar as is reasonably practicable and consistent with the child's welfare, to ascertain and give due consideration (having regard to the child's age and understanding) to the latter's wishes before providing accommodation. If that child is aged 16 or more and consents to being accommodated (and if this is judged to be necessary on welfare grounds), or to being discharged from accommodation, then a local authority is obliged to give effect to that consent regardless of any opposition from a parent or elsewhere. If anything, the legal situation has firmed since the decision in *Krishnan v. Sutton London Borough Council*,[23] when the court refused to discharge a child against her wishes to the care of her father.

The position regarding the ascertained wishes of a child aged under 16 is less certain. Much would depend on the extent to which such a child could be judged to be *Gillick* competent. However, given that this provision rests on the consent of all parties, it is unlikely that the wishes of a child under the age of 16 would be allowed to prevail in the face of parental opposition.

Child protection

Legislative concern to provide for the protection of children in circumstances of abuse or neglect at the hands of their parents or third parties represents the earliest expression of the welfare principle and continues the most basic function of the law relating to children. This function is essentially reactive and negative in nature as it is usually activated after the welfare threshold has been breached and a child harmed. It is most often given effect through the removal of the child concerned from a familiar environment (which may contain supportive as well as harmful relationships). As it is designed and utilised to deal with the effects of a welfare breach, in itself it does nothing to address the causes.

Children at risk of significant harm: the threshold for coercive state intervention

The principle of the welfare of the child has always required, as a basic minimum, that protection be given to the bodily integrity of a child. The role played by the principle in public family law proceedings commenced to secure protection for a child is now governed almost exclusively by the provisions in Part V of the 1989 Act. These authorise coercive state intervention in the affairs of a family by a local authority and/or certain others.

The phenomenon of child abuse is most often represented by domestic maltreatment in the form of a physical or sexual assault on a child by a

23 [1969] 3 All ER 1367.

member of that child's immediate family, a close relative or a family friend. The legal response in civil law is provided by s 43(1)(a) of the 1989 Act, which categorises a child as abused when he or she 'is suffering, or is likely to suffer, significant harm'. 'Harm', under s 31(9), encompasses both ill-treatment (which 'includes sexual abuse and forms of ill-treatment which are not physical') and the impairment of 'health' (i.e. physical or mental health) or 'development' (i.e. physical, intellectual, emotional, social or behavioural development).

The child

In this context a child is defined as someone who has been born but has not yet reached the age of 18 – a definition which caselaw has consistently held to exclude a foetus.[24] However, in recent years, this exclusion has been examined and significantly reinterpreted by the House of Lords in judgments which seem to indicate a trend with profound implications for extending the application of the welfare principle.[25] An emerging thread of logic suggests that harm inflicted upon a pregnant mother, and the subsequent birth of a child suffering ongoing impairment directly resulting from that harm, would be sufficient to ground proceedings against the perpetrator of the harm alleging liability for impairing the welfare interests of the child. There has also been much media speculation as to the prospect of maternal accountability for a child born with a health impairment caused by the mother's excessive smoking, drinking, etc. while pregnant. The viability of this approach received a setback with the decision of the Scottish courts in *Kelly v. Kelly*[26] that an estranged husband had no right to intervene – as 'next friend' of his unborn child – to prevent his wife from having an abortion. However, the trend towards viewing the welfare interests of a mother and her very young child as inextricably fused has been hardening.

While a breach of the welfare threshold will activate child protection proceedings, it also continues to attract criminal law sanctions. The 1989 Act, understandably, did nothing to lessen the fundamental conflict between the legal system's obligation to protect the welfare interests of a child and to ensure that the requirements of criminal justice are satisfied. The latter has always remained grounded on general considerations of public interest, has

24 See, for example, the judgment of Sir George Baker in *Patton v. Trustees of British Pregnancy Advisory Service* [1979] QB 276.

25 See *D (A Minor) v. Berkshire County Council* [1987] 1 All ER 33, where the House ruled that for the purposes of care proceedings, it may be appropriate to take into account a mother's treatment of her child while it was still a foetus in the womb. See also *Attorney-General's Reference (No 3 of 1994)* [1997] 3 WLR 421, which ruled that a cohabitee was guilty of manslaughter following the death of a child some three months after its premature birth due to injuries sustained when it was still a foetus in the womb.

26 [1997] 2 FLR 828.

assiduously guarded against any obscuring or diminution of a defendant's rights and has insisted on a high standard of proof to secure a conviction. This continues to sit uncomfortably alongside the individualised welfare interests of a child. Where, as is most often the case, a child is involved as a witness in criminal proceedings instigated against his or her alleged abuser, this conflict is glaringly evident, with welfare interests routinely subordinated to justice considerations and often seriously impaired as a consequence. More often than not, the interests of justice can be satisfied only by an examination of the evidence of the child concerned – including probing his or her character, motives and previous experience – as that child is the only witness to the alleged abuse. An inevitably distressing experience will be made harrowing where the child is required to give evidence against an abusing family member. Affording some immediate safeguards for the welfare interests of a child witness while also allowing for measures that will, in the long term, minimise the destruction of relationships upon which that child is psychologically dependent and permit rehabilitation within his or her family is among the most serious challenges now facing all professionals working in the field of child protection.

The professional response recognises and differentiates between four different types of abuse: neglect; physical abuse; sexual abuse; and emotional abuse.[27]

NEGLECT

The liability of a parent, a person with parental responsibility or someone with *loco parentis* standing for any harm which befalls a child as a consequence of their failure to afford him or her an adequate standard of care or protection is well established. Traditionally, this liability arose in circumstances where the failure in parenting was associated with low standards of care, maintenance or safety, due perhaps to poverty, immaturity or parental incapacity resulting from illness, injury or learning disability. The introduction of the 1989 Act saw this liability assimilated within the definition of 'harm' in s 31(9), allowing it to be grounded equally on the fault or default of a culpable person.

It has always been the actual consequences for the child – not the intentions of the carer – which are of primary concern to both local authority and court. The standard of child care required is judged objectively in the sense that the measure applied is that of a hypothetical caring parent: that is, no allowance can be made for the fact that the actual parent is too young, inexperienced or distressed to cope any better. The standard applied is also subjective in the sense that the level of care expected from such a parent is that

27 See *Working Together under the Children Act 1989: A Guide to Arrangements for Inter-agency Co-operation for the Protection of Children from Abuse*, London, HMSO, 1991.

actually required to meet the particular needs of the child in question: that is, the fact that the level of care provided would be adequate for an average child is irrelevant if the child in question requires a higher standard of care due to a disability, for instance.

Evidence of parental failure to provide, or permit others to provide, essential medical treatment for a seriously ill child has repeatedly been found sufficient to ground court intervention.

PHYSICAL ABUSE

As has been said: 'Physical abuse implies physically harmful action directed against a child; it is usually defined by any inflicted injury such as bruises, burns, head injuries, fractures, abdominal injuries or poisoning.'[28] This is the most frequently recorded form of abuse. The legal issues are most often relatively straightforward as evidence in the form of injuries and testimonies from victim and perpetrator are readily available. However, it is the deliberate harm inflicted by a well-intentioned parent, or someone acting on his or her behalf, for the purposes of disciplining a child that gives rise to most contention. The common law right[29] of a parent to administer 'moderate and reasonable chastisement' governed the law in this difficult area for centuries but it is no longer held to be justifiable for a parent in Scotland or in Wales[30] to demonstrate disapproval of a child's unacceptable behaviour and to discourage its repetition by physically chastising that child. Paradoxically, it was acceptance of its status as a legal incidence of parenthood that enabled the European Court of Human Rights to rule in favour of parent petitioners who objected to the use of corporal punishment in state schools.[31]

The issue as to if and when third parties have a right to administer such chastisement arose for consideration in an ECtHR[32] case concerning a seven-year-old boy who had been punished by his headmaster. The chastisement took the form of three strikes on his bottom, through his shorts, with a rubber-soled gym shoe. The boy alleged breach of Article 3 of the European Convention of Human Rights 1950. The ECtHR held that the following factors should be considered in determining whether or not a breach had occurred:

- the nature and context of the punishment;
- the manner and method of its execution;

28 See Kempe, C., Silverman, F., Steele, B., Droegmueller, W. and Silver, H., 'The Battered-Child Syndrome', *Journal of the American Medical Association, 181* (1962), pp 4–11.
29 See *R v. Hopley* (1860) 2 F&F 202.
30 Prohibited in Scotland since January 2020 and in Wales since 2022.
31 See *Campbell and Cosans v. UK* (1982) 4 EHRR 293.
32 See *Application No. 13134/87* (1993). Also note Article 37 of the UN Convention on the Rights of the Child, ratified by the UK in 1991.

- its duration;
- its physical and mental effects; and, in some cases,
- the sex, age and state of health of the victim.

It was decided, by a majority verdict of five to four, that the punishment had not been so severe as to constitute a breach of Article 3. The ECtHR also decided, this time unanimously, that the punishment had not adversely affected the child's physical or moral integrity to a degree that would have constituted a breach of Article 8 (respect for private and family life) and held that the applicant had an adequate route to a remedy under domestic law. The headmaster was found to have been acting within the scope of his *loco parentis* responsibilities, as, subsequently, was a child-minder[33] who admitted smacking a child in her care but with parental permission. However, a stepfather[34] who had beaten a nine-year-old boy on more than one occasion, causing bruising on his legs and bottom, was found to have inflicted excessive punishment that breached Article 3.

Despite these cases, in England[35] and Northern Ireland reasonable parental chastisement continues to be regarded as coming within the legally permitted parameters of Article 3.

SEXUAL ABUSE

This is recognised in s 31(9) of the 1989 Act as constituting a specific form of ill-treatment and has been defined as follows:[36]

> Sexual abuse is defined as the involvement of dependent, developmentally immature children and adolescents in sexual activities they do not fully comprehend and to which they are unable to give informed consent or that violate the social taboos of family roles.

It might be added that the definition of sexual abuse is not dependent upon comprehension on the part of the child; nor does the presence or absence of comprehension detract from the culpability of the abuser.

The media attention given to serious abuse by predatory paedophiles resulted in the introduction of the Sex Offenders Act 1997, with its mandatory requirement for the registration of all future convicted offenders. In fact, however, the perpetrators are more likely to be parents or other family members than strangers. The main legal problems in securing future protection for the welfare interests of a child victim of alleged sexual abuse have been related to satisfying the standard of proof and providing sufficient corroborative evidence.

33 See *London Borough of Sutton v. Davies (No 2)* [1995] 1 All ER 65.
34 *A v. United Kingdom (Human Rights: Punishment of Child)* [1999] 2 FLR 959.
35 The Children Act 2004, s 58.
36 See Schechter, M. and Roberge, L., 'Sexual Exploitation', in Helfer, R. and Kempe, C. (eds), *Child Abuse and Neglect*, Cambridge, MA, Ballinger, 1976, pp 127–142.

The normal standard of proof, resting on the balance of probabilities, applicable in all civil proceedings, also applies to cases of child sexual abuse. However, the courts have tended to place a heavy burden on the party alleging such abuse to produce a convincing weight and range of evidential material in support of the allegations. The House of Lords examined this approach in what became a leading case[37] on the standard of evidence applicable in cases of alleged sexual abuse. This was a case which rested on the single issue of whether the elder of four sisters had been sexually abused by her stepfather, who had been acquitted of rape on that issue. The court subsequently had to consider an application for care orders in respect of the other three sisters on the grounds that they were 'likely to suffer significant harm' (as per s 31(2)) if the orders were not made. Having considered different possible interpretations of the requisite standard and reviewed related caselaw, the House concluded that the correct rule was to apply the simple balance of probabilities test. The ruling in *In re H and R (Child Sexual Abuse: Standard of Proof)* also serves to underline the basic obligation of applicants in such cases to discharge the burden of proof lying on them to show that the child concerned is likely to suffer significant harm; this requires actual evidence.

In the absence of an admission of guilt, allegations of child sexual abuse present the court with greater difficulties than other forms of abuse. In the words of Browne-Wilkinson LJ: 'Child abuse, particularly sex abuse, is notoriously difficult to prove in a court of law. The relevant facts are extremely sensitive and emotive. They are often known only to the child and to the alleged abuser.'[38] There is a school of thought[39] which holds that this ruling has raised the threshold of proof by requiring a somewhat higher standard of evidence in sexual abuse cases and that this therefore works to the disadvantage of children's welfare interests. But, in fact, the courts have for some years been more assiduous in their demands for proof in this category of case than in relation to other abuse cases and this ruling seemed more likely to stem than increase any tendency towards incrementally raising the standard of proof. The grievousness of the consequences for the child, as much as for the perpetrator, of a finding of guilt in such cases cautions against any relaxation in the existing standard. Reliance solely on the testimony of a victim is particularly fraught with legal difficulties. Corroboration must be sought in the form not only of medical evidence but also in verifiable psycho-social disturbance.

A central issue in *In re H and R* was whether, even if abuse had occurred in respect of one child, it would provide sufficient evidence to ground a finding of risk of future abuse to that child's siblings. As Browne-Wilkinson LJ stated:[40]

37 See *In re H and R (Child Sexual Abuse: Standard of Proof)* [1995] 1 FLR 643.

38 *Re H (Minors) (Sexual Abuse: Standard of Proof)* [1996] AC 563 at para 8.

39 See Fortin, J., *Children's Rights and the Developing Law*, London, Butterworths, 1998, pp 383–387.

40 *Re H (Minors) (Sexual Abuse: Standard of Proof)*, op cit at para 4.

> If legal proof of actual abuse is a prerequisite to a finding that a child is at risk of abuse, the courts will be powerless to intervene to protect children in relation to whom there are the gravest suspicions of actual abuse but the necessary evidence legally to prove such abuse is lacking.

The House of Lords held that the issue of whether the girl's siblings were exposed to 'harm, or the likelihood of harm ... attributable to ... the care given to the child, or likely to be given to him if the order were not made, not being what it would be reasonable to expect a parent to give to him' (as per s 31(2)(b) of the 1989 Act) was not dependent upon the initial finding. The two parts of this provision may stand separately: 'the likelihood of future harm does not depend on proof that disputed allegations are true' (as per Lord Lloyd of Berwick). In principle, it was possible for the court to find that a risk of future abuse existed to a child's siblings despite there being insufficient evidence to confirm past abuse in respect of the child concerned.

EMOTIONAL ABUSE

This type of abuse was clearly intended for inclusion within the 'forms of ill-treatment which are not physical' for the purposes of s 31(9) of the 1989 Act. Like neglect, emotional abuse is more frequently a sin of omission than commission. Unlike neglect, it has gained legal recognition as a form of abuse, requiring coercive state intervention to protect a child's welfare interests, only comparatively recently. Whether resulting from deprivation or deliberation, emotional abuse, like all other forms of child abuse, is a consequence of the misuse by adults of the authority they bear as such in their relationships with children. Once the level of abuse breaches the threshold of significant harm it satisfies the grounds for coercive intervention by a local authority or 'authorised person'. The consequent problems in providing sufficient evidence to convince the court of a cause-and-effect linkage between a child's emotional disturbance and the particular conduct of a specific adult are well established. This form of abuse, which may take the form of an absence of normal behaviour rather than an infliction of the abnormal (e.g. parental refusal to talk to a child), can often present the most difficult challenge for the professionals and judiciary seeking to protect a child's welfare interests.[41]

Ascertaining child abuse

The intervention threshold is set by the legal benchmark 'significant harm', as defined in s 31(9) of the 1989 Act. Only a breach or suspected breach in this

41 See, for example, *Re M and R (Child Abuse: Evidence)* [1996] 2 FLR 195, CA, where the Court of Appeal upheld the finding of emotional abuse by the court at first instance and the making of interim care orders.

threshold will authorise representatives of the public interest in the welfare interests of children to investigate private standards of care.

INVESTIGATION

Both the court and a local authority may initiate an investigation. Under s 37 of the 1989 Act, the court in the course of any family proceedings may require a local authority to conduct an investigation of a child's circumstances with a view to determining whether grounds exist to make application for a care or supervision order. This is an important discretionary power which provides the judiciary with a capacity to direct intervention for child protection purposes. It is supplemented with a power to make an interim care or supervision order pending the results of the investigation. Under s 47 of the 1989 Act, a local authority has a duty to investigate when it has reason to believe that a child in its area is suffering, or is likely to suffer, significant harm.

Mandatory reporting of actual or suspected incidents of child abuse – an uncontroversial public law requirement for the protection of children's welfare interests in other modern western societies – is not part of the law in this jurisdiction.[42] However, failure to disclose knowledge of criminal conduct to the proper authorities is itself an offence. An informant is entitled to have his or her anonymity protected by the investigating local authority.[43] Once a referral has been received then, under s 47(9), certain specified agencies have a duty to assist a local authority in its enquiries 'by providing relevant information and advice'.

The child must be seen by the investigating officer from the local authority and, if the child is of sufficient age and understanding, should be interviewed in relation to the presenting issues. The stress of interview may further compromise a child's welfare. Butler-Sloss LJ offered guidance in the Cleveland Report on interviewing children[44] and subsequently observed: 'Generally, it is desirable that interviews with young children be conducted as soon as possible after the allegations are first raised, should be few in number and should have investigation as their primary purpose.'[45]

The decision whether or not to place the name of a child on the child protection register is taken at a multidisciplinary case conference after evidence has been heard from all professionals who have been involved with the child. Factors determining registration are: certainty that abuse or neglect has occurred; its seriousness; the characteristics of the parents indicating a future risk to the child; and chronic concern on the part of community agencies. The

42 Although local authority social workers and police officers are under a mandatory duty so to report.
43 See the House of Lords ruling in *D v. NSPCC* [1977] 1 All ER 589.
44 See *Report of the Inquiry into Child Abuse in Cleveland 1987* (Cmnd 412), London, HMSO, 1988.
45 See *Re M (Minors) (Sexual Abuse: Evidence)* [1993] 1 FLR 822.

main function of the register is to provide a central record of those children defined by a panel of inter-agency professionals as currently in need of an inter-agency protection plan.

As a means of facilitating the protection of a child's welfare interests, it is doubtful whether placing his or her name on such a register achieves very much. Research findings indicate that this practice provides little assurance that, thereafter, effective professional intervention will ensure either adequate protection for the child concerned or appropriate support services for the family.[46] The link between a local authority's investigative/coercive intervention duties and its powers under Part III (specifically, the link between ss 47 and 17 in which the circumstances described and the services are the same) may not be readily made.[47] Alternatively, s 17 enquiries are seen by some professionals as a 'passport to services'.[48]

ASSESSMENT

Under the 1989 Act, the legislative intent is to provide a local authority with a broad range of options at the conclusion of its protective procedures.

An investigating local authority may determine that a child is vulnerable but the significant harm threshold has not been breached. The local authority will then consider whether the circumstances are such as to require it to treat the child as coming within the definition of 'in need'. If so then this will give rise to a duty under s 17 to provide a 'range and level of services appropriate to those children's needs'. This, in effect, is a decision that the impairment of welfare interests does give rise to a public interest in the quality of care arrangements but is such as to require consensual rather than coercive intervention. Again, a local authority investigation may conclude that a child is vulnerable, the significant harm threshold has not been breached but no one person has parental responsibility for the child. Then, in keeping with the 'family care is best' principle, that authority could support a private proceedings application from a suitable member of the family for a s 8 order (e.g. a child arrangements order). The local authority itself has no right to apply for a s 8 order.

A local authority may decide that there is cause for concern and more time is needed for a thorough investigation. Under the 1989 Act, it will then consider whether an application for an interim care order or a child assessment order will best enable it to complete its enquiries. Although both orders are

46 See: Bell, S., *When Salem Came to the Boro*, London, Pan Books, 1988; Gough, D., *Child Abuse Interventions*, London, HMSO, 1993; and Corby, B., *Working with Child Abuse*, Milton Keynes, Open University Press, 1987.

47 See Gibbons, J. et al., *Operating the Child Protection System: A Study of Child Protection Practices in English Local Authorities*, London, HMSO, 1995, where a study of CPRs revealed that in more than 50 per cent of the cases, though a finding had been made of grave concern, no services were provided.

48 See Eekelaar and Dingwall, op cit, on the subject of 'diagnostic inflation'.

public family law measures, they each allow a local authority to hold a fairly neutral position in relation to the child and family and permit the *status quo* care arrangements to continue while enquiries are pursued.

Alternatively, it may decide that although there is sufficient cause for concern to warrant commencing proceedings under Part IV of the 1989 Act, it will not do so. A local authority has discretion to decide whether or not a child whom it has found to be in need of protection should be brought before the court. While s 47(8) places an onus on an investigating local authority 'to take action to safeguard or promote the child's welfare', this duty is conditional upon it being 'within their power' and 'reasonably practicable' for the local authority to do so. A local authority will, therefore, be justified in concluding that although the significant harm test is satisfied, it will not commence proceedings as it would not, for example, be in a position to allocate the necessary staff and/or resources to implement any order granted. It is clear that such an exercise of local authority discretion will not be open to judicial challenge.[49] Where it decides not to initiate any court proceedings, a local authority must nevertheless consider whether it should review the case at a later date. In the event of it determining that such a review would be appropriate then, under s 47(7), it must fix a date for that review.

This discretionary capacity of a local authority, enabling it to choose not to respond to a breach of the welfare threshold, was wholly new. The discretion appeared to give a local authority the ability to circumvent the public interest by not using coercive intervention powers in circumstances for which they were legislatively provided. The protection of children's welfare interests, in circumstances where they may have suffered or could be at risk of suffering significant harm, by the public agency specifically vested with child protection duties came to rest on the discretionary decision of the latter to bring the matter to court. The law could offer no protection to a child unless the relevant local authority elected to initiate proceedings, and it could impose no sanctions on the local authority which chose not to do so.

Where there is clear evidence of significant harm and it is 'within their power' and 'reasonably practicable' for it to do so, then the local authority is required to initiate the appropriate proceedings. It may do this by ensuring that appropriate care arrangements are made for the children concerned away from the family home. The local authority may achieve the latter either on a consensual basis by 'looking after' such children within the meaning of s 27, on a coercive basis by applying directly for a care order or supervision order, or it may need to intervene coercively and immediately using the powers of Part V.

49 See, for example, *Nottinghamshire County Council v. P (No 2)* [1993] 2 FLR 134, CA and *Re S and D (Children: Powers of Court)* [1995] 2 FLR 456, CA. But see also the implications arising from the judgment of the ECtHR in *Osman v. UK* [1999] 1 FLR 193.

Protection: the principles and consequences

As the Court of Appeal has firmly emphasised,[50] coercive intervention is not permissible unless and until the threshold criteria of 'significant harm' have been met. In many, if not most, cases, it will be found that this threshold has not been breached, or, if it has, that the breach is repairable and ongoing local authority intervention is unnecessary. Only when there is evidence to substantiate a breach sufficient to require displacement of parental or other authority will state intervention be justified. Welfare under the 1989 Act, unlike under the 1969 Act, is seen first and foremost as a matter for the family, not the state.

Proceedings commenced under Part V of the Children Act 1989 are excluded from the s 8(4) definition of 'family proceedings'. When hearing Part V proceedings the court is unable to make any s 8 order – neither on its own motion nor in response to an application. It can only make or refuse to make the order applied for with the exception that it may make an emergency protection order instead of a child assessment order. When considering an application for an order under Part V (rather than a s 8 order or an order under Part IV) the court must have regard to the paramountcy principle but is not required to apply the 'welfare checklist'. Child protection is statutorily set aside to facilitate urgent professional intervention and prompt judicial determination as to whether or not emergency powers should be used to secure a child's immediate protection. However, the actions of the court are governed by the 'no-delay' principle, the 'no-order' presumption and the requirement to draw up a timetable to expedite the proceedings.

The sense of urgency, characteristic of these proceedings, prompted the Court of Appeal[51] to rule that such applications should not be delayed by an unduly legalistic analysis of whether or not the presenting evidence fully satisfied the significant harm test. However, in a judgment which overturned the approach in *Newham*,[52] the House of Lords fully restored significant harm as a condition precedent in applications for an emergency protection order, a child assessment order or an order for the police to exercise their powers of protection.

REMOVAL FROM HOME

Traditional child protection practice, entailing the removal of the child concerned, ensured that it had at least one serious consequence for the subject's welfare interests. This 'child rescue' approach wrenched the child from his or her home and network of positive relationships as well as from the source of abuse. The following precipitate immersion in a strange new foster-care or

50 See *Nottinghamshire County Council v. P (No 2)* [1993] 2 FLR 134.
51 See Sir Stephen Brown P in *Newham London Borough v. AG* [1992] 2 FCR 119 at p 120.
52 See *In re H and R (Child Sexual Abuse: Standard of Proof)*, op cit.

residential-care setting could add trauma to the loss of relationships upon which the child, for better or worse, had been emotionally dependent. The 1989 Act sought to change this practice by clearly stating that local authorities should give preference to facilitating the removal of the abuser or suspected abuser, rather than the child.[53] The subsequent introduction of non-molestation orders and occupation orders under the Family Law Act 1996[54] served to emphasise the desirability of effecting such a change in practice by providing the means whereby family members can initiate the action necessary to remove the offender rather than the child from their home. Again, this could be viewed as another instance of a public law issue being redefined as private, which, when resulting in responsibility being borne by those victimised by criminal behaviour, may be neither just nor feasible.

The orders

The proceedings available under Part V of the 1989 Act are applications for a child assessment order, an emergency protection order, a recovery order and a police protection order. Part V also makes provision for the setting up and running of children's refuges.

CHILD ASSESSMENT ORDER

This order, like an emergency protection order, is a tightly defined grant of authority to an applicant, intended to license coercive intervention in family affairs for a specific purpose and for a restricted time period. It provides a less interventionist option than the emergency protection order, interim care order or interim supervision order. The legislative intent is to provide positive welfare intervention, to which all parties could give their agreement, and thereby forestall a judicial necessity to impose a more draconian protection order. Of all the orders designed to affect the welfare interests of a child directly, this one has the singular characteristic of being vulnerable to the veto of the child concerned. By refusing to cooperate, the child is quite legitimately able to assert his or her view of how his or her welfare interests should be advanced.

A child assessment order is available under s 43 of the 1989 Act on the grounds specified in s 43(1). Only a local authority or an 'authorised person' (as defined by s 31(9)) is permitted to apply. It may be utilised in conjunction with private but not public law orders (though it may coexist with an education supervision order). Its function is to authorise the means whereby a local authority can establish whether or not the subject is suffering, or likely to suffer, significant harm. By issuing a child assessment order, the court can permit an applicant to bring a child to a named assessor and ensure that such assessment as the court specifies is conducted by that assessor. A child

53 See Sched 2, para 5(1).
54 See ss 42(2)(a), 62(3) and 63, and s 33(3)(f), respectively.

assessment order does not give the applicant any degree of parental responsibility. Section 43 stresses the limitations of the authority conferred by this order: the court is prohibited from granting a child assessment order in situations where an emergency protection order would be more appropriate (para 4); the child, if of sufficient understanding to make an informed decision, may refuse to submit to the assessment (paras 7 and 8); and the child may be kept away from home only for the period or periods specified in the order (para 9).[55] The necessity for the child to be away from home will arise only if the court is convinced that this is necessary for the purposes of the assessment (and not, for example, to ensure the child's protection), can be limited to a period or periods less than the statutory maximum and can otherwise be accomplished within such directions as the court may decide to attach to the order, including directions regarding contact arrangements with family and others.

EMERGENCY PROTECTION ORDER

The tightly defined powers of an emergency protection order reflect the professional and public disquiet aroused by the Cleveland affair and the guidance offered in the subsequent Cleveland Report.[56] Unlike its predecessor – the place of safety order – an emergency protection order is of much shorter duration and focuses attention on the child, rather than the place. If, having located the child, the bearer of an emergency protection order should discover that he or she is no longer at risk then the child should not be removed. An emergency protection order allows for continued contact between child and family and is not to be used as an expedient means of commencing care proceedings. Available under s 44 of the 1989 Act, this order is intended to provide court authorisation for urgent protection to be given to a child by ensuring his or her immediate removal to, or retention in, a secure place. There are two sets of grounds. The first, specified in s 44(1)(a), rests solely on the test of prospective harm: evidence of past or present harm is insufficient but may be relevant to indicate the likelihood of a future occurrence; there is no requirement relating to fault for, or causation of, such harm. The second, under s 44(1)(b) and (c), is relevant only to applications from either a local authority or an authorised person where enquiries are being urgently pursued in relation to actual or suspected significant harm and those enquiries are being frustrated by access to the child being unreasonably refused. Under s 44 (9), the court may issue a warrant permitting a constable to accompany the applicant and to use such reasonable force as may be necessary to ensure

55 It may be queried whether both the CAO and the EPO are in accord with Article 51(d) of the European Convention on Human Rights; detention is not for the purposes of educational supervision, nor is it for the purposes of bringing the child before the competent legal authority.

56 *Report of the Inquiry into Child Abuse in Cleveland 1987*, op cit.

entry to premises or access to the child. The second set of grounds is restricted to applications from a local authority or an authorised person and represents a legislative response to the case of Kimberley Carlile and others.[57] In such circumstances, s 47(6) places a strict duty on a local authority or an authorised person to apply for an emergency protection order, or other public law order, unless satisfied that the child's welfare may be otherwise safeguarded.[58]

The court is also required to make an emergency protection order, in the context of proceedings for a child assessment order, where it considers that the grounds for the former exist. It is significant that the court has been given the power to question a local authority's grounds for optimism, which may lie behind the latter's application for a child assessment order, and is empowered of its own motion make instead an order giving absolute priority to the protection of the child concerned. On the other hand, even if the grounds are satisfied, the court need not make an emergency protection order. Rather, it may conclude, after applying the paramountcy principle and the no-order presumption, that the child's interests would be best served by not granting the order sought. This is an important judicial discretion enabling the court to avoid licensing coercive intervention even though the welfare threshold has clearly been breached.

The power vested in the holder of an emergency protection order to exercise parental responsibility is hedged around with restrictions. There is a requirement to establish and take into account the views of the subject of an emergency protection order. The s 44(13) provision requiring contact arrangements to be facilitated is framed more as a right of the child rather than of the parent or other persons. The total possible period of retention is 15 days (as opposed to 15 weeks under a place of safety order). Indeed, an important principle behind this order, as is clear from s 44(5)(b), is that discretionary action is limited to the minimum necessary to 'safeguard the welfare of the child'. It would, therefore, be inappropriate to seek to make any decisions which would have a long-term effect on the child's life. Similarly, s 44(10) and (11) place an onus on the bearer of an order to arrange for the child to return home to the care of the person from whom he or she was removed, or returned to a parent, a person with parental responsibility or someone judged (by the bearer of the order and the court) to be appropriate as soon as this is reasonably practicable.

57 *Report of the Commission of Inquiry into the Circumstances Surrounding the Death of Kimberley Carlile, a Child in Mind: Protection of Children in a Responsible Society*, London, London Borough of Greenwich Social Services, 1987.

58 Ensuring prompt access to a child suspected of being abused was a primary legislative objective following publication of the Kimberley Carlile report (ibid) and two others: *A Child in Trust: The Report of the Panel of Inquiry into the Circumstances Surrounding the Death of Jasmine Beckford*, London, London Borough of Brent, 1985; and *Whose Child: Report on the Death of Tyra Henry*, London, London Borough of Greenwich, 1987.

RECOVERY ORDER

There is no legislative precedent for this order, introduced with the 1989 Act, which represented another tightening up of the public law regime to permit direct and immediate coercive intervention to retrieve a child whose status as being in need of protection was not in doubt. Where the court has confirmed a breach of the welfare threshold it can now prescribe the manner of his or her recovery. The order is available under s 50 of the 1989 Act and applies to a child defined in s 49 as being in care, the subject of an emergency protection order or in police protection who needs to be physically retrieved. It authorises a constable to enter and search specified premises for the child, using reasonable force if necessary.

POLICE PROTECTION

Again, this power was new to statute law and illustrated the legislative intent to ensure that welfare in the context of protection was afforded prompt recognition followed by direct coercive intervention. Under s 46 of the 1989 Act, this power may be used in circumstances where either the police are the first to discover that a child is suffering or likely to suffer significant harm or the urgency is such that immediate intervention is required. As there are no powers to search, it may be used only where the police have already located the child. Having taken the child into police protection, a constable may, under s 46(3)(f), remove him or her to accommodation provided for such children under s 21.[59] Although the police do not thereby acquire parental responsibility, they must nonetheless do all that is reasonable to safeguard and promote the child's welfare while he or she remains in their care. In addition, such steps as are reasonably practicable must be taken to ascertain the wishes and feelings of the child s 46(3)(d).

REFUGES

By enabling a local authority to ensure the provision of a safe haven for children whose welfare is threatened, this provision sought to broaden an authority's protective capacity. Once a child's safety was secured by means of an emergency protection order, for example, the local authority could give effect to its duty to provide reception and accommodation facilities by means of provision within a designated refuge for children at risk.

Child-care proceedings and looked after children

The 1989 Act imposed some firm and clear lines of demarcation in the law relating to children: between the remit of court and local authority; between

59 Section 21:

(2) Every local authority shall receive, and provide accommodation for children –
(a) in police protection whom they are requested to receive under section 46(3)(f).

care and offence proceedings; and between the jurisdiction of the family proceedings court and all other courts. It narrowed the scope for judicial discretion while increasing that of local authorities. It introduced definite thresholds for coercive and consensual intervention and proscribed conduct and circumstances construed as likely to cause a breach. It underpinned judicial interpretation of welfare issues with a checklist of indicators and reinforced the court's welfare focus by requiring compliance with a number of governing rules and presumptions. In such ways this legislation substantively altered the law relating to child care and protection. Other changes, such as providing for a child's interests to be represented by a solicitor and guardian *ad litem* (see, further, Chapter 6), and the ability of the court to grant an order or orders other than that applied for, especially private law orders, broadened the scope to tailor court disposal options to suit the needs of the child concerned.

However, the inability of the court to affect planning for a child's future welfare after the issue of a care order, except in the context of proceedings for a child arrangements order, remained a serious gap. This was compounded by the lack of any formal mandatory procedure for ensuring that a child's rights and welfare interests are represented in any decision-making processes affecting him or her while the subject of a care order. The record of local authority care for children in the United Kingdom is sufficiently well documented to warrant legislative provision of independent safeguards to protect, monitor and review the welfare interests of children while in care.

The roles of court and local authority

The Children Act 1989 radically adjusted the role and weighting given to the principle of the welfare of the child in public family law. This affected the roles and responsibilities of both court and local authority.

Local authority

The relationship between local authority and parent, in a public family law context, is governed by the principle stated in the 1989 Act that the interests of children will be best served if the former make every effort to achieve a partnership with the parents. When this is considered in conjunction with the directive in s 17(1)(b) of the 1989 Act to 'promote the upbringing of such children by their families', the 'no-order' presumption of s 1(5) and the absence of any requirement to give priority to the separate interests of a child, the cumulative effect is to place an onus on a local authority to safeguard the welfare interests of a child by maintaining that child in parental care wherever possible. Moreover, even where the 'significant harm' threshold has been breached a local authority, under s

47(8), has discretion to waive its power to instigate care proceedings if they should view such proceedings as not 'reasonably practicable'.[60]

NON-INTERVENTION

The legislative synchronisation of the roles of court and local authority in relation to the welfare interests of a child is far from seamless (see also 'Care plan' below). As Sir Stephen Brown P stated in *Nottinghamshire*: 'if a local authority doggedly resists taking the steps which are appropriate to the case of children at risk of significant harm it appears the court is powerless'.[61]

The fact that initiating action to secure the safety of a child known to be at risk became a local authority discretion rather than a duty left a child's welfare interests at this stage more vulnerable under the 1989 Act than they had been under the 1969 Act; welfare was to be seen first and foremost as a matter for the family, not the state.

A local authority, it would seem, had no statutory obligation to apply the paramountcy principle. This principle, as stated in s 1(1) of the 1989 Act, was to be binding on the judiciary, not on a local authority. There was no specific statutory requirement on a local authority under this legislation that it should give any priority to the welfare interests of a child,[62] though, in due course, some contrary judicial guidance emerged. Indeed, if a local authority were required in the course of its family support duties to give automatic precedence to the interests of children, this would be in conflict with the whole partnership ethos. The legislative intent, seemingly, was to leave a local authority free to negotiate the best compromise possible between the conflicting interests of family members which still enables it to safeguard and promote the welfare of any children involved. Only when conciliation had failed, the issues had been transferred to the court and the latter was then required to consider changes in the legal status of a child did the paramountcy principle come into play. Paradoxically, a local authority may now find the court employing this principle to restrain rather than facilitate its intervention. In circumstances where, according to the statutory grounds, a local authority could intervene and is entitled to be granted a care order the court may rule that it should not do so and decline to grant the order sought. This may occur, for example, where the court determines that it is of paramount importance not to cause further damage to the psychological bond between child and parent.

60 Such was the conclusion of the court in *Nottinghamshire County Council v. P (No 2)* [1993] 2 FLR 134 at p 148.
61 Ibid.
62 In fact, the 1989 Act explicitly *reduced* the onus on a local authority when it removed the obligation placed on it by s 18(1) of the Child Care Act 1980 to give 'first consideration' to welfare interests.

Court

Judicial determination of issues concerning parental responsibilities in most court proceedings was significantly altered by the 1989 Act. This upgraded the principle of the welfare of the child to paramountcy status and comprehensively applied it to guide judicial decision-making on matters affecting a child's upbringing. It reinforced this new normative approach with a battery of ancillary welfare-related directives, including s 1(3)'s 'welfare checklist', which for the first time provided a statutory specification that identified the content of the welfare principle (see, further, Chapter 4). While in private family law the checklist has a mandatory application only to contested cases, in all public proceedings the court is required to have particular regard to:

a the ascertainable wishes and feelings of the child concerned (considered in the light of his age and understanding);
b his physical, emotional and educational needs;
c the likely effect on him of any change in his circumstances;
d his age, sex, background and any characteristics of his which the court considers relevant;
e any harm which he has suffered or is at risk of suffering;
f how capable each of his parents, and any other person in relation to whom the court considers the question to be relevant, is of meeting his needs;
g the range of powers available to the court under this Act in the proceedings in question.

Coercive intervention by a local authority under Part IV proceedings will not be authorised until the court has applied the checklist criteria to the particular circumstances giving rise to the local authority application and is then satisfied that an order is necessary.[63]

Three other statutory directives, ancillary to the welfare principle and having a direct bearing on both court and local authority, are the 'no-order' presumption, the 'no-delay' requirement and the 'limited litigation' principle.

NO-ORDER

Section 1(5) of the 1989 Act stipulates that, when considering an application for an order, a court 'shall not make the order or any of the orders unless it considers that doing so would be better for the child than making no order at all'. This places a firm onus on a local authority applicant not only to satisfy the court that the specified statutory grounds can be met but also to convince it that in the particular circumstances not to grant an order would result in greater harm to the child than to do so. That is, definite evidence has to be

63 See *Humberside County Council v. B* [1993] 1 FLR 257.

produced to rebut the presumption that no order is best. This approach has been neatly summarised in an observation made by Templeman LJ:[64]

> The best person to bring up a child is the natural parent. It matters not whether the parent is wise or foolish, rich or poor, educated or illiterate, provided that the child's moral and physical health is not in danger. Public authorities cannot improve on nature.

NO-DELAY

This principle is declared in s 1(2) of the 1989 Act in the following terms:

> In any proceedings in which any question with respect to the upbringing of a child arises, the court shall have regard to the general principle that any delay in determining the question is likely to prejudice the welfare of the child.

In itself, this places no onerous burden on the courts: while they are required to have regard to the principle and presumably to act in accordance with it wherever possible, they are also free to act otherwise whenever circumstances dictate. It is, however, given teeth by s 32, which imposes a mandatory duty on a court hearing an application for an order under Part IV to draw up a timetable 'with a view to disposing of the application without delay'. The importance of this directive was emphasised by the Court of Appeal when it overturned the decision of the court at first instance to adjourn care proceedings pending the outcome of a criminal trial.[65] One reason for this statutory requirement was to address the problem of local-authority-orchestrated delay which, by favouring a continuation of the settled care arrangements provided by an applicant, effectively pre-empted judicial discretion and did not necessarily permit a decision which would best promote the long-term interests of the child concerned. Now, once an application is lodged in court, it will in theory be for the court, not a local authority, to determine the pace at which proceedings progress. However, adhering to the time constraints continues to prove problematic for local authorities.

NO UNNECESSARY LITIGATION

The limited litigation principle is declared in s 91(14) of the 1989 Act in the following terms:

> On disposing of any application for an order under this Act, the court may (whether or not it makes any other order in response to the

64 See *Re KD (A Minor) (Ward: Termination of Access)* [1988] 1 AC 806 at p 812.
65 See *Re TB (Care Proceedings: Criminal Trial)* [1995] 2 FLR 80.

> application) order that no application for an order under this Act of any specified kind may be made with respect to the child concerned by any person named in the order without leave of the court.

Although more directly relevant to private family law proceedings, this provision also serves to remind local authority applicants that the court will not permit repeated litigation on the same issues as this is not conducive to the stabilisation necessary for promoting a child's welfare interests.

The parties

Any person with parental responsibilities and the child concerned are automatically parties in care proceedings instigated under the 1989 Act. Other persons may apply, or the court may direct that they be joined, to become parties to such proceedings.

The applicants are restricted, under s 31 of the 1989 Act, to a local authority or an authorised person. No others may apply for a care order or a supervision order. For the purposes of this Act, 'authorised person' is restricted to mean an officer of the NSPCC. The respondents to a care order application are each parent with parental responsibility for the child concerned. Any other parent and certain other persons must be notified and may then elect to become respondents: an unmarried father or person currently caring for the child, for example, must be notified and may then decide to apply to be joined to the proceedings.

The subject of such proceedings can be any child below the age of 17 (or 16, if married). Any such person may be the subject of proceedings instigated to obtain a care, supervision or interim order. Under s 41(6), any such proceedings are designated 'specified proceedings' and the child concerned is, therefore, automatically made a party. This will be the case regardless of whether the child does or does not wish to make application for any of these orders.

REPRESENTATION

The 1989 Act introduced important provisions providing representation for a child in Part IV proceedings. This is to be provided by: a guardian *ad litem* (subsequently a Cafcass officer) in respect of welfare interests; a solicitor as regards legal interests; and a local authority social worker in relation to his or her home and other factual circumstances (see, further, Chapters 6 and 7).

THE WELFARE THRESHOLD

Significant harm is declared a threshold condition for Part IV proceedings by s 31(2) of the 1989 Act:

> A court may only make a care or supervision order if it is satisfied –

(a)that the child concerned is suffering, or is likely to suffer, significant harm ...

Section 31(9) defines 'harm' as 'ill-treatment or the impairment of health or development' and states that 'ill-treatment' 'includes sexual abuse and forms of abuse which are not physical'. The latter term clearly allows for the inclusion of emotional abuse within the definition of 'harm'.[66]

The first requirement of this provision is that 'harm' or the 'likelihood of harm' exists. It is evident that 'ill-treatment', the 'impairment of health' and the impairment of 'development' are each independent and alternative conditions all or any one of which would be sufficient to establish 'harm' or the 'likelihood of harm' and thus satisfy the terms of this requirement. The court considered the meaning of harm in a case[67] where a 15-year-old girl had obdurately refused to attend school for three years. The court made a care order holding that harm included social, educational and intellectual development.

The degree to which such conditions must exist in order to constitute 'significant' harm and thereby satisfy the 'significance' test is problematic: how bad does the harm have to be for it to be judged 'significant'? Clearly, at one extreme, if the harm can be considered very grave, as in a case[68] where the 'harm' involved the death of an abused child (see below), then there is little difficulty. However, the uncertainty increases in proportion to the decrease in gravity of harm. The 1989 Act does not provide any definition for the term 'significant'. The only statutory guidance available is that this be determined by making a comparison with a 'similar' child. Again, the exact meaning of 'likelihood' has given rise to considerable contention. It has been held[69] that the 'likelihood' test would be satisfied by evidence that there was a real risk of future harm. The House of Lords has consolidated this view in a judgment which has significantly eased the threshold test by rejecting the argument that 'likelihood' should be equated with 'probability'. The fact that the mere 'likelihood' of a future occurrence of harm could be sufficient to justify coercive intervention provides an important extension to the protective reach of a local authority's statutory powers.

Under s 31(2)(b)(i) of the 1989 Act, the 'harm' or 'likelihood of harm' must be attributable to 'the care given to the child, or likely to be given to him if the order were not made, not being what it would be reasonable to expect a parent to give to him'. Later, the section states:

(10)Where the question of whether harm suffered by a child is significant turns on the child's health or development, his health or development shall be compared with that which could reasonably be expected of a similar child.

66 See *Report of the Inquiry into Child Abuse in Cleveland 1987*, op cit, p 4.
67 See *Re O (A Minor) (Care Order: Education: Procedure)* [1992] 2 FLR 7.
68 See *Re D (A Minor) (Care or Supervision Order)* [1993] 2 FLR 43.
69 See *Newham London Borough Council v. AG* [1993] 1 FLR 281.

The requirement, therefore, is that the 'harm' or 'likelihood of harm' is attributable to, rather than caused by, either an unreasonable standard of parenting or the child being beyond parental control. In the former instance, the standard of parental care will be judged by an objective application of the 'reasonableness' test: that is, not what *that parent* in those circumstances could be expected to provide but what a *reasonable parent* would provide. However, it has been held[70] that the statutory reference to 'care' (as in s 31(2)(b)(i), above) referred to the actual parent or carer whose lack of care caused the harm, not to the hypothetical reasonable parent in that situation.

Parental fault or default is not the issue; it is the bare fact that there has been a breach of the significant harm threshold, whether by child or parent, which is of concern to the court (see, further, the discussion of 'beyond parental control' in 'Intervention in a care context', below). The tenses used in this provision gave rise to considerable uncertainty as they refer only to present and prospective harm. However, in *Re M (A Minor) (Care Order: Threshold Conditions)*[71] it was found that the operative time for adducing evidence of significant harm is not the date of hearing. In the words of Lord Mackay: 'the relevant date with respect to which the court must be satisfied (that the child is suffering significant harm) is the date at which the local authority initiated the procedure of protection under the Act'. The spirit behind this ruling, and the authority attached to it, became evident in *M v. Birmingham City Council*,[72] where the Court of Appeal held that the court was not to be tied to the facts existing at the time of the hearing but could consider the state of affairs – in the past, present or future – according to the context in which it fell to be applied.

The orders

Responsibilities in relation to the welfare interests of a child are transferred, in varying degrees, from a parent to an authorised body by the issue of one of the court orders available under the Children Act 1989. The order made by the court will be the one affording the minimum degree of coercive intervention in the affairs of a family necessary to safeguard the welfare interests of the child concerned.[73] Care orders are governed by Part IV of the 1989 Act.

CARE AND SUPERVISION ORDERS

Both care and supervision orders are available under the 1989 Act if the two stages of the application process are completed. Firstly, the threshold criteria

70 See *Re S and R (Minors) (Care Order)* [1993] Fam Law 43.
71 [1994] 2 FLR 577. See: www.swarb.co.uk/c/hl/1994re-m-threshold.html.
72 [1994] 2 FLR 141.
73 See dicta to that effect in *Re O (Care or Supervision Order)* [1996] 2 FLR 755 and *Re B (Care or Supervision Order)* [1996] 2 FLR 693.

of s 31 must be met. Secondly, the court must also be satisfied that the order, if made, would be compatible with the child's welfare interests; this is ascertained by applying s 1(2), (3) and (5).

The 1989 Act upholds the spirit of the *Liverpool*[74] ruling by preventing the court from exercising any discretionary power to supervise, review or in any way intervene in a local authority's exercise of the powers granted to the latter by a care order or supervision order.[75] The legislative intent is that it should be for a local authority, not the court, to implement the authority conferred by a care order or supervision order, subject only to the power reserved to the court by s 34(1). In the words of Butler-Sloss LJ: 'After a care order is made, the court has no continuing role in the future welfare of the child.'[76] Nevertheless, she goes on to acknowledge that this statement is subject to some specific exceptions (e.g. applications for contact or leave to refuse contact, for the discharge of care order or for a child arrangements order).

Before the court passes responsibility to a local authority by way of a care order, however, it has been held[77] that it should satisfy itself that all the facts are known as fully as possible. Such facts should be presented to the court by way of a 'care plan' dealing with contact arrangements and addressing the headings outlined in the Regulations.[78] If the court is not satisfied that the care plan is in the child's best interests then, the advice of Wall J[79] is that the court may refuse to make a care order or supervision order. In such circumstances the court very often issues an interim care order, or perhaps a series of such orders, until such time as it is satisfied that an appropriate and effective care plan has been formulated. The court may conclude that a local authority has provided sufficient evidence to establish that the significant harm threshold of s 31 has been breached but, because its care plan is insufficient to meet the requirements of the welfare test in s 1, the order sought cannot be granted. The fact that a local authority has applied for a supervision order will not prevent the court from instead issuing a care order[80] or from making an

74 See *A v. Liverpool City Council* (1982) FLR 222.

75 See, for example: *Re W (A Minor) (Care Proceedings: Wardship)* [1985] FLR 879; *Re B (Minors) (Care: Contact: Local Authority's Plans)* [1993] 1 FLR 543; *Kent County Court v. C* [1993] 1 FLR 308; *Re T (A Minor) (Care Order: Conditions)* [1994] 2 FLR 423; and *Re S (Contact: Prohibition of Applications)* [1994] 2 FLR 1057.

76 See *Re B (Minors) (Contact: Local Authority's Plans)* [1994] 1 FLR 543 at pp 550 and 551.

77 See *C v. Solihull Metropolitan Borough Council* [1993] 1 FLR 290 and *Hounslow London Borough Council v. A* [1993] 1 FLR 702.

78 See *Manchester City Council v. F* [1993] 1 FLR 419.

79 See *Re J (Minors) (Care: Care Plan)* [1994] 1 FLR 253 at p 258F–G.

80 See *Re D (A Minor) (Care or Supervision Order)* [1993] 2 FLR 423, where the court made such a substitution because it considered that the risk to the children of a current relationship, posed by a father who had previously abused his own children (causing the death of one), was too great to warrant a supervision order.

interim care order on application for a care order.[81] The determining factor will be a combination of the gravity of the prospective harm and the likelihood of it occurring. So, to a considerable extent, the court also has discretion in the exercise of its statutory powers even where satisfied that the threshold conditions of s 31(2)(a) and (b) have been met. This discretion is provided by the welfare principle.

The making of an order ends court involvement in responsibility for decisions affecting the welfare of the child. The local authority is thereafter free to change or abandon its care plan without leave of the court. The principle judicially expressed in the *Liverpool* decision has now been given full legislative endorsement.

A care order, like a supervision order, is available only on evidence of a breach of the significant harm threshold. Their functions in relation to the welfare interests of a child are therefore essentially negative. The supervision order imposes reciprocal legal obligations on three parties: the supervisor (most often a local authority social worker); the child or young person; and the 'responsible person', who is usually the person with parental responsibility for the child. This order provides the means whereby an offer of broad professional support to parents and to a child, supplemented by certain specific powers, may be sufficient to maintain the latter in the community. Because it leaves all parental responsibilities with the parent, its capacity to further a child's welfare interests remains dependent upon parental cooperation.

IN CARE, A 'LOOKED AFTER' CHILD

Under s 33(1), a care order places a duty on the named local authority to take the child concerned into its care whereupon he or she becomes a 'looked after' child. The order vests parental responsibilities for the child concerned in the local authority not to the exclusion of those responsibilities that remain with the parents but to the exclusion of any further court responsibility. This is in keeping with the principle under the 1989 Act, unlike the position previously, that a clear line be drawn between the responsibilities of the court and those of the local authority.

Under s 22(a) of the 1989 Act, the making of a care order gives the named local authority the duty to safeguard and promote the welfare of the child concerned. It is significant that decisions taken by a local authority, unlike those of the court, are not statutorily governed by the paramountcy principle. The clear legislative intent is not to impose as onerous a burden on a local authority as is placed on the court, but the former is now required to meet specified welfare standards. Whereas previously it was statutorily required to apply the primacy of the welfare principle in relation to children in care,[82] the

81 See *Re M and R (Child Abuse: Evidence)* [1996] 2 FLR 195, where the court substituted interim orders for the sought care orders even though satisfied that the s 31 requirements had been met.

82 See s 12(1) of the 1948 Act and s 20(1) of the 1969 Act.

current reference to the basic threshold of 'safeguard' implies that if a local authority strives to ensure the health and safety of a child in its care then it is fulfilling an important statutory duty that was not always attended to within the previous broad discretionary duty. Should it fail in that duty, however, it is clear from the ruling of the House of Lords in *X v. Bedfordshire CC*[83] that a local authority will escape liability: it cannot be liable for a breach of statutory duty,[84] for negligence, nor even for a breach of the common law duty of care. This and subsequent rulings[85] constitute a significant setback for welfare interests. If a breach of the most basic threshold by the public authority specifically and statutorily entrusted with safeguarding it cannot ground an action by or on behalf of the child concerned then the latter's welfare interests have been seriously devalued. The litany of public inquiries into the gross and long-term abuse of children in local authority care by local authority staff throughout the United Kingdom strongly suggests that the welfare interests of children in care need to be amenable to external monitoring.

The concept of partnership in the context of care arrangements has been operationalised through the following approach: all children in respect of whom a local authority provides away-from-home care, whether or not under the terms of a court order, are now regarded as being 'looked after' by that local authority; and any parent whose child is being 'looked after' retains parental responsibility for that child. The effect of the first presumption is, essentially, that a local authority must be guided by the same principles when making arrangements for a child who is the subject of a care order as for one for whom it is merely providing accommodation. This, for example, requires a local authority to give due consideration to the wishes and feelings of a child (depending on his or her age and understanding) and those of certain others before taking any decisions in respect of that child. Under s 22(5), it must also respect the child's religious persuasion, racial origin and cultural and linguistic background.

The 1989 Act, more so than previous legislation, placed an obligation on a local authority to maintain and facilitate the relationship between a child in

83 [1995] 2 FLR 276. See also *Nottinghamshire County Council v. P (No 2)* [1993] 2 FLR 134, CA and *Re S and D (Children: Powers of Court)* [1995] 2 FLR 456, CA.

84 But see *Osman v. UK*, op cit.

85 See *H v. Norfolk County Council* [1997] 1 FLR 384, where the plaintiff had been sexually abused by his foster-father while in care, and *Barrett v. Enfield London Borough Council* [1997] 2 FLR 167, where a young man who had spent 17 years in care alleged that he had been left with psychological and psychiatric problems as a result of the local authority's 'catalogue of errors'. However, in the more recent decision of the Court of Appeal in *W v. Essex County Council* [1998] 2 FLR 278 there is evidence of a retreat from the virtual blanket immunity for any local authority liability implied in the *Bedfordshire* ruling. In the *Essex* case the court was prepared to hold that a local authority could be liable for the abuse of children in foster care caused by the wrongful placing of a known abuser in the foster home without informing the foster-parents of his abusive record.

care and his or her family of origin because of the presumed importance of that relationship to the continued welfare of the child, as highlighted in several rulings by the ECtHR. Therefore, insofar as it is practicable and consistent with the child's welfare, under s 23(7), a local authority must ensure that the accommodation it provides is near to the child's home and caters also for any other sibling that the local authority might be looking after. Also, under s 23(6), a duty is placed on a local authority to return any child which it may be looking after to family care unless this would not be reasonably practicable or consistent with his or her welfare. The effect of this second directive is to impose upon both parent and local authority a sense of shared responsibility for important decision-making in respect of any child subject to a care order. Parents do not wholly shed responsibility for their children on the making of an order, and a local authority does not thereby attain exclusive rights to determine matters affecting the welfare of the children concerned. Initially it seemed probable that these statutory presumptions, together with the partnership ethos, combined to produce unforeseen effects which worked to the detriment of the welfare interests of many children: they reduced the likelihood of children in care being placed for adoption, which in turn prompted recourse to the strategy of 'concurrent placements' whereby local authorities sought to circumvent constraints on placing a 'looked after' child for adoption by designating certain family placements with the dual status of both foster and adoption homes. Despite evidence that local authority care at best places children at a disadvantage relative to their peers[86] (even according to such basic indices as health and education) and at worst exposes them to serious risk of abuse, and that the number of prospective adopters was far greater than that of children waiting to be adopted, in the years following the introduction of the 1989 Act only a very small minority of children in public care became available for adoption.

The power of the court to make a contact order (subsequently known as a 'child arrangements order') in respect of such a child also illustrates the legislative intent to safeguard relationships judged to be of importance to the welfare of the child concerned. Indeed, by exercising its powers under s 34(5) and (7), the court may of its own motion require a local authority to permit contact between a child and parent, and by attaching specific conditions can,

86 See Utting, Sir W., 'Putting Children First', NFM Lucy Faithfull Memorial Lecture, 13 November 1997, who cites the following statistics from the Social Services Inspectorate report for that year:

1. More than 75 per cent of care leavers have no academic qualifications of any kind.
2. More than 50 per cent of young people leaving care after the age of 16 are unemployed.
3. 17 per cent of young women leaving care are pregnant or already mothers.
4. 10 per cent of 16–17-year-old claimants of DSS severe hardship payments have been in care.
5. 23 per cent of adult prisoners and 38 per cent of young prisoners have been in care.
6. 30 per cent of young single homeless people have been in care.

if necessary, significantly alter a care plan to ensure that this aspect of the child's welfare is appropriately provided for.

Finally, the absence of any statutory duty requiring local authorities to provide specific after-care services for children was rapidly identified as a serious deficit, leaving the latter's welfare interests particularly vulnerable. The eligibility, under s 24(2) of the 1989 Act, of a person under the age of 21 who was in care after he or she became 16 to claim advice and assistance from the relevant local authority places a weak and inappropriate onus on the wrong party; the local authority should be charged with a specific duty to provide a service programme tailored to facilitate the particular rehabilitation of each child being discharged from care.

Care plan A care plan is the means whereby a local authority formulates its strategy in respect of a child it is looking after. A care plan must be drawn up before a child becomes 'looked after', or as soon after that event as is possible, or in circumstances where a care order is being sought. It may cover only a few days. Thereafter, it may be changed only at a formal review. Changes made to a care plan do not need to be notified to the court.

The design and contents of a care plan should conform to an agreed format which, in addition to including the usual material relating to child and family profile and agency formalities, should address the following questions:[87]

- Were the child/young person and family known to the social services department/voluntary agency prior to the date of placement? If so, the following issues should be covered: day care, previous accommodation episodes, social work support, help from other agencies.
- Indicate the legal basis for current work with this child/young person.
- Why does the child/young person need to be looked after now?
- What attempts have been made to arrange for the child/young person to live with a relative or close friend as an alternative to accommodation?
- If additional resources were available, would accommodation be necessary? If no, why is the local authority being asked to provide a placement?
- Which agencies, relatives and other interested people have been consulted concerning the child/young person's situation and the formulation of this plan? Give details and attach any written reports.
- What is the overall plan for this child/young person? Choose from following options: time limited assessment; remaining with family through provision of support services including respite care; return to birth family within either one month, six months or other specified number of months; live with relatives/friends; supported living in the community; independent living; special residential placement (e.g. hospital unit); long-term

87 As drawn up by the Dartington Social Research Unit, approved by the Department of Health and issued as part of the *Looking after Children* series.

placement with foster carers (no return to birth family anticipated); adoption; other, please specify.

- Explain the reasons why this particular plan has been chosen.
- What needs to be done before this plan can be achieved? Please identify what are the key tasks, say who will be responsible and give a target date.
- What long-term needs does the child have which the placement must meet? Consider the following issues: ongoing physical and mental health conditions, illnesses or disabilities; education; contact with relatives; ethnic/racial origin; religion; language; culture.
- If it is not possible to meet all the above, which should be the priority needs and how should they be addressed?
- What type of placement is proposed (e.g. foster care, residential unit)?
- What is the contingency plan if the preferred placement is not available or breaks down?
- For how long will the child/young person need to be looked after by the local authority/voluntary organisation?
- If the child/young person is accommodated, what has been agreed for ending this episode?
- What steps will be taken if any party wishes to alter this plan?
- State date for first review of plan.
- This plan has been discussed with the following who have recorded whether or not they agree: child/young person; mother; father; other/s with parental responsibility; other/s e.g. other agency carers; other interested relative (if applicable); social worker; team manager/reviewing officer.
- If any of the above have not been consulted please explain why.
- Please give details if any of those above disagree with any of the provisions of the plan.

Placed for adoption The flow of children from local authority care into the private law adoption process has been a relatively recent development. For many generations, when care in the family of origin failed, whether due to criminal abuse perpetrated by a culpable parent or neglect by a well-meaning but inadequate parent, children have entered the public care system and remained there. However, research had demonstrated that long-term residential care in children's homes was damaging to the welfare interests of the tens of thousands of such children placed there by court orders,[88] while those placed for adoption had much better outcomes.[89]

88 See, for example, Waterhouse, R., *Lost in Care: Report of the Tribunal of Inquiry into the Abuse of Children in Care in the Former County Council Areas of Gwynedd and Clwyd since 1974*, London, HMSO, 2000.

89 See, for example: Rowe, J. and Lambert, L., *Children who Wait*, London, British Association of Fostering and Adoption, 1973; and Goldstein, J., Freud, A. and Solnit, A.J., *Beyond the Best Interests of the Child*, New York, Free Press, 1974.

Under the Adoption Act 1976, local authority adoption responsibilities rested on several planks: forming and maintaining a local adoption service; linking adoption to other child-care services; managing its own work as a registered adoption agency; carrying out certain supervisory duties in relation to all adoption placements; utilising the 'freeing order' process under s 18; and providing post-adoption support. These were increased under the 1989 Act, which introduced substantive amendments to the Adoption Act 1976. Consequently, 'freeing for adoption' became central to local authority policy: this process came to be used exclusively in respect of a child in care and for whom the court was satisfied that a 'freeing order' would be in his or her 'best interests', as required by s 6 of the 1976 Act.

While it remained a difficult judgment as to whether the welfare interests of a child committed to long-term local authority care could be best furthered by plans to rehabilitate him or her with his or her family of origin or by plans for adoption, the principles and ethos of the 1989 Act exercised an influence, not present in earlier legislation, towards a preference for the former option (see, further, Chapter 9).

INTERIM ORDERS

Under s 38(1) of the 1989 Act, the court is empowered to grant either an interim care order or an interim supervision order when:

(a) in any proceedings on an application for a care or a supervision order, the proceedings are adjourned; or
(b) the court gives a direction under section 37(1).

The principal effect of this order is to provide a holding operation, permitting a local authority to carry out its enquiries, gather evidence and prepare reports so as to bring a case before the court in as short a time as possible. The court must restrict itself to maintaining the *status quo* between the parties by authorising and controlling the minimum level of intervention required in the circumstances for a local authority to prepare its case.[90] A local authority will be entitled to an interim care order in circumstances where its need to carry out the initial investigations necessary to establish whether or not a child is at risk of significant harm is being obstructed by a lack of parental cooperation.[91]

90 See *Re G (Minors) (Interim Care Order)* [1993] 2 FLR 839 at p 846, where Waite J stated that 'Parliament intended the regime of an interim care order to operate as a tightly run procedure closely monitored by the court and affording to all parties an opportunity of frequent review closely monitored by the court and affording to all parties an opportunity of frequent review as events unfold during the currency of the order.' See also Brasse, G., 'A Tightly Run Procedure? Interim Care Orders under Strain', *Family Law*, 24 (1994), pp 261–264.
91 See *Re B (A Minor) (Interim Care Order: Criteria)* [1993] 1 FLR 815.

An interim care order can allow the court, for a limited period, to impose its own care plan on a local authority instead of granting a care order application by that authority. This is achieved by the court making an interim care order subject to directions designed to provide the information necessary for a valid care plan to be compiled. The court is thereby placed in a position to decide, once the interim care order has run its course, whether the making of a full care order would be in the child's best interests.[92] This discretionary judicial power – to make the order considered by the court rather than the applicant to be most appropriate to the welfare of a child – has also been used to give preference to interim care orders instead of child assessment orders at the early stages of coercive intervention. It offers the court a last opportunity to require a professional evaluation of the welfare interests of a child, and submission of evidence that such interests are being or are in danger of being so impaired as to justify a care order, before full responsibility for decisions relating to those interests passes to a local authority with the issue of a care order.

The court may make an interim supervision order linked to a residence order (subsequently amended to child arrangements order), instead of making an interim care order. It must do so when making a child arrangements order in care proceedings, unless satisfied that this is unnecessary. However, it cannot use an interim supervision order to achieve objectives statutorily reserved to an interim care order.[93]

In keeping with the full care and supervision orders, an interim order has a negative functional relationship with welfare. The 'reasonable grounds for believing' test may not require evidence of an actual breach of the welfare threshold but grounds must still exist before the order can be made. However, in practice, the functions of the interim care order are quite complex. It has a proven capacity to act as a judicial bridgehead into local authority decision-making affecting the welfare interests of the child concerned. This, together with the judicial power to add such discretionary conditions as it sees fit to the order, makes an interim order a potentially very powerful exercise of authority in respect of a child's welfare interests. However, as Professor Hayes has succinctly stated:[94]

> a care order is still a care order, whether it is an interim or a final order. By drawing a distinction between the two orders the courts are in grave danger of blurring the law and departing from the clear principles relating to the proper exercise of judicial power which were established in *A v. Liverpool City Council.*

Although, if such a departure allowed the court to exercise a degree of ongoing monitoring of arrangements agreed with a local authority then, arguably, this would only benefit the welfare interests of the children concerned.

92 See *Re R and G* [1994] 1 FLR 793.
93 See ibid.
94 Hayes, M., 'The Proper Role of Courts in Child Care Cases', *Child and Family Law Quarterly*, 8(3) (1986), pp 201–216.

EDUCATION SUPERVISION ORDER

This is the only interventionist order that is not grounded on 'significant harm' as a basic prerequisite, a fact that reflects the distinctive nature of the legal relationship between parental responsibilities and welfare interests in the context of compulsory education. Arguably, it is in this context – a matter of undoubted importance to the welfare of children – that the law remains most ambivalent about whether it is primarily pursuing public or private functions. All statutory duties to comply with compulsory education requirements rest on parents, rather than children. All formal opportunities for choices to be made and consents given are for parents, not children. The formal requirement that local authority social workers at least seek and take into account the views of children where decisions are to be taken affecting them would seem to have no counterpart when teachers take such decisions. The law has not moved far from its traditional respect for the core parental right to decide matters relating to the education of children.

Under s 36 of the 1989 Act, the court may, on the application of a local education authority, make an education supervision order in respect of a child where that child 'is of compulsory school age and is not being educated'. Proceedings for an education supervision order are defined as 'family proceedings' under s 8(3) and (4) of the 1989 Act. The court must, therefore, apply the paramountcy principle, the welfare checklist, the no-delay principle and the no-order presumption. The fact that they are designated 'family proceedings' also means that the court is free to exercise its discretion and make any s 8 order instead of an education supervision order. It may call for welfare reports and for a hearing to be adjourned for preparation of such reports. The order does not carry any attached directions from the court but instead delegates the power to make such directions to the supervisor; these may be made at any time while the order is in force.

In *Re O (A Minor) (Care Order: Education: Procedure)*[95] the court considered the possible bearing of the 'significant harm' threshold on a situation of chronic non-attendance. It found that where a child was not attending school without good reason he or she was then either suffering harm due to a lack of adequate parental care or was beyond parental control. In that case it was held that the court at first instance had been right to impose a care order rather than an education supervision order where the 15-year-old child had been truanting for three years and had attended school for only 28 days in the previous year. This important ruling endorsed the pre-1989 Act view of Denning MR in *Re S* that 'if a child was not being sent to school or receiving a proper education then he was in need of care'.[96]

The fact that there should now be an order which solely addresses school non-attendance marks a significant change in the legislative approach to non-

95 Op cit.
96 [1978] QB 120.

attending children. Previously, any child with a record of poor school attendance was statutorily defined as vulnerable, the behaviour indicative of welfare needs and the court required to consider a care disposal option. Under the 1989 Act, such a child is viewed as ill-disciplined, the behaviour indicative more of deviancy than of care needs and as such warranting a regulatory form of supervision.

DISCRETIONARY PRIVATE ORDERS

Of considerable importance is the fact that the court may respond to an application for a care or supervision order by instead making a s 8 – or 'child arrangements' – order. The court did not possess this discretionary power – to reinterpret public law proceedings as providing grounds for exercising private law remedies – under previous legislation and it cannot exercise it in reverse. For example, in *Re B (Care: Expert Witness)*[97] the Court of Appeal held that the rejection of a care order application by a local authority and the substitution of a child arrangements order with attached conditions in favour of the child's parents was an appropriate response to the particular welfare interests of the child.

Control: civil and criminal law

'Control', as a legal function in the context of child welfare, is essentially negative, rooted in private family law and owes its origins to the doctrine of parental rights. As such, it acknowledges that the recipient of parental care has a corresponding duty to the provider not to obstruct or make impossible by wilful behaviour the provision of such care. This continues to be a matter for the civil jurisdiction of the courts. But 'control' also represents a public law interest in the protection of third parties from the unreasonable behaviour of children and young persons inadequately supervised by their parents. This public law dimension, a natural corollary to the parental duties of care and protection, has grown to become a significant and contentious area for modern social policy.

The responsibility to exercise control, so as to ensure that the behaviour of a child or young person does not breach socially acceptable norms, is in law distributed with some uncertainty between child, parent and state. Once such a breach has occurred then the role to be played by the welfare principle will depend very much on whether the issues of liability for the consequences and imposition of measures to provide for future control arise for judicial determination in civil or criminal proceedings. A particularly revealing dimension to the evolving legal role of the welfare principle is provided by the history of its application to the criminal behaviour of children and young persons. An in-depth examination of the law relating to juvenile justice is, however,

97 [1996] 1 FLR 667.

outside the scope of the present study, which confines itself to considering areas of overlap between the civil and criminal jurisdictions, to identifying the role of the welfare principle in relation to 'control' in an 'offence' context and to comparing the defining characteristics of the welfare principle in both.

Control: the law and the principles

Responsibility for controlling the behaviour of children and young persons, and liability for any harm or loss incurred as a consequence of a failure to exercise such control, has long been governed by both civil and criminal law. The welfare principle has played a critical role within each and in managing the interface between both. Other principles have also played a part. However, by the end of the twentieth century there had been a quite dramatic and comprehensive change in the law relating to control: new legislation had carefully teased apart the legal response to such behaviour occurring in 'care' and 'offence' contexts, resulting in two distinct and largely separate systems – one for child care and another for youth justice – though some provisions have had the effect of bridging the two, most notably those relating to remand and secure accommodation.

At first sight, as a consequence of this change, the role of the welfare principle would seem to have been wholly eclipsed by that of justice, supplemented by considerations of punishment, proportionality and deterrence. The creation of a specific Youth Court, the extension of its remit at either end of the age range, the removal of the care disposal option and the increase in the number of powers available to it have all served to consolidate a much more coherent and independent justice model than existed previously. There is also the inescapable fact that once proceedings are under way there is far less scope for the principle in the Youth Court than in the Family Proceedings Court to influence the course of events, the decision made and the disposal option chosen. The difference in the representation available to the child is particularly apparent, as is the shift from a focus on the offender in isolation to a broader approach that holds parents accountable for their failure to exercise adequate control by making room in proceedings for the views of victims and by requiring offenders to make direct reparation. This is balanced by a welfare-led focus on preventative intervention, spearheaded by a new and comprehensive youth justice service, intended to reduce the numbers of children and young persons charged with criminal offences.

The law

Ultimately, differentiating between behaviour in terms of its relative appropriateness to civil or criminal proceedings varies according to prevailing social values and falls to be determined by the social policy of the government of the day.

CIVIL LAW

In civil law, responsibility for the consequences of a child's behaviour was traditionally held to rest solely with the parent but is now best viewed as shared between child and parent, with the proportional distribution varying in accordance with the age and understanding of the child. Uncertainty regarding the grounds for apportioning responsibility between them is particularly apparent in the caselaw relating to the legal capacity of minors in matters of contract, torts and property. Family law reflects the same uncertainty as that prevalent in the broader civil jurisdiction of which it forms a part.

The body of legislation comprising successive Children and Young Persons Acts has provided the statutory framework for resolving control issues arising in a public family law context. The role of the principle in relation to the control function broadly follows the typical pattern of such other functions as 'care' and 'protection' (see above). The threshold of coercive and mandatory intervention by a local authority is legislatively set in prescriptive terms. The grounds underpinning the threshold are objectified: what matters is that the behaviour is uncontrolled; the fact that either parent or child is too ill or otherwise too disabled to exercise adequate control is beside the point. Judicial determination provides adjudication on the issues but is discretionary in relation to disposal. The disposal options are essentially of a treatment and rehabilitative nature, the choice of which is governed by considerations for the welfare interests of the child concerned.

CRIMINAL LAW

In criminal law, responsibility for the consequences of a child's behaviour was traditionally held to rest solely with the child unless parental involvement, as accomplice or through the usual rules governing the acts of principal and agent, could be proven. Children found guilty of criminal activity were treated by the legal system as adults and flogged, imprisoned, transported overseas or hanged in accordance with the prevailing statutory tariff for criminal offences. More recent legislation has broadened liability to hold parents also accountable for the criminal activity of their children.[98]

The age of the child concerned plays a crucial part in determining criminal liability. In England and Wales, in keeping with traditional common law rules, the commission of a crime requires that the *actus reus* (or physical act) be accompanied by the appropriate *mens rea* (or malicious intent). The *doli incapax* presumption sets the age of criminal

98 Signalled by the White Paper *Crime, Justice and Protecting the Public* (Cmnd 965), London, HMSO, 1990, in which the government indicated its resolve to place the responsibility for controlling wayward children firmly on parents by making it a criminal offence if they should 'fail to prevent their children from committing offences'.

responsibility at 10 years,[99] below which a child cannot be held to have the requisite *mens rea* to commit a crime, and proceedings, if appropriate, must be of a civil nature. A child between the ages of 10 and 14 was presumed to be incapable of committing a crime, although that presumption could be rebutted by evidence[100] demonstrating that he or she knew the activity was wrong; the younger the child, the stronger the presumption.[101] A reverse presumption applied in respect of a young person aged between 14 and 16: that is, from the age of 14, a person was presumed to have intended the consequences of his or her actions. Thereafter, young persons were held to have full capacity and to be as criminally liable for their actions as any adult. The Criminal Justice Act 1991 reasserted the *doli incapax* presumption: children below the age of 10, not possessing the *mens rea* necessary for criminal intent, were to be deemed incapable of committing criminal offences. The same Act altered the law to the extent that the presumption of wrongful intent was extended to the age of 17: all children and young persons between the ages of 10 and 17, inclusive, were held to possess the necessary *mens rea*, are therefore liable for their criminal conduct and fall within the jurisdiction of the Youth Court. However, on conviction, they may be treated differently than fully mature adults. The Crime and Disorder Act 1998 abolished the rebuttable presumption favouring those aged 10 to 14, effectively making all offenders aged between 10 and 17, inclusive, amenable to the Youth Court.

The law relating to juvenile offenders is to be found mainly in that body of legislation comprised of successive Criminal Justice Acts. While an assessment of the role and functions of the principles governing the criminal justice system is outside the scope of this study, some of its more prominent distinguishing characteristics and their effect on the welfare principle can be noted. The threshold for coercive and mandatory intervention is legislatively explicit. The grounds underpinning the threshold are objective: once the uncontrolled behaviour results in a crime then prosecution must follow. The judicial role is

99 At common law this was initially fixed at aged seven, which was raised to eight in 1933 and to ten in 1963.

100 As in *JM (A Minor) v. Runeckles* (1984) 79 Cr App Rep 255.

101 See *X v. X* [1958] Crim LR 805. The law on this matter was well scrutinised by the courts in *C v. DPP* [1994] QBD 3 All ER 191, which concerned a 12-year-old boy charged with the offence of tampering with a motor vehicle. He was convicted in the Magistrates' Court, it being held that on the evidence the presumption of *doli incapax* was rebutted. He appealed to the Divisional Court by way of case stated on the issue of whether there was any or sufficient evidence that he knew his act to be seriously wrong at the time. The appeal was denied, it being held that the *doli incapax* presumption was outdated and could no longer be regarded as a part of the law of England. But see *C v. Director of Public Prosecutions* [1995] 1 FLR 933 HL, where on appeal to the House of Lords the *doli incapax* presumption was reaffirmed: it may be rebutted only by showing clear positive evidence – not consisting merely in the evidence of the acts amounting to the offence itself – that the child knew the act was seriously wrong.

firmly adjudicatory; there is little, if any, scope for discretion. Disposal options are governed by considerations of justice and public protection: they are preset in accordance with a 'tariff' which matches orders available with crimes on a proportionality basis and have a definite punishment and deterrent orientation.

WELFARE NEEDS AND CRIMINAL BEHAVIOUR

Justice and welfare are the two competing frames of reference governing the legislative response to the problem of a child whose behaviour is both out of parental control and criminal. The extent to which the welfare needs of such a child should be taken into account by the criminal justice system, if at all, is determined by a social policy which periodically oscillates between placing an emphasis on welfare or justice. As has been observed, 'our juvenile justice system tends to swing uneasily between the "justice" and "welfare" models'.[102] The present firm endorsement of the justice model is the result of just such a swing.

The Children and Young Persons Act 1969 made a significant shift from the traditional approach of treating juvenile offenders as simply young adults, deserving of little more than a diluted interpretation of the same criminal justice system. Instead, it established the principle that it was inappropriate to apply a rigid differentiation on the basis of needs and deeds and ascribe welfare- and justice-oriented disposals, respectively. This approach was considerably influenced by the principles expressed in the White Paper *Children in Trouble*, which stated, for example:[103]

> It has become increasingly clear that social control of harmful behaviour by the young, and social measures to help and protect the young, are not distinct and separate processes. The aims of protecting society from juvenile delinquency, and of helping children in trouble to grow up into mature and law-abiding persons, are complementary and not contradictory.

In particular, 'discretion' as a *modus operandi*, justified by the concept of individualised justice and the principle of the welfare of the child, was developed as an appropriate and sufficient rationale for judicial disposal in proceedings for compulsory care and juvenile justice. The welfare principle was employed, at judicial discretion, to permit a treatment order to be made under the Children and Young Persons Acts rather than a punishment order under the Criminal Justice Acts. This occurred where, in relation to a particular instance of criminal behaviour, the welfare of the child was of more

102 See Hoggett, B., *Parents and Children*, 4th ed., London, Sweet & Maxwell, 1993, p 215, where she references 'Parsloe, 1978; cf. Priestly, Fears and Fuller, 1977; Taylor, Lacey and Bracken, 1979; Morris, Giller, Szwed and Geach, 1980'.

103 See Home Office, *Children in Trouble* (Cmnd 3601), London, HMSO, 1968, p 4; see also Home Office, *The Child, the Family and the Young Offender* (Cmnd 2742), London, HMSO, 1965.

pressing concern to the court than satisfying the requirements of justice by rigorously applying the tariff of punitive sanctions. Ironically, however, the indeterminate duration and intrusiveness of the welfare option was often less welcome to child and family than the fixed penalty approach of juvenile justice.[104] The 1969 Act also generated controversy among the professionals involved because of its perceived failure to deal adequately with 'criminal' juveniles. Squaring the circle between an approach emphasising the needs of the individual child (favoured by the social work profession) and one affording greater weight to the interests of the general public (favoured by magistrates) proved difficult.

PROBATION SERVICE

In existence since 1907 and reorganised under the Criminal Justice and Court Services Act 2001, the Probation Service has a general duty to manage offenders released from prison on licence and those on community sentences. In so doing, it has a limited brief for those who enter the youth justice system and for preventing children and youths from being at risk of breaching the 'significant harm' threshold by engaging in anti-social or criminal behaviour. However, by the 1990s, the Probation Service had become decidedly less welfare oriented and more distinctly correctional in its policy towards child offenders: priority was given to the protection of the public and the reduction of reoffending; the functions of promoting and protecting the welfare of children were essentially devolved to local authority social workers.[105]

Changes in the legislative framework

Proceedings relating to controlling the behaviour of children and young persons were reorganised into two distinct sets of statutes. The Children Act 1989 governed the civil family proceedings jurisdiction. The Criminal Justice Act 1991, together with such ancillary legislation as the Criminal Justice and Public Order Act 1994 and the Crime and Disorder Act 1998, structured the equivalent criminal jurisdiction. These provided – and largely continue to provide – the broadly separate and alternative 'care' and 'offence' contexts in which the legal system defines and responds to the uncontrolled behaviour of children and young persons.

THE 'CARE' CONTEXT

By abolishing care orders in criminal proceedings, s 90 of the Children Act 1989 made a clear and firm legal distinction between care and criminal

104 See Parker, H., *Receiving Juvenile Justice*, Oxford, Blackwell, 1981.
105 Not until the Children Act 2004 was there a clear specification of Probation Service responsibilities for child welfare.

behaviour. Those whose uncontrolled behaviour was such as to indicate state intervention on care grounds were to be the subject of proceedings governed by the 1989 Act. All other children and young persons aged 10 or older who were the perpetrators rather than the victims of criminal offences would be the subject of proceedings governed almost exclusively by other legislation.

THE 'OFFENCE' CONTEXT

The clear legislative intent to define the uncontrolled and criminal behaviour of children and young persons as a matter to be governed more by justice than by welfare considerations found expression in the Criminal Justice Act 1991. The perpetrators of such behaviour were presumed to have intended the consequences of their actions. The responsibility for exercising control and liability for failure to do so were seen as rooted in the family of origin rather than attributable to a more general social malaise. Both child and parent were to be held accountable before the court. The prevailing ethos of the 1989 Act – returning responsibilities to the family – was also evident in the 1991 Act. The latter required a parent to accompany their child,[106] aged between 10 and 16 and accused of a criminal offence, to the court hearing and to pay any fines and/or costs.[107] The parent may be bound over by the court,[108] with or without recognisances,[109] to exercise control over such a child. This approach, designed to hold parents responsible for exercising proper control over juveniles and make them financially accountable for the consequences of failing to do so, has since been reinforced.[110]

The Crime and Disorder Act 1998 built upon the established principle of parental responsibility by introducing the 'parenting order', enabling the court to require the parent of every convicted juvenile to attend counselling programmes and, if necessary, control the future behaviour of the juvenile in a specified manner. Where the juvenile is aged between 16 and 18 the court will hold him or her, rather than the parent, directly responsible and accountable for criminal offences.

OVERLAP OF CARE AND CRIMINAL JURISDICTIONS

The behaviour requiring control may bridge both care and offence contexts. The standard of 'significant harm' is the determinant of whether otherwise criminal behaviour will be treated by the legal system as more appropriately

106 Criminal Justice Act 1991, s 58.
107 Ibid, s 57.
108 Ibid, s 58(1)(a).
109 Ibid, s 58(2) and (3).
110 See Home Office, *No More Excuses – a New Approach to Tackling Youth Crime in England and Wales* (Cmnd 3809), London, HMSO, 1997. Note also the Criminal Justice and Public Order Act 1994, which extended the judicial power to bind over parents.

dealt with by care proceedings. Usually this arises in individual cases where a child's uncontrolled behaviour – resulting in criminal harm, damage or loss – becomes the subject of proceedings under the 1989 Act instead of the 1991 Act because clear evidence exists that the behaviour also harmed or threatens to harm the welfare interests of that child to a significant degree. This will also be the outcome where the harm, damage or loss results from the uncontrolled behaviour of a child below the age of 10 and therefore falls outside the legal definition of 'criminal'. The child is then treated as in need of care, not as an offender. The same logic applies to categories of behaviour per se, rather than just to their individual manifestations. While the process of criminalising and decriminalising categories of behaviour is a general process legislatively calibrated in accordance with the changing priorities of unfolding social policy, it has become particularly evident in the context of the law governing adolescents and sexual activity. Child prostitution, for example, has been removed from the statute books as a criminal activity, and children engaged in prostitution are amenable only to care proceedings. Homosexual relations have been decriminalised for those aged 16–18. On the other hand, rape, offences involving sexual intercourse and buggery have become criminal activities for boys aged 14 and under.[111]

Control: preventing anti-social behaviour

The consequences of the uncontrolled behaviour of a child or young person may give rise to either civil or criminal proceedings. Accordingly, the statutory duty to put in place measures designed to reduce the likelihood of children and young persons becoming the subjects of proceedings due to their behaviour being out of control is one which falls on both local authorities and the police. However, this duty is only to assist those with primary responsibility – parents and the children at risk of offending – to cope more effectively with problematic behaviour.

Local authorities

Under the Children Act 1989, local authorities have a duty to assist parents in exercising control over children and young persons by making such provision as is likely to prevent the latter from entering the youth justice system. Under Sched 2(7), of the 1989 Act:

> Every local authority shall take reasonable steps designed –
> (a) to reduce the need to bring –
> ...
> (ii) criminal proceedings against such children
> ...

111 Sexual Offences Act 1993.

(b) to encourage children within their area not to commit criminal offences; and
(c) to avoid the need for children within their area to be placed in secure accommodation …

This specific statement requires local authorities to be proactive in their prevention duties. As such, it complements and gives focus to their general duty under s 17(1)(b) to provide 'a range and level of services appropriate to those children's needs'. However, there is no indication of any overall strategy nor of precisely what services they might deploy in giving effect to those duties. But s 20(3) does link a preventative duty to specific objectives and services:

> Every local authority shall provide accommodation for any child in need within their area who has reached the age of sixteen and whose welfare the authority considers is likely to be seriously prejudiced if the authority does not provide him with accommodation.

By requiring local authorities to provide accommodation for such young persons 'in need', this provision offers the possibility of assistance being made available to those at risk of being drawn into the youth justice system.

The Crime and Disorder Act 1998 places further preventative duties and confers certain powers on local authorities. Section 39 requires every local authority to set up at least one 'youth offending team' in its area, while ss 38–41 specify that youth justice services must be made available. The legislative intent is that such teams and services would be deployed so as to maximise the opportunities for preventing youths from committing offences and being drawn into the criminal justice system. In addition, local authorities have been given the power under s 14 to create local child curfew schemes which can be used to designate specified public places 'out of bounds' to children below the age of 10 unless accompanied by a responsible adult; this curfew can be enforced by the police. It is of considerable significance that the lead role for this preventative strategy has been given to local authority social workers rather than the Probation Service or the police. The governing principle for crime prevention in relation to children and young persons is to be welfare rather than justice, supported by an infrastructure of professionals and services.

Police

The strategy to prevent children and young persons entering the criminal justice system has for some time rested on a diversionary policy. The former centrepiece of this policy was a scheme for the administration of a formal police caution to any child or young person guilty of a minor offence as an alternative to criminal proceedings. Because it rested on the consent of all parties, particularly that of the parents, it was viewed as a discreet means of reinforcing the latter's responsibility and powers in relation to the control of minor offenders. It was ended by the Crime and Disorder Act 1998, which substituted a scheme for administering a formal police reprimand and final warning, together, where appropriate, with an offer of a place in a programme designed to dissuade offenders from reoffending. This scheme differs from its predecessor in that it is enforced by stiff sanctions for any failure to comply.

Intervention in a care context

The Children Act 1989 provides the governing authority for such intervention. Under s 31(2)(b)(ii), the threshold of 'significant harm' may be breached where the 'harm' or the 'likelihood of harm' is attributable to 'the child's being beyond parental control'. The requirement, therefore, is that the 'harm' or the 'likelihood of harm' is attributable to, rather than caused by, the child being beyond parental control. A child may be in need of control because the 'significant harm' threshold has been or is being breached either by the child's own conduct or by the fault or default of a parent. It is the bare fact that the child is found to be beyond parental control which is all important.[112] This may arise, for example, from drug or alcohol abuse, sexual promiscuity or anorexia nervosa.

THE GROUNDS FOR INTERVENTION AND THE ROLE OF WELFARE

The welfare principle may well come into play at an early stage by identifying a child as being 'in need' within the definition of the 1989 Act. This will trigger local authority service provision duties. The principle is also given effect by s 11 of the Crime and Disorder Act 1998, which enables the court to make a 'child safety order' in respect of a child below the age of 10 whose behaviour is giving rise to a concern that he or she is in danger of becoming engaged in activities which would be criminal for an older child.

Once the threshold of 'significant harm' is breached, however, then the relevant local authority has a corresponding duty to consider bringing care proceedings. The courts have held that this threshold may be breached by a child's persistent refusal to attend school. A distinctive characteristic of local authority powers at this point is that it has discretion not to commence proceedings.

THE COURT, JUDICIAL OPTIONS AND THE ROLE OF WELFARE

The Family Proceedings Court is the appropriate forum for hearing issues relating to the behaviour of a child who is out of control in a care context. Where the behaviour is such that the ''significant harm threshold has been

112 See, for example, *Re O (A Minor) (Care Order: Education: Procedure)*, op cit, where it was considered to be irrelevant to determine whether this established fact was attributable to the fault of child or parent.

breached then, normally, proceedings will be commenced under s 31(2)(b) of the 1989 Act. In making this determination the court will have regard to a further provision in the same section:

> (10) Where the question of whether harm suffered by a child is significant turns on the child's health or development, his health or development shall be compared with that which could reasonably be expected of a similar child.

In so doing, the Court of Appeal has held that the court is not tied to the facts existing at the time of the hearing; rather, the term 'being beyond parental control' should be viewed as describing a state of affairs – in the past, present or future – according to the context in which it fell to be applied.[113] The conduct of proceedings, role of the parties, provision of reports and representation and weighting of the child's welfare interests will be as for other care proceedings.

LOCAL AUTHORITY OPTIONS AND THE CHILD IN CARE

The issue of a care order vests parental responsibility in a local authority, which thereby also acquires responsibility for controlling the behaviour of the child concerned. Many adolescents, having become the subject of care orders because of their uncontrolled behaviour, pose serious management problems for the staff of children's homes. For local authorities, the recurring dilemma of how to impose reasonable restraints on the activities of a *Gillick* competent minor who has chosen to behave in a way that threatens their welfare interests or those of others is well documented.[114] Since the introduction of the 1989 Act, the secure accommodation provisions have provided judicial protection for all parties when formal recourse must be had to constraint measures (see below).

Intervention in an offence context

A child may be in need of control because his or her criminal behaviour is endangering others. The governing legislation is provided by an array of statutes including not only the Criminal Justice Act 1991, the Criminal Justice and Public Order Act 1994 and the Crime and Disorder Act 1998 but also the residual provisions of statutes such as the Children and Young Persons Acts 1933 and 1969.

THE GROUNDS FOR INTERVENTION AND THE ROLE OF WELFARE

Police intervention may initially have been in pursuance of their preventative duties and may have concluded in a formal reprimand (see above). A decision

113 See *M v. Birmingham City Council* [1994] 2 FLR 141.

114 See, for example, Levy, A. and Kahan, B., *The Pindown Experience and the Protection of Children*, Stafford, Staffordshire CC, 1991.

to arrest for criminal activity will be taken purely on the basis of whether evidence exists to satisfy the prescriptive grounds for the alleged crime, and the resulting procedure will be governed by the provisions of the Police and Criminal Evidence Act 1984. Any decision not to bring an offending child before the court, unlike the equivalent decision in respect of a child with welfare needs, is amenable to judicial review. A local authority is free to choose not to initiate care proceedings where the 'significant harm' threshold has been breached and will be shielded by the ruling in *Liverpool*[115] from having to account to the court for that decision. The Crown Prosecution Service, however, may find itself judicially challenged should it choose not to initiate criminal proceedings where a juvenile has committed, or is suspected of committing, a criminal offence.[116] In both instances the public interest in ensuring that the welfare of a child is fully taken into account by those charged with responsibility for deciding on the appropriateness of court proceedings may be avoided.

From the time of arrest, the welfare principle has a role to play in moderating the approach of the criminal justice system towards juveniles. The special requirements differentiating the treatment of juveniles and adults include measures for: notifying parents and the relevant local authority; an 'appropriate' adult to be present during police questioning; keeping juveniles apart from adult offenders; being held on remand in local authority accommodation; and a presumption of entitlement to bail.

THE COURT, JUDICIAL OPTIONS AND THE ROLE OF WELFARE

The Youth Court[117] is the appropriate forum for hearing issues relating to the behaviour of a child out of control in an offence context. In contrast to the pre-1989 era, the court will not hesitate to prosecute child offenders, is permitted to do so in relation to those aged 10–14 and is also now unable to order a care disposal on the grounds of a child's particular welfare interests. These justice-oriented changes have been slightly offset by the rule that those aged 17 are to be made amenable to the Youth Court instead of, as formerly, facing prosecution as adults. The procedures of this specialised Magistrates' Court, established to deal with charges of criminal activity brought against juveniles in the 14–17 age group, are governed by special rules differentiating the treatment of juveniles from adults in the criminal justice system. Protection is given to juveniles by measures that confer anonymity, limit those who

115 Op cit.

116 See, for example, *R v. Chief Constable of Kent and Another ex parte L* [1991] Crim LR 841, where the decision of the police to institute criminal prosecution, rather than comply with the recommendation that a caution was sufficient, in respect of a juvenile who had allegedly inflicted serious injuries on his victim was judicially reviewed and upheld.

117 The Juvenile Court was renamed the Youth Court under s 70 of the Criminal Justice Act 1991.

may be present, impose reporting restrictions and make adjustments to the use of language. It has jurisdiction to hear and determine summary offences and also has authority to deal summarily with indictable offences (except murder) if it is considered expedient to do so by the court and with the agreement of parents and subject. However, where a child is charged with a very serious offence then he or she will be tried by judge and jury in the Crown Court in accordance with the same procedures as apply to adults. For example, any child aged 10 or older who is charged with murder or manslaughter will be exposed to the full rigour, formality and ritual of the legal system in a manner which makes little allowance for his or her welfare interests.

The manner in which the welfare interests of a juvenile are brought before the Youth Court is important. The court will always have the benefit of a 'welfare report', which provides factual information on the child, his or her family and home surroundings and some general guidance as to which disposal options might be most appropriate. The report is usually filed by the relevant local authority following mandatory service of the notice of prosecution, though, in particular circumstances, it may be compiled by a probation officer or court welfare officer. The juvenile's interests will not be represented by a guardian *ad litem* nor necessarily by a solicitor; he or she has no entitlement to legal aid or legal representation.[118] The child must, however, be given copies of all reports and/or the court must explain the issues to the child. The court may then make such order as would have available to it if the case had been tried on indictment. In reaching its decision the court is obliged 'to have regard to the welfare of the child or young person'.[119] By not requiring it to give either first consideration or paramount weighting to the latter's welfare interests, the legislative intent is to leave the court free to give overriding priority to the interests of justice.

The orders

Depending on the nature of the uncontrolled behaviour and its consequences, the response may be a matter for either the civil or the criminal jurisdiction.

IN A CARE CONTEXT

In this context the appropriate judicial disposal option will be a public or private family law order, or a combination of orders, available under the 1989 Act, except in exceptional circumstances where urgent recourse to wardship is indicated. A care order is not available in respect of children who have committed offences or are only in breach of statutory education requirements.[120]

118 The court has discretion to direct that legal aid be made available; and under r 5 of the 1992 Rules, it has discretion to permit a parent or other person to represent the child.
119 Children and Young Persons Act 1933, s 44(1).
120 But see *Re O (A Minor) (Care Order: Education: Procedure)*, op cit, where the court ruled that obdurate and persistent school refusal, maintained over a period of years, constituted a breach of the 'significant harm' threshold.

It is available in respect of a child beyond parental control, but 'significant harm' must first be established. The full authority of a care order is often necessary where the behaviour constitutes a possible threat to the general public. The narrowly defined and explicitly control-oriented disposal options may be sufficient; these include the child assessment order and supervision order in public law proceedings, and the prohibited steps order or specific issue order in private proceedings. The more generic scope of the child arrangements order with attached directions, perhaps accompanied by other orders, may also offer the basis for an overall package of statutory authority tailored to control the behaviour of a particular child in particular circumstances.

IN A CRIMINAL CONTEXT

A critical test for the way in which the legal system relates to children is the role permitted the welfare principle in determining the appropriate sentence for young children convicted of serious criminal behaviour.[121] Given its pivotal role across the centuries – identifying, articulating and giving weight to the developmental needs of children in the context of legal issues affecting their upbringing – what part does it now play in inducing the judiciary to take into account the welfare needs of very young criminals? The House of Lords had cause to consider the role played by the welfare principle in the sentencing policy governing convicted juveniles.[122] It concluded that a clear historical strand of legislative intent could be detected, differentiating between the rationale for sentencing juveniles and adults, which required the principle to be taken into account in relation to the former.[123] Their lordships held that the Secretary of State had been wrong to advise that an inflexible application of the tariff system would be sufficient in computing the sentence for two ten-year-old offenders; their needs as children required a different approach. Unlike adults, the sentencing of juveniles necessitated making provision for a regular review of their needs and allowing for the possibility of welfare considerations contributing towards their early release.

The disposal options available in respect of offending juveniles are, in the main, set out in the Criminal Justice Act 1991.[124] The majority of offenders are the subjects of 'diversion policy' options. They are formally reprimanded and diverted away from the juvenile justice system in circumstances where the

121 See, for example: *R v. Fuat and Others* (1973) 57 Cr App R 840; *R v. Fairhurst* [1986] 1 WLR 1374; and *R v. Wainfur* [1997] 1 Cr App R (S) 43.

122 See *R v. Secretary of State for the Home Department ex parte Thompson and Venables* [1997] 2 FLR 471.

123 Evident in the Children Act 1908 and the Children and Young Persons Act 1933, s 44.

124 But see also the Children and Young Persons Act 1933, the Powers of Criminal Courts Act 1973, the Magistrates' Courts Act 1980, the Criminal Justice Act 1982 and the Crime and Disorder Act 1998.

offence is a first and/or minor transgression and either guilt has been admitted or may be readily proven. Many others found guilty of minor offences will be absolutely or conditionally discharged or they and/or their parents will be the subject of directions requiring the payment of fines, compensation or deprivation of all rights to offence-related property. The Crime and Disorder Act 1998 introduced a new focus on reparation, whereby an offender may be required to make amends directly to the victim; in addition, the latter's views will be taken into account by the court prior to sentencing. It also provided that an 'action plan' would be required from the offender explaining how he or she intends to 'mend their ways'. Only those found guilty of serious or repeated offences will, following determination, be retained within the system by an order requiring that they undertake treatment in either a community or custodial setting. The court will then draw from the tariff of disposal options available under the criminal justice legislation, ranging from supervision in the community to long-term custodial confinement.

Community treatment options The wide range of community disposal options introduced by the 1991 Act allows the rehabilitation of juvenile offenders to be individually tailored to a greater extent than ever before. These include community service orders, attendance centre orders, curfew orders, supervision orders, combination orders and probation orders. In practice, the majority of juvenile offenders are made the subject of supervision orders with attached judicial directions suited to individual circumstances. As providing supervision is a duty which falls to local authority social workers who are professionally more concerned with the needs than the deeds of juveniles, it may be construed that most offenders continue to benefit more from welfare-oriented than punishment-oriented disposals.

Custodial treatment options These options are reserved for those young offenders who persistently reoffend or whose offences are so grave that no other option is justified.[125] The courts have increasingly relied on custodial sentences[126] since the introduction of the Criminal Justice and Public Order Act 1994, which reduced the age of the children amenable from 14 to 10. Of these options, the courts resort most frequently to detention in a young offenders' institution where the offender is over the age of 15. Another alternative, again introduced by the 1994 Act, was the secure training order, which provided for the detention of persistent offenders aged 12–14 in a secure training centre followed by supervision in the community. This option

125 Criminal Justice Act 1991, s 1(2).

126 In a 1995 Green Paper, the Home Secretary indicated that, while the range of community disposals in England and Wales would remain as they are, the custodial options may well be strengthened. See Home Office, *Strengthening Punishment in the Community* (Cmnd 2780), London, HMSO, 1995.

was broadened by the Crime and Disorder Act 1998 to become a detention and training order, which replaced other custodial orders and is now the basic disposal option for all young offenders. The most extreme custodial option, available under s 53(1) of the Children and Young Persons Act 1933 and reserved for convictions of murder, is detention 'at Her Majesty's pleasure'. Other custodial options include detention for treatment under the Mental Health Act 1983 and detention in secure accommodation.

Secure accommodation

There are two different forms of secure accommodation: for children and young persons being 'looked after' by a local authority; and for those convicted of, or on remand in relation to, a criminal offence. Both can be accessed only by order of the court and result in the imposition of serious constraints upon the welfare interests of the children concerned.

SECURE ACCOMMODATION IN A CARE CONTEXT

Any child already being accommodated by a local authority is eligible for a judicially sanctioned removal to, or retention in, secure accommodation. This is so whether the accommodation is provided on a voluntary basis or as the consequence of a care order and regardless of the type of accommodation provided (foster home, psychiatric hospital, hostel, children's home, etc.). In *A Metropolitan Borough v. DB*[127] Cazalet J held that a hospital maternity ward, which was kept locked and to which the only inmate (a 17-year-old pregnant crack-cocaine addict) had no key, met the definition of secure accommodation.

Authority to provide secure accommodation is to be found in the Children Act 1989 and supporting regulations.[128] Under s 25(1) of the 1989 Act 'secure accommodation' means 'accommodation provided for the purpose of restricting liberty'. Whether or not a particular place or practice meets the terms of this definition is ultimately a matter for the court to determine. Any practice which prevents a child from leaving a room of his or her own volition, however, could amount to a restriction of liberty. It has been held[129] that a behaviour modification unit in a hospital, where the programme entails a restriction on personal liberty, is a form of secure accommodation.

Under s 25(1), a child who is being looked after by a local authority may not be placed (or, if placed, may not be kept) in secure accommodation unless it appears:

127 [1997] 1 FLR 767.

128 See the Children Act 1989, s 25, the Children (Secure Accommodation) Regulations 1991, the Children (Secure Accommodation) (No 2) Regulations 1991 and the Children (Secure Accommodation) Amendment Regulations 1995.

129 See *R v. Northampton Juvenile Court, ex parte London Borough of Hammersmith and Fulham* [1985] FLR 193.

(a) that –
  (i) he has a history of absconding and is likely to abscond from any other description of accommodation; and
  (ii) if he absconds, he is likely to suffer significant harm; or
(b) that if he is kept in any other description of accommodation he is likely to injure himself or other persons.

Intended as a 'last resort',[130] there are thus only two types of situation in a care context which justify secure accommodation.

The role of the welfare principle can be seen in the restrictions placed on the use of secure accommodation. It is never justified as a punishment,[131] nor by the lack of an alternative. Under regulations provided for in s 25(7), the Department of Health has excluded certain categories of children and young persons from eligibility for placement in secure accommodation:

- no child being accommodated for 24 hours or less;
- any child already detained under the Mental Health Act 1983;[132]
- no child under the age of 13 years without the prior approval of the Secretary of State;
- no child convicted of a grave offence whose detention is subject to the discretion of the Home Office; and
- no young person aged between 16 and 21 years who is being provided with accommodation by a local authority in order to safeguard or promote that person's welfare, or who is the subject of a child assessment order and is being kept away from home pursuant to that order.

Under s 25(2), provision is made for regulations to specify a maximum period during which a child may be retained in secure accommodation without recourse to the court.[133] A previous prohibition on the use of secure accommodation in a voluntary or registered children's home has been abolished.[134]

The court has an important role in safeguarding the welfare interests of children. Where a child is to be detained in secure accommodation for a period exceeding 72 hours then authority to do so must be sought from a

130 See the Children Act 1989, Guidance, vol 4, 'Residential Care', para 8.5.
131 See the Children Act 1989, Regs, vol 4, para 8.5.
132 In this context, the decision of Wall J in *Re C (Detention: Medical Treatment)* [1997] 2 FLR 180, concerning a suicidal 16-year-old girl suffering from anorexia nervosa, should be noted. Faced with resistance from the hospital for a detention order under the 1983 Act and from the local authority for a care order under the 1989 Act, Wall J used the court's inherent *parens patriae* jurisdiction to authorise detention in the hospital.
133 Under Reg 10(1), a child in care may be so retained for a maximum period of 72 hours in any period of 28 days, unless a further period has been sanctioned by the court. See also the Children (Secure Accommodation) Regulations 1991 and Reg 11(3) for exceptional arrangements at weekends and during public holidays.
134 See the Children (Secure Accommodation) (Amendment) Regulations 1995, Reg 6.

Family Proceedings Court (or a County or High Court where a secure order is made in the course of civil proceedings being heard in either court). As stated in the Guidance: 'It is the role of the court to safeguard the child's welfare from inappropriate or unnecessary use of secure accommodation.'[135] However, as Butler-Sloss LJ observed in *Re M (Secure Accommodation Order)*,[136] the action of the court in making such an order 'may be inconsistent with the concept of the child's welfare being paramount'. She then ruled that welfare is a relevant but not a paramount consideration in determining whether or not a secure accommodation order should be made and that the welfare checklist had no application. The court also held that the no-order presumption had no role to play in such proceedings. This finding had the effect of reversing the presumption that the court is required to make the order sought once it is satisfied that all formal requirements have been met. This is an interesting deviation from the usual rule that once threshold requirements are met, the making of an order (whether or not the one sought) is a matter of judicial discretion to be determined on the basis of the particular welfare needs of the child concerned. Instead, this provision deals with the control function of welfare in a prescriptive manner.

The role of the welfare principle may be constrained in the context of secure accommodation proceedings but the normal rules for acknowledging and representing a child's welfare interests in family proceedings must be respected. The court has ruled that the child concerned must be given the opportunity to present their case properly. In *Re AS (Secure Accommodation Order)*[137] an appeal was allowed because the 12-year-old boy had not been notified of the proceedings and a guardian *ad litem* had not been appointed. In *Oxfordshire County Council v. R*[138] the court advised that as secure accommodation proceedings were family proceedings for some purposes of the 1989 Act, hearsay evidence was therefore admissible. Under s 41, they are also 'specified proceedings' and therefore the court must appoint a guardian *ad litem* unless satisfied that it is not necessary to do so in the interests of the child. Having determined that the criteria for detention are met, then it is for the court, under s 25(4), to 'make an order authorising the child to be kept in secure accommodation and specifying the maximum period for which he may be so kept'.[139] Before so doing, however, the court must, under s 25(6), ensure that legal representation is provided for the child 'unless, having been informed of his right to apply for legal aid and having had the opportunity to do so, he refused or failed to apply'.[140]

135 Children Act 1989, Guidance, vol 1, para 5(7).
136 [1995] FLR 418 at pp 423–442.
137 [1999] 1 FLR 103.
138 [1992] 1 FLR 648.
139 Under Reg 13(2), the order may authorise the retention of a child for a period not exceeding three months. Under Reg 13, on subsequent applications, a local authority may seek six-month extensions.
140 Legal aid for secure accommodation proceedings is provided for under Part IV of the Legal Aid (General) Regulations 1989.

Once the criteria cease to be met, the child should be removed. After placement in secure accommodation, the welfare interests of the child fall to be protected by the local authority, not the court. Thereafter, it is most unlikely that those interests will be represented by a guardian *ad litem* or solicitor and they will not arise for review before the court.

In addition to the responsibilities it has in respect of all children whom it is looking after, a local authority has other duties which are specific to children in secure accommodation. In particular it must establish a review panel of at least three members, at least one of whom must not be employed by the local authority, which shall conduct a review of every child in secure accommodation within one month of a child's admission and at not less than three-month intervals thereafter. In addition to addressing matters relating to the child's welfare, as detailed in s 26, the panel must satisfy itself that the criteria for retention in secure accommodation are still being met. When making its deliberations, it is required to ascertain and take into account the wishes and feelings of the child and those of any person bearing parental responsibility or having had care responsibility in respect of him or her. All involved must be advised of the outcome of the review and proper records must be maintained.

SECURE ACCOMMODATION IN AN OFFENCE CONTEXT

Section 23(5) of the Children and Young Persons Act 1969[141] provides authority for children and young persons held on remand, or following committal, in respect of a criminal offences to be placed in secure accommodation. It states that before making such an order the court must first satisfy itself that it is necessary for the protection of the general public from serious harm. Specifically, to be eligible, a juvenile should have been either:

1. detained by the police under section 38(6) of the Police and Criminal Evidence Act 1984; or
2. remanded to local authority accommodation under s 23 of the Children and Young Persons Act 1969;
   (a) having been charged or convicted of an offence of violence (or having been previously convicted of such an offence); or
   (b) having been charged with or convicted of an offence which would be imprisonable for fourteen years or more if they were aged twenty-one or over.

The eligibility criteria were broadened by interim arrangements put in place by s 60 of the Criminal Justice Act 1991. This enabled a court, after it had consulted with the local authority or Probation Service, to remand a 15- or

141 As amended by the Criminal Justice Act 1991 and supplemented by the Children (Secure Accommodation) Regulations 1991.

16-year-old with a 'security requirement' to local authority secure accommodation where the juvenile:

1. is charged with, or convicted of, a violent or sexual offence or an offence punishable, in the case of an adult, with imprisonment for fourteen years or more; or
2. has a history of absconding while remanded to local authority accommodation and is charged with, or has been convicted of, an imprisonable offence alleged or found to have been committed while he was so remanded.

The welfare principle comes into play in a negative sense by restricting access to secure accommodation. In either of the above cases the court must be convinced that protecting the public from serious harm is possible only by so remanding the juvenile. As s 60 became fully implemented it replaced s 23 of the 1969 Act and the above judicial power became available together with conditions which can be attached when remanding juveniles. The maximum period a young offender may be retained in secure accommodation is for the duration of the remand or 28 days, whichever is longer. Thereafter, court authorisation must be sought.

SECURE ACCOMMODATION AND WELFARE INTERESTS

The welfare principle has a very restricted role in the judicial determination of an application for a secure accommodation order: no paramount weighting; no checklist; and no no-order presumption. It is also compromised by the fact that the order can be made in respect of children whose behaviour requires control for very different reasons. Local authority use of secure accommodation is, in theory, for the welfare of the child concerned: to protect him or her from the possibility of self-inflicted harm. In practice, it is most often utilised to protect others from the possibility of harm being inflicted upon them by the child. These are very different sets of needs: the introverted anorexic and the belligerent vandal have little in common with each other and require very different regimes from that which is appropriate for the criminal youths referred by the youth justice system. Secure accommodation facilities can meet the welfare test only if they appropriately differentiate between these different sets of needs, in particular by providing a safe, therapeutic environment suited to the healthcare needs of children at risk of self-harm.

Conclusion

The law and practice relating to child protection traditionally served to fence off society's fundamental need to preserve the life and safety of children from a more general concern for their growth, development and well-being. In this context, children were more the objects of intervention rather than parties to a legal process.

The Children Act 1989 challenged that approach by requiring adjustments to accommodate the principle of partnership with parents, presuming that care in the family of origin is in a child's best interests and making provision for those interests to be both prioritised and represented in any decisions taken regarding his or her upbringing. Child protection and family care were not to be legislatively addressed as separate entities and positioned as alternatives. Instead, local authorities were directed by the provisions of the 1989 Act to consider modes of consensual intervention that might pre-empt or bridge any such gap and prevent a 'child in need' from becoming a child at risk of 'significant harm' while also preventing, if possible, any further step towards non-consensual adoption. A feature of the Act was the moral authority vested in the presumption favouring family care, preferably in the family of origin, but otherwise with foster-parents or adopters rather than in residential care. The fact that the functions of prevention and promotion were given statutory recognition, underpinned by the concept of 'children in need', was a very significant step forward for the welfare interests of children. Both functions, with their firmly positive bearing on welfare, represented an entirely new departure in child-care law, with certain provisions going a step further by linking these functions to specified family support services. Nonetheless, a lack of sufficient resources ensured that the pressures on local authorities to give urgent attention to those children whose welfare interests may be critically impaired following a breach of the 'significant harm' threshold always worked to the disadvantage of those who should have received the support necessary to forestall a breach of the 'children in need' threshold.

Under the 1989 Act, as before, the functions of care, protection and control continued to be the primary means by which local authorities and the courts gave effect to the welfare principle. The Act drew a firmer and clearer line between their respective remits, clarifying their respective areas of authority, in particular confining that of the court, while also drawing an equally firm line between welfare and criminal matters, consigning the latter to the youth justice system. It established a checklist of indices, together with the paramountcy weighting, as the legally designated process for interpreting and applying the welfare principle when determining issues that required balancing parental responsibility against the needs of children. Perhaps most importantly, this formative child-care statute brought specificity to the concept and responsibilities associated with what had formerly been the nebulous and somewhat paternalistic principle of the welfare of the child.

9 Private family law

Contested and uncontested proceedings

Introduction

Family law has always had difficulty in disentangling public and private interests. By the latter half of the twentieth century, the principle of the welfare interests of a child had been accepted as representing a threshold sufficient to warrant state intervention into private family affairs across the broad front of family proceedings. When parent-initiated consensual proceedings alerted the court to the fact that decisions likely to impact significantly upon a child's best interests were to be taken, then the intervention threshold was crossed by a judicial, if not also a social work, scrutiny of the welfare implications arising from those decisions. The court would require the outcome of a parent's proceedings to be at least compatible with the welfare interests of any child involved. It might even become the decision-maker in respect of any welfare-related issues. Ultimately, it could become the arbiter of a child's welfare by directing that he or she be committed into the care of a local authority.

The introduction of the Children Act 1989 signalled the beginning of the end of such extensive state policing of the welfare threshold. As traditional family structures and accompanying social mores ceded ground under pressure from the myriad challenges of modern society, resulting in an unprecedented volume of family law cases coming before the courts, bringing with them a disparate range of attendant parenting disputes, the state began its staged withdrawal from intervention in families where child protection was not a presenting issue.

This chapter considers the law relating to child welfare, in the context of private family law proceedings, during the closing decades of the twentieth century.

Uncontested proceedings

Uncontested proceedings, initiated by a parent/parents or a substitute, involving decisions determining the future care arrangements for a child or children, had, by the closing decades of the twentieth century, been largely

DOI: 10.4324/9781003268512-13

reabsorbed into private family law. It was a period which witnessed state withdrawal across a broad front of such proceedings. Whereas previously child welfare would have been submitted to judicial scrutiny, usually supplemented by that of other professionals, this had become a rare occurrence. A legal presumption had been established that responsibility for ensuring future care arrangements for children would satisfy their welfare interests was a private matter for parents. This presumption was rebutted by notice that proceedings would be contested.

Welfare in the context of parental agreement

At the end of the twentieth century, the law would seem to have been set on confining the function of welfare and making it more a matter for administration than adjudication. In uncontested proceedings, decisions regarding the future upbringing of children were – and continue to be – very largely left to parents rather than reserved to the courts. The legislative intent – to replace the 'winners and losers' approach to issues concerning the future care arrangements for children arising in the context of matrimonial proceedings with one which instead presumes that the parties should be able to make their own arrangements outside the court – radically altered the welfare threshold. In practice, the presumption now operates to re-privatise most welfare-related decisions taken in this context. This in itself gives rise to questions about the logic and equity of treating contested applications differently from uncontested applications in private law proceedings – and treating both differently from public law proceedings – in relation to the common benchmark of the welfare principle. It is not evident that a causal relationship necessarily exists between parental agreement and satisfying the welfare test.

The parties

In uncontested proceedings which involve parental decisions to make, break, suspend or significantly alter the legal ties of family membership, the legal focus on the future care arrangements for a child is limited.

THE CHILD

The definition of 'child' in the 1989 Act is restricted to mean a person below the age of 16 years for the purposes of making a s 8 order,[1] below 17 when making a care or supervision order[2] and otherwise below the age of 18 years. A child will be a 'child of the family' when in the care of a person who has parental responsibility for him or her, or in the care of any other person with

1 See s 9(6).
2 See s 31(3).

whom he or she has been living,[3] and, for the purposes of any proceedings, is the child who is the subject of those proceedings.[4]

A child may, in private law proceedings and with leave of the court, acquire full party status. The Family Proceedings Rules make provision for a solicitor to provide representation in private proceedings. The child concerned may independently initiate some proceedings (e.g. for a residence order, or child arrangements order, as it would subsequently become) and his or her wishes may in others (e.g. where an adoption order is made subject to a contact condition) have a determining effect on any decision regarding his or her welfare. The role a child plays in proceedings is dependent upon a 'competence test' (see, further, Chapter 6).

The significance of the landmark decision by the House of Lords in *Re D (A Minor)*,[5] in terms of the light shed on the judicial rationale for distinguishing between the welfare of the child and the legal interests of the mother, is difficult to judge. It may, perhaps, be seen as a logical extension of the judicial view that the younger the child, the more fused are mother/child interests; the greater, therefore, is the maternal obligation to safeguard her own well-being as only by doing so will her child's interests be protected. This interpretation would seem to have been reinforced by a subsequent decision of the House in *Attorney-General's Reference (No 3 of 1994)*,[6] where a cohabitee was found guilty of manslaughter when the child, which he had wounded while it was a foetus in the womb, died some months after its birth. In its judgment the House referred to mother and foetus as 'two distinct organisms living symbiotically', which expresses the high degree of interdependence that the courts have customarily held to be characteristic of the maternal bond.

In relation to adolescents, the two landmark decisions which have done most to shape the modern role of the child in proceedings affecting his or her welfare are *J v. C*[7] and *Gillick v. West Norfolk and Wisbech Area Health Authority.*[8] The first firmly established that a child's welfare must be judicially treated as the factor of paramount importance in any case affecting the care, custody or upbringing of that child. The second held that the decision of a 'mature minor' could prevail over the contrary views of a parent and be binding on a third party (see, also, Chapter 4). It is significant, however, that English statute law continues not to give a child of any age the right to be consulted by his or her parents in relation to decisions taken by the latter which may affect his or her welfare interests. In the context of uncontested

3 See s 17(10). See *Re A (Child of the Family)* [1998] 1 FLR, where a grandchild was held to be a 'child of the family' for the purposes of s 41 of the Matrimonial Causes Act 1973 in the context of divorce proceedings commenced by grandparents who had cared for the 18-month-old child since birth.
4 See *Birmingham City Council v. H (No 2)* [1993] 1 FLR 883.
5 *Re D (A Minor) (Wardship: Sterilisation)* [1976] 1 All ER 326.
6 [1997] 3 WLR 421.
7 [1970] AC 668, HL.
8 [1986] 1 AC 112, HL.

proceedings, the absence of such a right may place a child who is unhappy about the agreed arrangements in the position of having to contest them in order to have his or her welfare interests taken into account. This contrasts with legislation in Scotland which imposes a duty on any person exercising parental responsibilities to have regard to the views of the child concerned when making any major decision.[9]

THE PARENT/S

Perhaps the most significant development of the welfare principle by the end of the twentieth century was its withdrawal from areas of law where it had previously played an important role. In a sense the welfare threshold in private family law had been raised to leave a greater range of parenting decisions to parents, or at least to raise the presumption that they would not require judicial scrutiny.

One example of this trend can be seen in the way that child support legislation has absorbed the duty of a divorced or separated parent on low income to provide maintenance for his or her child. This circumstance is now catered for by state machinery which calibrates maintenance in accordance with standardised rules and provides uniform methods for its collection and payment rather than it being left to the discretion of parent or court, where the role of welfare could, and often did, lead to wide variations in levels of payment. In effect, this system provided statutorily benchmarked standards for the payment of maintenance which were recognised as welfare-proofed levels for the guidance of all parents.

Another example was the resurgence of judicial interest in the 'blood tie' as the rationale for preferring first-party to third-party care arrangements for a child. The presumption in the 1989 Act that the welfare of a child is best furthered by care within his or her family of origin, deeply rooted in family law, had come to acquire broad acceptance as a benchmark for giving effect to the welfare principle. As Waite J stated in *Re W (A Minor) (Residence Order)*: 'the welfare of the child is indeed the test, but there is a strong supposition, other things being equal, that it is in the interests of the child to be brought up by his natural parents'.[10] This reliance on the blood tie as the welfare rationale for removing children from third-party carers and returning them to their natural parents was also very evident in cases such as *Re B (Adoption: Child's Welfare)*[11] and *Re M (Child's Upbringing)*.[12]

Again, an example of the state leaving welfare matters to parents can be seen in its disinclination to eliminate the common law right of a parent to chastise his or her child by administering reasonable corporal punishment.

9 See s 6(1) of the Children (Scotland) Act 1995.
10 [1993] 2 FLR 625 at p 639.
11 [1995] 1 FLR 895.
12 [1996] 2 FLR 441.

This was left untouched by the 1989 Act. Its continuance was demonstrated in a case[13] where a registered child-minder, authorised by the mother, smacked a child and the resulting case caused the Department of Health to revise its guidelines to advise staff that such authorised chastisement was permissible. Subsequently, the case of *Costello-Roberts v. United Kingdom*,[14] where a seven-year-old was chastised by the headmaster of a private school, using a gym shoe, confirmed that parentally authorised corporal punishment in non-state schools was, until then, not prohibited.

It may also be argued that the state has in effect withdrawn from the more fundamental issues affecting welfare interests. Whether children are conceived by artificial means and whether they are born, rather than aborted, are now essentially matters of private choice. A comprehensive genetic counselling service is available to inform such choices. Accessing treatment in circumstances where without it a grievously ill child may die is also a matter which, as caselaw has demonstrated, is a responsibility resting on a parent rather than the court.[15] If a parent fails to give effect to this responsibility by seeking medical advice then he or she may be guilty of criminal neglect, but having received that advice it will remain a private matter between parent and professional as to whether the treatment is provided, unless either party chooses to involve the court.

Needless to say, the court can only take decisions where proceedings have been instigated. These will be lodged by parent, child, person or body with parental responsibility or a professional and grounded on evidence that the decision of one of them, on a matter affecting the upbringing of the child, is invalid because it is not in the child's best interests. Most often, the parties are parents and medical practitioners; the issue is whether or not vital treatment should be available to a child; and the decision is one which the medical practitioners want the court to make. It would seem that such cases, invariably involving very difficult and painful choices, are being brought before the court with increasing frequency. This should not, however, obscure the fact that the vast majority of decision-making in this area does not reach the court. Only where the child involved suffers from a severe learning disability and invasive treatment is being proposed, or where parent or medical professional chooses to disengage from such treatment on grounds of religion/conscience, is there a requirement that court authorisation be sought. Otherwise, life-and-death treatment decisions affecting foetuses, neonates, newborns with complex health problems and seriously ill children are constantly being taken jointly – and privately – by parents and medical staff. Decisions to prescribe

13 See *Sutton London Borough Council v. Davis* [1994] 1 FLR 737.

14 [1994] ELR 1. But see *A v. United Kingdom (Human Rights: Punishment of Child)* [1998] 2 FLR 959, where the ECtHR held that English law did not provide sufficient protection for the human rights of a nine-year-old boy who had been beaten with a stick by his stepfather.

15 See, for example: *Re R v. Cambridge District Health Authority, ex parte B* [1995] 1 FLR 1055; and *Re T (Liver Transplant: Consent)* [1997] 1 FLR 502.

palliative care seldom come before the courts. Where there is no disagreement about treatment and welfare interests, the decisions remain private and confidential. The question has to be raised as to whether this should be so. Should a decision that is manifestly crucial to a child's welfare interests warrant court attention only when decision-makers disagree? Given the accompanying context of shock, trauma, distress and exhaustion within which parents have to take such decisions, are the best decisions always reached, even if they accord with medical opinion? If professional independent representation is seen as necessary for children in 'care' cases, and possibly in 'custody' cases, should it not also be available in 'life-or-death' treatment cases? The possibility of guardians *ad litem* in paediatric units is perhaps far fetched, but there is a case to be made for 'the child's voice to be heard' through the provision of independent representation in all life-or-death treatment decisions affecting children, irrespective of whether parents and medical staff are in agreement.

The general health, treatment and religious upbringing of children are entrusted to parental care, at least until adolescence. In addition, the compulsory requirement to ensure the education of children, to a standard and an age set by statute, falls on parent rather than child, though considerable discretion is left to parents to choose how best to give effect to this duty.

Parental responsibility The 1989 Act replaced the concepts of 'parental rights' and 'parental duties', which for centuries have formed the basic constructs of family law in the United Kingdom, with the composite term 'parental responsibilities'. Section 3(1) of the Act defines these as: 'all the rights, duties, powers, responsibilities and authority which by law a parent of a child has in relation to the child and his property'. This change signalled a profound difference of approach from a proprietary frame of reference to one implying that parental use of authority would be valid only if employed for the benefit of the child. It also suggests that such responsibilities are exclusively attributes of parenthood which may be temporarily met by other persons or bodies but can never be wholly shed by a parent – to whom, by definition, they must continue to attach. An unmarried father, however, is not to be considered a parent per se for the purposes of the above provision. Arguably, this withholding of parental status unfairly differentiates between marital and non-marital children, the latter's welfare interests being compromised by the non-entitlement to automatic inclusion in a fully legally constituted two-parent family.

As explained in the 1989 Act, '"parental responsibility" means all the rights, duties, powers, responsibilities and authority which by law a parent of a child has in relation to the child and his property'.[16] The responsibilities of a parent may be held by someone other than the parent of the child

16 Children Act 1989, s 3(1).

concerned and more than one person may hold such responsibility in respect of the same child at the same time. The role of this 'parental responsibilities' legal construct has the effect of clarifying who is entitled to take what decisions in respect of a child's welfare interests at any point in time. One clearly discernible legislative intent underpinning the 1989 Act was to leave such decisions with the bearers of parental responsibility and to minimise intervention, whether by local authority or court, in private family law matters.

Another clear legislative intent was to introduce discretionary judicial options enabling the most appropriate order, or combination of orders, to be made as indicated by the particular needs of a child rather than as determined by the nature of the proceedings instigated by a parental applicant. The availability of s 8 orders under the 1989 Act, together with supplementary powers to attach conditions, directions, time frames, etc., has introduced a capacity for considerable judicial discretion to be exercised in private family law proceedings.

Blood tests Traditionally, the importance of conducting blood tests to determine a child's paternity was twofold. Firstly, it provided the means whereby the status of the child as legitimate or illegitimate could be ascertained. Secondly, it provided the evidence for holding a putative father liable for the maintenance of his child. Both have now ceased to be important. An application for court leave for blood tests to be undertaken is currently most likely to arise in the context of contact proceedings initiated by a man whose claim to paternity is denied by the child's mother. In responding to the application, or in deciding to act of its own motion, the court will apply the welfare test only insofar as it is presumed to be in the best interests of the child concerned that the truth regarding paternity is clearly established; welfare is not the paramount consideration. Where it appears that this information would be unlikely to affect existing care arrangements, or may adversely affect them, then the court will be more inclined to take the view that the test is not justified.[17] Where it decides that the test is in the child's best interests but parental cooperation is not forthcoming, the court may then order the child to be delivered to the Official Solicitor to ensure that the test is conducted.[18]

The proceedings

In uncontested proceedings for guardianship or divorce or nullity or judicial separation, and in a number of circumstances in which adults may carry immediate care responsibility, decisions will be taken regarding the welfare interests of any child involved. The principles, decision-makers and bearers of parental responsibility will then determine the welfare of the child. The

17 See, for example: *S v. S, W v. Official Solicitor* [1970] 3 All ER 107; *Re F (A Minor) (Blood Test: Paternity Rights)* [1993] Fam 314.
18 See *Re R (Blood Test: Constraint)* [1998] 1 FLR 745.

judicial power to redefine a private law issue regarding future care arrangements for a child, whether arising in a consensual or contested application, as a matter for coercive public law intervention, was removed by the 1989 Act. The discretion of the court to make an order, in the course of matrimonial and other private law proceedings, committing a child into the care or supervision of a local authority, was ended. Instead, under s 37, it may request a local authority to carry out an investigation of a child's home circumstances. The Act also introduced a new judicial option by providing a power, under s 16, to make a family assistance order, requiring a local authority to provide short-term support to a family.

The most important principle introduced by the 1989 Act was that when determining any issue affecting the upbringing of a child the court must, as stated in s 1(1), regard the welfare of that child as the paramount consideration. There was – and is – no requirement that the welfare checklist, as stated in s 1(3), be considered in any uncontested private family law proceedings. So, for example, in an uncontested adoption application the court is not obliged to refer to the checklist and therefore is not under a duty to consider alternative orders.

PARENTAL RESPONSIBILITY ORDER

This provides the means whereby an unmarried father, who is unable or unwilling to acquire parental responsibility for his child by making a voluntary agreement with the mother, may be vested with such responsibility by the court under s 4(1) of the 1989 Act. The making of an order is clearly a matter of judicial discretion to be exercised according to the welfare interests of the child concerned. The order vests parental responsibility in the bearer, though not necessarily to the exclusion of others. It lasts until terminated by the court on the application of any person with parental responsibility for the child or, with the leave of the court, the application of the child concerned (see also Chapter 4). The court has decided[19] that where the following tests are satisfied then it would *prima facie* be in the child's best interests for a parental responsibility order to be made:

a the degree of commitment which the father had shown to the child;
b the degree of attachment which existed between them; and
c the reasons of the father for applying for the order.[20]

Where a father has been previously convicted of violence against the mother and of cruel behaviour towards the child,[21] or where he is in

19 See *Re H (Illegitimate Children: Father: Parental Rights) (No 2)* [1991] 1 FLR 214.
20 This approach was later endorsed by the court in *Re G (A Minor) (Parental Responsibility Order)* [1994] 1 FLR 504.
21 As in *Re T (A Minor) (Parental Responsibility: Contact)* [1993] 2 FLR 450.

prison and there is little evidence of attachment,[22] then the court will refuse his application for this order.

GUARDIANSHIP ORDER

Guardianship has its origins at the heart of private family law. A guardianship appointment is most likely to be uncontested and, whether made by parent or court, confers a *de jure* duty of care on a named adult in respect of a specific child. This distinguishes it from a number of other *de facto* care relationships (see, 'Carers', below). Such *de facto* arrangements can leave the responsibility for safeguarding the welfare interests of a child in some uncertainty. This problem was addressed first by the Law Commission[23] and then by the Children Act 1989.

The law of guardianship is now wholly governed by ss 5 and 6 of the 1989 Act. A guardian may be appointed by the court or by a parent. The court may make such an appointment either on application or of its own motion in any family proceedings. A parent appointment may be made under s 5(3): 'A parent who has parental responsibility for his child may appoint another individual to be the child's guardian in the event of his death.' The provision requires the appointment to be made by will or deed or by means of some other such properly attested legal document: that is, no special document is needed.

Guardianship has been statutorily assimilated, along with wardship, into that category formally defined in the Children Act 1989 as 'family proceedings' (for all practical purposes). It now shares with other such proceedings some specific characteristics in relation to welfare. For example, the criteria governing appointment are statutorily prescribed, the common welfare threshold of the paramountcy principle determines any change in the child's status in relation to the applicant and, if granted, the order vests parental responsibility in the applicant.

To be appointed guardian, whether by parent or court, is to be vested with full parental responsibility for the child. Just like a parent, the guardian must ensure that the child's welfare interests are catered for by providing adequate food, clothing, medical aid and lodging and by making appropriate arrangements for the child's education and religious upbringing. The role of the guardian is to 'stand in the shoes of the parent' and undertake responsibilities for the child to the extent and in the manner that the parent would have done. Therefore, under s 3(1) of the 1989 Act, the guardian assumes the role of the parent in relation to 'all the rights, duties, powers, responsibilities and authority which by law a parent of a child has in relation to the child and his property'. Like a parent, a guardian will be liable to criminal charges for any

22 See *Re P (Parental Responsibility Order)* [1997] 2 FLR 722.

23 See *Law Commission Report No. 91 Review of Child Law: Guardianship*, London, HMSO, 1985.

neglect, ill-treatment or failure to educate the child. Again, like a parent, if parental responsibility is shared between a number of guardians, or between a parent and a guardian, then each has an equal and independent right of action and right of access to the court to resolve disputes. In a sense, guardianship is unique in that it does not divest a parent of authority; rather, it is a trust relationship which empowers an appointed person to act for the parent.

However, there are limits on the extent to which a guardian 'stands in the shoes of the parent'. A guardian is not expected to shoulder the full private family law responsibilities of a parent. The public sector provides a 'guardianship allowance' to defray maintenance expenses and special provision is also made in the Child Support Act 1991 for guardians. Nor are they permitted to benefit from their appointment by, for example, inheriting the property of a deceased child. A guardian has no rights of succession. Nor will the appointment have the effect of conferring on the child the citizenship of the guardian. Among the attributes of parental authority which vest in a guardian, but not in the holder of a child arrangements order, are the right to consent or withhold consent to adoption and the right to appoint a testamentary guardian.

Where the parents are divorced and the one with care and possession of the children wishes to ensure that in the event of his or her death the other does not remove them, then a guardianship appointment could be made in favour of a third party (perhaps a grandparent on that side of the family). This will have the effect of placing the guardian on the same legal footing as the surviving parent, who, of course, retains parental responsibility. He or she will then be able to resist any threatened peremptory removal by that parent, at least until the matter is brought before the court. This, in fact, was more or less what occurred in a case[24] where the Court of Appeal, overturning a decision favouring a surviving divorcee, ordered that the children remain with the appointed guardians pending an assessment by a social worker.

DIVORCE, NULLITY AND JUDICIAL SEPARATION ORDERS

Prior to the introduction of the 1989 Act, parties to a marriage breakdown had a general expectation that legal proceedings would conclude with a judicially brokered package, including orders in respect of their children (for custody or access). This expectation owed a lot to s 41 of the Matrimonial Causes Act 1973. The court then had a strict duty, before making absolute any decree of nullity or divorce, to be satisfied that the parties' proposed arrangements in respect of the future welfare interests of their children were 'satisfactory' or 'the best that could be devised in the circumstances' or that 'it is impractical for the party or parties appearing before the court to make any such arrangements'. Effectively, this gave the judiciary the power and duty to

24 See *Re H (A Minor) (Custody: Interim Care and Control)* [1991] 2 FLR 109.

play a very positive role in respect of a child's welfare; the private interests of the parties could be realised only if they first undertook to satisfy a public interest in ensuring the future welfare interests of that child. Arguably, welfare interests in private proceedings could only benefit from the mandatory representation provided in public proceedings by solicitor and guardian *ad litem*.

However, s 41 was amended by the 1989 Act to remove the mandatory welfare test. With the test has gone the assumption that proceedings need necessarily conclude with judicial orders in respect of any children of the marriage. Its removal has combined with the additional influence of the 'no-order' presumption contained in s 1(5) of the 1989 Act to produce the result that in consensual proceedings, for divorce or nullity or for judicial separation, the court no longer has a strong positive function in relation to welfare. What was previously a strict duty, central to the 'welfare proofing' of future care arrangements, has been significantly watered down. The link is broken between the private right of parents to obtain an order dissolving the legal basis of their spousal relationship (or settling the terms of their separation) and the duty of the court to ensure that the exercise of that right is compatible with the public interest in adequate care arrangements being made for the future welfare of any children concerned.

Instead, two discretionary powers have been introduced, each with a marginal capacity to affect a child's welfare interests: a power under s 37 to request a local authority investigation into a child's circumstances; and a power under s 16 to make a family assistance order.

SECTION 8 ORDERS: JUDICIAL INITIATIVE

The court has a power, under s 10(1)(b) of the 1989 Act, to intervene and on its own initiative make a s 8 order in 'any family proceedings in which a question arises with respect to the welfare of a child'. In theory, this provides a powerful safety net to ensure that private law proceedings are concluded in a manner compatible with the welfare interests of the children involved. However, the opportunity for such intervention is dependent upon information being placed before the court alerting it to the existence of grounds for concern regarding welfare matters. This may not happen.

Even the full formal divorce process offers no guarantee that the court will scrutinise care arrangements for children. Under s 41 of the Matrimonial Causes Act 1973 (as substituted by the Children Act 1989, Sched 12, para 31) the court is still prevented from making absolute a decree of divorce, nullity or separation unless, by order, it declares itself satisfied that: there are no children of the family; or the arrangements for the welfare of the children that have been made are satisfactory or the best that can be made in the circumstances; or it is impracticable for the party or parties appearing before the court to make any such arrangements for the children. The court will initiate enquiries only where a disclosure of information obviously calls into question the adequacy of proposed arrangements and such a disclosure will inevitably delay proceedings, which both parties will usually wish to avoid. If the court is able to make a finding of satisfaction, it may then issue an order to that effect and need not be concerned about the possible bearing of the provisions available under the 1989 Act. This will follow almost automatically where the proceedings are uncontested.

Because most divorces are uncontested, and proceedings are conducted entirely on the basis of affidavits, the judge will usually see only the plaintiff's 'statement of arrangements for children'. This statement is frequently perfunctory, with few details, and there is no means whereby the court can check the accuracy of the facts presented therein. Even where the facts give rise to some judicial disquiet in relation to proposed care arrangements, the no-order presumption of s 1(5) will militate against any initiative by the court to exercise its discretionary power under s 10(1)(b) to issue a s 8 order. There will very seldom be any opportunity for the court to hear the views of the children concerned.

The Family Law Act 1996 This situation was reinforced by the Family Law Act 1996, which by removing the fault grounds for divorce, leaving only the ground of irretrievable breakdown and emphasising the importance of mediation, ensured that fewer divorce proceedings would be contested.

The 1996 Act introduced very little in the way of change to the role played by the welfare principle in divorce proceedings. Allowance was made for the welfare interests of any children involved to affect the length of the waiting period. The nine-month waiting period required between the filing of the statement of marital breakdown and the hearing was compulsorily extended by a further year where divorcing parents have a child below the age of 16. This extended period can be waived in circumstances where the court is satisfied that such a delay would be significantly detrimental to the welfare of a child. Where the offer of mediation is accepted or directed by the court, and is being provided under the legal aid scheme, the mediators are required – under s 13B(8) of that scheme – to have arrangements designed to ensure that the parties are encouraged to consider:[25]

1. the welfare, wishes and feelings of each child; and
2. whether and to what extent each child should be given the opportunity to express his or her wishes and feelings in the mediation.

This provision did no more than meet the basic requirements of Article 3 of the European Convention on the Exercise of Children's Rights. When the matter comes before the court and consideration is given to whether the provisions of the 1989 Act need to be utilised, the court is then required, under s 11(4), to have regard to a checklist of factors which includes the child's wishes

25 As inserted by s 27 of the Family Law Act 1996.

and feelings, the parties' conduct in relation to the upbringing of the child and the general principle that the child's welfare is best served by promoting a good continuing relationship with both parents. These new welfare provisions did not add significantly to the existing law, nor were they readily operationalised.

SECTION 8 ORDERS: PARENTAL INITIATIVE

Before the introduction of the 1989 Act, the parties to a marriage breakdown when seeking an order governing the future status of their marital relationship would also petition the court for orders in relation to the future care arrangements for their children. Often the latter were simply requests for a judicial endorsement to confirm care arrangements already privately agreed and these would be routinely granted. Since the 1989 Act, orders relating to children are granted only where there is an actual dispute regarding care arrangements. There is no scope for a parental initiative to obtain a s 8 order in uncontested proceedings; most divorce proceedings are uncontested.

Carers In public law, there is now a proliferation of care relationships (baby sitters, child-minders, foster-parents, playgroup organisers, teachers, supervisors in crèche and nursery school facilities, etc.) which are not individually endorsed by a specific grant of authority. In private law, the more complex relationships associated with the modern role of the family in society, particularly those resulting from second and third marriages, have also generated many care relationships (most obviously, step-parents and cohabitees) that are similarly ill-defined in law.

The introduction of custodianship orders under the Children Act 1975 gave the judiciary access to a statutory means of protecting and providing ongoing security for established care relationships. The legal construct 'parental responsibilities', introduced by the 1989 Act, is now central to identifying the rights and duties of carers. As stated in s 2(9) of that Act:

> A person who has parental responsibility for a child may not surrender or transfer any part of that responsibility to another but may arrange for some or all of it to be met by one or more persons acting on his behalf.

This provision allows informal arrangements to be made whereby parental responsibility may be shared with another person. The person with care of the child but without full parental responsibility is required, under s 3(5)(b), to do 'what is reasonable in all the circumstances of the case for the purpose of safeguarding or promoting the child's welfare'. This will include taking decisions such as to remove a child in need of protection to a safe place and to authorise treatment in the event of an accident. The act of delegation will not affect the continuing liability of the delegator for ensuring the safety and well-being of the child concerned.

Care by a relative is defined by s 105(1) of the 1989 Act, which states: '"relative", in relation to a child, means a grandparent, brother, sister, uncle or aunt (whether of the full blood or half blood or by marriage or civil partnership), or step-parent'. Arguably, one reason for this definition is to mark a legislative distinction between the *locus standi* of those entitled to be heard by the court on a matter affecting the welfare of a child and those not so entitled, though there are no provisions explicitly to that effect. Unarguably, it serves to place the respective rights of all those mentioned on an equal footing.

In general the courts look more favourably on arrangements which keep responsibility for the care of a child within the family, albeit the extended family, rather than arrangements which require local authority involvement. The 1989 Act, with its statements of principle requiring the courts and local authorities to give preference to family-based care and through the s 8 range of orders, enables the judiciary to give security to carers and child, alike.

Grandparents, in common with all others defined as 'relatives', are entitled to apply for child arrangements orders under the 1989 Act. Where the child has lived with them for a minimum of three years, and they have the consent of anyone with parental responsibility, then the application may be made without leave of the court; otherwise, leave must be obtained. In private family law proceedings, an application by a grandparent for such an order will stand a greater chance of success if supported by a birth parent and, conversely, will be more likely to fail if contested by such a parent. Where the evidence demonstrates that contact would be to the child's best interests, even where the child is in care, then the court will need to be dissuaded from making an order.[26]

A step-parent has long been denied recognition as coming within the legal definition of 'parent'.[27] The fact that such a person lacked legal rights in respect of their spouse's children, despite voluntarily undertaking maintenance and other responsibilities, has often been the subject of judicial concern. However, legislative unease about the use of adoption by a step-parent to acquire with a spouse joint exclusive custodial rights to the latter's children of a previous marriage has also been apparent. The s 8 orders were created with the circumstances of step-parents very much in mind.

Child arrangements orders are seen as offering an enduring degree of status, protection and security commensurate to the care responsibilities of a step-parent and not necessarily foreclosing a child's relationships with the 'other side of the family'. Where a child is 'a child of the family', as defined by the 1989 Act, then a step-parent is entitled without leave to apply for a residence or contact order (both now subsumed into the child arrangements

26 See: *Re F and R (A Minor) (*Section 8 *Order: Grandparent's Application)* [1995] 1 FLR 524; and *Re M (Care: Contact: Grandmother's Application for Leave)* [1995] 2 FLR 86.

27 See *Re N* [1974] 12 All ER 126.

order) and with leave to apply for a specific issue or prohibited steps order. The effects of such orders are the same as for any carer.

The position of a child who is unrelated in any way to a third party into whose care or under whose supervision he or she has been placed has been considerably improved by the 1989 Act. Providers of child-minding and day-care services, private foster-parents and schoolteachers are now all under a firmer duty than formerly to safeguard the welfare interests of any child in their care.

Contested proceedings

The modern role of the welfare principle is most evident in contested private law proceedings. These are usually brought for judicial determination of an aspect of a child's upbringing, the contesting parties are parents or a parent and a carer of the child concerned and the outcome is the issue of a s 8 order or orders. However, by the time the 1989 Act came into effect, private family law in the UK had become a good deal more complex. This was evident in the range and volume of litigation and litigants appearing before the courts. For example, the child may be both applicant and subject in a dispute concerning his or her welfare interests and need not have any blood relationship with the contesting parties. Proceedings regarding where a child is to live may be disputed not by a first party but by a grandparent, step-parent, foster-parent or any person with either parental responsibility or an established direct care relationship with the child concerned. The type of issues which attract litigation in a modern and more fluid world (in terms of relationships, careers, homes, etc.) are no longer concerned almost exclusively with where and with whom a child is to live but extend to include issues regarding names, healthcare, travel arrangements, variety of relationship contacts, etc.

By the close of the twentieth century, the nature, role and weighting of the welfare principle – as defined largely, but not exclusively, under the Children Act 1989 – had become a significant factor in the judicial determination of contested private family proceedings.

Principles, parties and proceedings

The role played by the welfare interests of the child is explicitly articulated in certain principles, is apparent in the rules governing the *locus standi* of the parties and has been largely consolidated in contested private proceedings by the 1989 Act.

Principles

The most important principle introduced by the 1989 Act is that when determining any issue affecting the upbringing of a child the court must, as stated in s 1(1), regard the welfare of that child as the paramount consideration. There are other significant duties arising in the context of contested proceedings. The welfare interests of a child are to be ascertained by reference to a stated checklist of considerations. The concept of parental responsibilities, rather than parental rights, will guide judicial determination of any such contest. No parent is to lose or be wholly absolved of future responsibility for a child, other than by way of a third-party adoption. At any time, more than one person may hold parental responsibility in respect of a child. An order shall not be made in respect of a child unless it would be better for the child to make the order than to make no order at all. Any order must be made with the minimum of delay and litigation should be the least required in the circumstances.

Parties

The range of persons who may now appear as parties in private contested proceedings has greatly changed from the time when family law meant the law relating to the marital family unit. Now, the 'child of the family' who is the subject of the contest need not necessarily have a blood relationship with the contesting adults. The latter may include grandparents, foster-parents, uncles and aunts, the partner of a parent, or any person who, although unrelated, has an established care relationship with the child in question. In fact, the boundaries constituting 'family' – the forum within which, or in reference to which, the law has always sought to determine the welfare of the child – have now become so wide and fluid as to defy definition. This generalised deconstruction is also apparent in the function of proceedings that are now more likely to address and adjust specific aspects of care arrangements, such as contact, rather than simply deal with long-term custody.

Under s 10(4) of the 1989 Act, the following are entitled to apply for any s 8 order without leave of the court:

(a) any parent, guardian or special guardian of the child;
 (aa) any person who by virtue of section 4A has parental responsibility for the child
(b) any person who is named in a child arrangements order that is in force with respect to the child, as a person with whom the child is to live.

Then, under s 10(5), there are those who may apply only for a residence or contact order (both now known as a child arrangements order). Such persons are any party to a marriage (whether or not subsisting) in relation to whom the child is a child of the family and any person with whom the child has lived for a period of at least three years. This category also includes those who make application with the consent of a person in whose favour a child arrangements order has been made – or the local authority in whose favour a care order has been made – in respect of the child concerned. Any and every person who has parental responsibility for such a child will always be so entitled. Also, under s 10(2)(b), an application for a s 8 order with respect to a child may be made by any person who 'has obtained the leave of the court to make the application'.

Where the child is the applicant then, under s 10(8), in determining whether or not to grant leave, the court may do so only when satisfied that he or she 'has sufficient understanding to make the application'. This provision has proven to be a powerful legal tool for positively advancing the welfare interests of children.

Where the applicant is a person other than the child concerned then, under s 10(9), the court is required to have particular regard to:

(a) the nature of the proposed application for the section 8 order;
(b) the applicant's connection with the child;
(c) any risk there might be of that proposed application disrupting the child's life to such an extent that he would be harmed by it; and
(d) where the child is being looked after by a local authority –
  (i) the authority's plans for the child's future; and
  (ii) the wishes and feelings of the child's parents.

That s 10(9) does not present a finite checklist of factors was emphasised in *Re A (A Minor) (Contact: Leave to Apply)*.[28] The court may not, however, apply the paramountcy principle. A s 10(9) applicant must demonstrate a sufficiently strong case to give a reasonable chance of success, if leave is granted.[29]

Section 9(3) prohibits any person who is, or has been within the previous six months, a local authority foster-parent from applying for any s 8 order unless that person has the consent of the local authority, is a relative of the child in question or the child has lived with him or her for at least one year preceding the application.

BIRTH PARENTS

The law clearly differentiates between the *locus standi* of unmarried parents in respect of their child. A birth mother is held to be inherently vested with full parental responsibilities for the child. A birth father will have no parental responsibilities unless he acquires them or they are vested by court order in him. As an ever-increasing proportion of annual births occur in a non-marital family context, this disparity between the legal positions of a child's parents is an important factor in any resulting private law dispute between them, or between either of them and a third party, on a matter concerning the upbringing of that child.

The increased importance of the welfare principle in such disputes is particularly evident where the contest lies between first and third parties. It

28 [1995] 3 FCR 543.
29 See *G v. Kirklees Metropolitan Borough Council* [1993] 1 FLR 805 per Booth J.

would seem, for example, to be displacing the legal weighting traditionally attached to the 'blood link'. This is no longer as determinative a factor as formerly in judicial determination of disputes between first and third parties.[30] Indeed, in such disputes, there is some evidence to show that the judiciary will also discount the bearing of legal status; parental responsibilities, whether vested inherently or by court order, will not outweigh the judicial importance attached to the child's welfare interests.[31]

Where the contest lies between first parties then, unless an unmarried father can demonstrate the existence of a relationship bond with his child, the presumption that a mother with care should continue in that role will be very difficult to refute. As the House of Lords (now the Supreme Court) has advised, there is a particular onus on an unmarried father to show that an order made in his favour would bring benefits to the child concerned.[32]

CHILD OF THE FAMILY

The proceedings, whether uncontested or otherwise, may apply in respect of any child of either of the parties, or a child treated as one of the family, who is aged less than 16 (though the court may direct that an older child be included).

Most obviously, a child of the parties is one born to both spouses during the course of their marriage. The child of either spouse, or one adopted by either or both, or who has lived with them in the family home, also meets this definition. Conversely, a child of either spouse who has been adopted into another family, as opposed to being placed by them in a private foster-care arrangement, can no longer be regarded as a child of the parties. The anomalous common law rule that the father is the natural guardian of his legitimate child[33] was removed by s 2(4) of the 1989 Act.

The term 'child of the family' remained largely unchanged by the 1989 Act except that, in relation to children in the care of a local authority and fostered with a family, it was interpreted as applying to children who are 'placed' rather than 'boarded-out'. The relevance of related caselaw, which previously defined the boundaries of this term, remained applicable. So, for example, an unborn child would not be included within this definition. This was the effect of the ruling in a case[34] where a pregnant wife left her husband within a week of their marriage and it was proven that he was not the father of the resultant child. Bagnall J held that there was no sense in which the deserted spouse could be regarded as having treated the then unborn child as a child of the

30 See, in particular, the House of Lords rulings in both *Re KD (A Minor)* [1988] AC 806 and *S v. M (Access Order)* [1997] 1 FLR 980.
31 See, for example, *Re O (A Minor) (Custody: Adoption)* [1992] 1 FLR 77.
32 See *Sanderson v. McManus* 1997 SLT 6.
33 See s 2(4): 'The rule of law that a father is the natural guardian of his legitimate child is abolished.'
34 See *A v. A (Family: Unborn Child)* [1974] Fam 6, [1974] 1 All ER 755.

family. The duration of the marriage may be very short, as in a case[35] where it lasted only a fortnight, yet still allow children to fall within the definition. However, there must be proof that the family unit actually existed before a child can be regarded as having been treated as a member of it.

Proceedings

The 1989 Act brought a new coherence to private family law proceedings. By far the majority of all private family law disputes concerning a child's welfare interests were subsequently brought before the court in the form of applications for s 8 orders. These usually occurred in the course of proceedings for divorce, separation or nullity, though they also occurred as freestanding applications, for example by grandparents, step-parents or foster-parents, under the 1989 Act. Sometimes disputes could, instead, be the subject of wardship proceedings. At other times welfare interests were addressed by applications for certain 'hybrid' orders.

By the end of the twentieth century, the law governing contested arrangements for children arising in the context of proceedings for divorce, nullity or separation was as stated in the Family Law Act 1996 together with s 44 of the Matrimonial Causes Act 1973, as amended. Only in 'exceptional circumstances' would the court delay the granting of a decree absolute. In most instances the court determined a divorce application without examining the parties on the detail of their proposed care arrangements. Later, in fresh proceedings, most typically for child arrangements orders, perhaps combined with other s 8 orders, one of the parties may bring this matter before the court. In that small minority of cases, where there is clear conflict regarding proposed care arrangements, the court will issue a s 7 direction to the local authority or a probation officer requesting a report on the welfare of the child or children concerned.

When proceedings come before the court, the fact of contest establishes the welfare threshold and triggers the mandatory judicial scrutiny of proposed care arrangements. This will not necessarily lead to a rigorous examination and testing of the parties' plans, nor definitely involve the children having their views represented before the court. It does, however, provide for the possibility of the child concerned being fully engaged as a party to proceedings, with attendant representation. Normally, the court will wish to hear from any child involved if he or she is sufficiently mature to have formed a considered view regarding future care arrangements, though such views will not be regarded as determinative. This marks a significant advance for the role of welfare interests in private law. The mandatory application of the paramountcy principle to determine issues relating to upbringing is also an important safeguard for those interests in this context.

35 See *W v. W (Child of the Family)* [1984] FLR 796, CA.

Under s 10(1)(b), in any family proceedings in which a question arises with respect to the welfare of any child, the court may make a s 8 order with respect to the child if 'the court considers that the order should be made even though no such application has been made'. Under s 11(3), it may make such an order at any stage during the course of family proceedings even though not in a position to finalise the proceedings. It may even do so in respect of a child in care, though this is restricted to the making of a child arrangements order.

The court will resort to using the powers of wardship only where statutory powers are unavailable or inappropriate to assist mainly parent applicants negotiate equitable arrangements for the upbringing of their children or to determine a particular issue affecting the welfare interests of a child. Before the introduction of the 1989 Act, and despite the greater reporting of public law wardship cases, the majority of wardship applications were private. It then also provided a forum where the legal interests of persons (such as an unmarried father, grandparent, step-parent, etc.) who would have had difficulty in finding representation in statutory proceedings could be taken into account when determining matters of custody or access. It also offered any applicant with an interest a 'court of last resort' when a particularly urgent, unusual or complex issue arose in relation to the welfare of a child. Since the 1989 Act, which imposed no constraints on private applicants, wardship has continued to offer a limited role for determining contested issues affecting a child's welfare interests.

Finally, some private law disputes concerning a particular aspect of a child's welfare can be addressed through narrowly defined proceedings for orders which are neither wholly public nor private in nature. These include parental responsibility orders, orders for financial relief and orders relevant in contexts such as domestic violence and child abduction and directions for local authority investigations.

The s 8 orders

Private family law orders, in relation to contested arrangements for children are available under s 8 of the 1989 Act and may be sought with or without leave of the court or following intercession by the court. Each order may be made for a specific or an unlimited period of time and otherwise end on the child's 16th birthday unless exceptional circumstances require an extension. Unlike their predecessors, these orders are intended to be flexible and a number may be made to provide a comprehensive package tailored to fit the particular circumstances of an individual child. Under s 11(7), conditions may be attached, additional judicial directions given and their duration specified. The s 8 orders and the ability to attach conditions provide wide opportunities for tailoring a disposal option to match the needs profile of a particular child. They permit a real shift in the judicial role in contested private proceedings from an adjudicative to an adjustive function. Instead of a s

8 order, the court may make a parental responsibility order, a family assessment order or an order appointing a guardian.

Residence orders and contact orders were both eventually replaced by the current child arrangements orders.[36]

RESIDENCE ORDER (NOW CHILD ARRANGEMENTS ORDER)

This, the first and most significant of the s 8 orders available to the court, was defined by s 8(1) as 'an order settling the arrangements to be made as to the person with whom a child is to live'.

It gave parental responsibility for a child, most often accompanied by actual physical possession, to a named person or persons, and replaced the previous custody order.

A residence order was usually made in favour of one person – a parent. Under s 10(4) and (5), a parent or guardian could be applicants as of right. Under s 9(3) all others required leave of the court. A local authority foster-parent could also apply but, depending on duration of care, would require the authority's permission before seeking leave of the court. An order could be made out to two or perhaps more persons, none of whom need be a parent.[37] Thus, grandparents, foster-parents, uncles and aunts or any combination of same, whether living together or not, could be eligible for such an order. Section 9(1) of the 1989 Act enabled the court to make a residence order in respect of a child in the care of a local authority which would have the effect of discharging the latter. In contrast, a local authority was prohibited by s 9(2) from being either an applicant or recipient in respect of such an order. This lack of reciprocity across the private/public divide demonstrated the different weighting statutorily allocated to the welfare principle in the two sectors.

Significantly, a residence order could also be made in favour of a child applicant.[38] This possibility at first attracted considerable media speculation that it would provide the means whereby children in this jurisdiction would be able to emulate the example set by their counterparts in the United States and, in effect, 'divorce their parents'. However, in cases such as *Re C (A Minor) (Leave to Seek Section 8 Orders)*,[39] where a 14-year-old girl sought a residence order to allow her to live with her friend's family, the court indicated that it would not license unilateral use of this order by children when to do so would threaten the interests of the family as a whole. It has to be said that this is a challenging proposition when viewed in the context of rights – those of parents to divorce and of *Gillick* competent children to make decisions. Despite the ruling in *Gillick* and the international thrust towards

36 See O'Halloran, K., *Children and the Law: European Perspectives on Welfare and Rights*, Abingdon, Routledge, forthcoming.
37 See, for example, *A v. A* [1994] 1 FLR 669, where a residence order was used to achieve a sharing of parental responsibilities.
38 See *Re AD (A Minor)* [1993] Fam Law 43.
39 [1994] 1 FLR 26. See also *Re O (Minors) (Leave to seek Residence Order)* [1992] 1 FLR 172.

recognising children's rights, the courts still hold to the view that the welfare interests of a child are best assured by protecting the legal integrity of the family unit, in the absence of grounds which prove otherwise. Significantly, the local authority saw no sufficient reason to treat the matter as one giving rise to issues of public law and therefore did not apply for either a care or a supervision order.

Under s 12(2), the making of a residence order automatically vested parental responsibility in the person named in the order. Its primary effect was to decide where a child should live and it was usually made in favour of one person – a parent. However, a residence order did not vest parental responsibility exclusively in the bearer. As between first parties: where one parent was granted an residence order, both would nonetheless retain full parental responsibility, and with it the capacity to take most decisions independently of each other in regard to the child concerned. As between first and third parties: s 12(2) provided that a parent or guardian with parental responsibility would not lose it on the making of a residence order in favour of a non-parent. Finally, s 2(6) provided that in any circumstance a person with parental responsibility would not lose it merely because a residence order had been granted to another.

The scope of authority vested by a residence order was not equivalent to its predecessor – the custody order. In particular, s 13(1) prevented the child's removal from the jurisdiction, though the courts were be prepared to recognise exceptional circumstances when this would be permissible.[40] The Court of Appeal held[41] that the law governing this issue remained the same as before the introduction of the 1989 Act. It confirmed the views earlier expressed by Bracewell J[42] that, while the welfare test was to be satisfied by reference to the checklist, it was not necessary methodically to apply and satisfy each item on that list.

Section 13 also prevented any change being made to the child's surname without the consent of all those with parental responsibility. This particular prohibition was subsequently judicially endorsed.[43] The singular importance attached to this matter was apparent in the comment jointly made by Thorpe and Hurst LJJ in *Dawson v. Wearmouth*: 'the registration or change of a child's surname is a profound and not a merely formal issue, whatever the age of the child'.[44] The court would apply the paramountcy principle to determine whether or not a child's surname should be changed. Caselaw reveals that little judicial weight would then be given to the views of the child concerned.[45]

40 See: *Re K (A Minor) (Removal from the Jurisdiction)* [1992] 2 FLR 98; and *M v. M (Minors) (Removal from the Jurisdiction)* [1992] 2 FLR 303 CA.

41 See *H v. H (Residence Order: Leave to Remove from the Jurisdiction)* [1995] 1 FLR 529.

42 See *M v. A (Wardship: Removal from Jurisdiction)* [1993] 2 FLR 715.

43 See: *Re B (Change of Surname)* [1996] 1 FLR 791; and *Re P (Change of Surname: Parent's Rights)* [1997] 2 FLR 730.

44 [1997] 2 FLR 629 at p 635.

45 See, for example: *W v. A (Minor: Surname)* [1981] 2 WLR 124, where the children were aged 12 and 10; and *Re B (Change of Surname)* [1996] 1 FLR 791, where they were aged 16, 14 and 12.

The hallmark of a residence order was that it authorised more than one person to hold parental responsibility for a named child at the same time: in keeping with the principle of parental responsibility, it did not vest authority exclusively in the named party. The other parent continued to hold and share with the named party all responsibilities in respect of the child, except for those covered by the order. Section 12 directed that where any court was making a residence order in favour of a father who did not yet have parental responsibility the court should then also make an order under s 4 of the 1989 Act giving him that responsibility; where the person vested with a residence order was not a parent or guardian then, under s 12(4), that person should have parental responsibility for the duration of the order and thereafter until revoked. Each parent retained the right to act independently of the other and the right to delegate their responsibility to another (e.g. a child-minder).

Under s 11(7), the court could attach conditions to a residence order. These could be in relation to matters such as blood transfusions, medical treatment or specific living arrangements. In respect of the latter, if the court issued a joint residence order, it could specify the periods the child was to spend in each household. It could also specify the duration of the order. The use of shared residence orders proved contentious.[46] Section 11(5) provided that a residence order should cease to have effect if the parent in whose favour it was made lived together with the other parent for a continuous period of six months or more. Under s 91(10), it would cease when the child concerned attained the age of 16 (or 18 in exceptional circumstances).

The residence order became a vitally important mechanism for giving effect to the principle of the welfare of the child in contested private family law proceedings. It offered the primary means for determining the major issue for child welfare – identifying the place the child would call 'home' – following family breakdown. Accessed by meeting threshold criteria which permit a wide range of applicants, it allowed the court to exercise a broad ambit of discretion in determining the party or parties in whose favour the order should be made, the variety of directions and conditions to be attached and their duration. Most applications, however, were uncontested. Only in that small minority of divorce, nullity or separation cases where the parties disclosed a disagreement in relation to future care arrangements for a child would the welfare test be judicially applied to determine in whose favour the order should be made. This seldom occurred because such a disclosure would inevitably delay the legal dissolution of the marriage.

CONTACT ORDER (NOW CHILD ARRANGEMENTS ORDER)

The second most significant s 8 order, in terms of degree of authority, was the contact order. In numerical terms, however, it was the one that was most

46 See, in particular, *A v. A (Minors) (Shared Residence Order)* [1994] 1 FLR 669. See also: *Re H (A Minor) (Shared Residence)* [1994] 1 FLR 717; and *G v. G (Joint Residence Orders)* [1993] Fam Law 615.

frequently made. This order gave recognition to the authority of Article 8(1) of the European Convention on Human Rights and Fundamental Freedoms, which states: 'Everyone has the right to respect for his private and family life, his home and his correspondence.' It was defined by s 8(1) of the 1989 Act as follows:[47]

> a 'contact order' means an order requiring the person with whom a child lives, or is to live, to allow the child to visit or stay with the person named in the order, or for that person and the child otherwise to have contact with each other.

It had a more comprehensive and flexible application than its predecessor – the access order – and was more assiduously enforced, usually in favour of a non-resident parent, by the courts.

Under s 10(4) and (5), any parent or guardian or any other person with a residence order in respect of the child concerned could apply as of right for a contact order. Under s 9(3), others were required first to seek leave of the court. A local authority could not apply. In the case of grandparent applicants, there was a requirement under s 10(1)(a) that leave of the court had to be obtained before an application was made. Having been granted leave, however, the courts would not recognise any presumption entitling a grandparent to contact: the applicant had to show good reason.[48]

Like the access order, a contact order vested rights in a named adult. It allowed defined contact or communication between the child and a named person or persons; that person need not be a parent or relative; and more than one contact order could be in effect at the same time in respect of the same child. Contact could be direct, providing for person-to-person meetings, at such times and perhaps places as specified by the court. Contact could also be defined as indirect, which could take the form of communication by letter or phone instead of or as well as person-to-person meetings.[49] It could allow for overnight stays, specify visiting arrangements and provide for 'reasonable contact' or contact at such intervals as determined by the court. A contact order made under s 8 differed from a contact order made under s 34. The former was a positive order, enabling contact between a child and a named

47 Section 8(1), as amended, now states:
'child arrangements order' means an order regulating arrangements relating to any of the following –
(a)with whom a child is to live, spend time or otherwise have contact, and
(b)when a child is to live, spend time or otherwise have contact with any person.

48 See *Re A (A minor) (Contact Application: Grandparent)* (1995) *The Times*, 6 March, CA.

49 See: *Re O (A minor) (Contact: Imposition of Conditions*) [1995] 2 FLR 124, where the contact was in the form of school reports; and *Re M (A Minor) (Contact: Conditions)* [1994] 1 FLR 272, where permission was given for contact by post between an unmarried father in prison and his two-year-old son.

person, and could not be made in respect of a child who was the subject of a care order; the latter limited, removed or redefined such contact. Under s 11 (7) of the 1989 Act, the court could attach conditions or make such directions as it considered fit, which allowed this order to be a particularly flexible and directive mechanism for the court to address the welfare interests of a child. Section 11(6) provided that the order would cease to have effect if the parent in whose favour it was made returned to live with the other parent for a continuous period of at least six months. Under s 91(10), it would cease when the child concerned attained the age of 16 (or 18 in exceptional circumstances). A care order discharged a contact order.

Continuing contact with both parents is presumed to be beneficial for a child's emotional stability. The contact order was a strategically important means of giving effect to the welfare principle in contested private family law proceedings. Its modern welfare significance has its roots in the decision in *M v. M (Child: Access)*,[50] when the court held that access was essentially a right of the child rather than of the parent. Caselaw has since continued the presumption that the inherent right is that of the child to maintain relationships.[51] In maintaining a child's presumed right to parental contact, the courts have been very alert to any initiative by one parent intended to deprive the other of contact. The Court of Appeal ruled that even 'eccentric, bizarre behaviour' should not deprive a father of contact with his children unless this behaviour presented a risk of harm.[52] The fact that a father was in prison, that he was not recognised as such by his son and that the mother and her family refused to cooperate did not deter the court from making an order for indirect contact on the grounds that this was in the child's long-term welfare interests.[53] However, as Balcombe LJ has observed,[54] the essential point is not whether contact is beneficial for the child but whether there is any good reason why the child should not have access. Where the application for contact occurred against a background of violent behaviour from the applicant towards the child's mother, with a real prospect of this recurring in the future, then the court would be justified in denying the father's request for contact with that child.[55] As before the introduction of the 1989 Act, disputes relating to contact continued to present the courts with the most litigated and hotly

50 [1973] 2 All ER 81.

51 This principle has been repeatedly asserted in such cases as: *Re S (Minors: Access)* [1990] 2 FLR 166; *Re H (Minors) (Access)* [1992] 1 FLR 148, CA; *Re R (A Minor) (Contact)* [1993] 2 FLR 762; and *Re M (Contact: Welfare Test)* [1995] 1 FLR 274.

52 See *Re B (Minors: Access)* [1992] 1 FLR 142.

53 See *A v. L (Contact)* [1998] 1 FLR.

54 See *Re M (Minors) (Access)* [1992] Fam Law 152.

55 See: *Re D (Contact: Reasons for Refusal)* [1997] 2 FLR 48; *Re H (Contact: Domestic Violence)* [1998] 2 FLR 42; and *Re A (Contact: Domestic Violence)* [1998] 2 FLR 171. See also Hester, M. and Radford, L., 'Domestic Violence and Child Contact Arrangements in England and Denmark', *Journal of Social Welfare and Family Law*, 14(1) (1992), pp 57–70.

contested problems in the law relating to children; and such problems were exacerbated when one of the parties refused to comply with the order.

The parent with a residential order, or with possession, who flatly refused to comply with contact arrangements agreed by the court fundamentally challenged the capacity of the latter to safeguard the welfare interests of the child concerned. In the pre-1989 Act era the judicial response was expressed with typical good sense by Ormrod LJ, who observed,[56] when ruling out enforcement by imprisonment: 'These cases are exceedingly intractable. They can only be dealt with by tact not force. Force is bound to fail.' Following the introduction of the 1989 Act, however, such cases came to be governed more firmly by the rule that access between child and parent was presumed to be in the welfare interests of the child concerned, and the court would not flinch from using imprisonment where it believed that an obdurate parent was obstructing contact. As Balcombe LJ stated,[57] the test to be applied was: '[A] re there any cogent reasons why a child should be denied the opportunity of access to his natural father?' Where the conditions were satisfied, the welfare checklist had been applied and contact was found to be in the child's interests then it would seem the court must make the order;[58] conversely, where the benefit of contact to the child was not clear then the order should not be made.[59] The principle was that though a parent may ultimately frustrate the court's intentions, he or she could not be permitted to foreclose the court's duty to make an order giving effect to the child's best interests. However, there is a very fine line to be drawn between the parent who is plainly and simply obstructing the court and the parent who by doing so is also prejudicing the welfare of the child to the point where an order would be counterproductive. For example, a mother's implacable hostility, fuelled by the attitudes of her mother and her second husband, was such that the court considered it to be futile to make an order which would only place the child concerned under considerable additional pressure.[60] Although questioned by the Court of Appeal, this view was ultimately allowed to prevail. Should the parent flagrantly and persistently refuse to comply with court orders allowing contact then the court might well treat this as contempt.[61]

The court could buttress contact orders in the face of parental hostility by issuing specific issue orders or prohibited steps orders, attaching conditions to a residence order, or directing a court officer, constable or local authority social worker to undertake and supervise contact arrangements.

56 See *Churchard v. Churchard* [1984] FLR 635 at 638 F–H.
57 See *Re D (A Minor) (Contact: Mother's Hostility)* [1993] 2 FLR 1.
58 As in *Re W (A Minor) (Contact)* [1994] 2 FLR 441 and *Re H (A Minor) (Contact)* [1994] 2 FLR 776.
59 See the judgment of the House of Lords in *Sanderson v. McManus*, op cit.
60 See *Re J (A Minor) (Contact)* [1994] 2 FLR 729.
61 See *A v. N (Committal: Refusal of Contact)* [1997] 1 FLR 533, where the Court of Appeal upheld a sentence of six weeks imposed on the parent concerned.

A child who refused to comply with the court's contact arrangements presented a double problem. Firstly, was the refusal a genuine reasoned or felt response emanating solely from the child or had it been produced as a result of pressure or prejudice from the child's carer? Secondly, in either case, would the child's welfare be best furthered in the long term by continuing, readjusting or severing the contact? The Court of Appeal ruled[62] that the following test should be applied: is the fundamental emotional need of every child to have an enduring relationship with both parents outweighed in this case by the depth of harm which the child will be at risk of suffering as a consequence of the court making the contact order? In this way the court raised a presumption of contact, underpinned by the welfare principle, evidenced by a basic tenet of developmental psychology,[63] to be displaced only by evidence that such contact would breach the 'significant harm' threshold.

SPECIFIC ISSUE ORDER

This order enables the parties, usually parents, to appear before the court to seek direction in relation to a specific aspect of parental responsibility. It is defined by s 8(1) of the 1989 Act as follows: 'an order giving directions for the purpose of determining a specific question which has arisen, or which may arise, in connection with any aspect of parental responsibility for a child'. The aim, however, is not to give one parent or the other a general 'right' to make decisions about a particular aspect of the child's upbringing. Instead, it is to enable a particular dispute over such a matter to be resolved by the court, including the giving of detailed directions, where necessary. Under s 10(4), a parent, guardian or special guardian may apply as of right, as may any person with parental responsibility or who has a child arrangements order in respect of the child concerned. All others may do so only with leave of the court.

The order directs that the named party or parties behave in a specified manner with regard to the issue raised. It replaces the flexible powers previously available to the judiciary in wardship proceedings with a narrower discretionary power which may be applied to any specific difficulty between the parties. It may be made in conjunction with a child arrangements order and may be made instead of the latter where its comprehensive authority is unnecessary to resolve a limited area of contention. The court may attach conditions.

The specific issue order has a limited application to a child's welfare interests but, because of its directive nature, is often of vital importance in circumstances where such interests are in need of urgent protection. Like a prohibited steps order (see below), it is confined to dealing with narrow issues relating to specific aspects of parental responsibility. Most commonly, such issues have concerned a child's education[64] or their return to the

62 See *Re M (Contact: Welfare Test)* [1995] 1 FLR 274, CA.
63 See Bowlby, J., *Attachment*, London, Penguin, 1969.
64 As in *Re P (A Minor) (Education)* [1992] 1 FLR 316, CA.

jurisdiction.[65] An extreme example of an aspect of parental responsibility, which has in the past from time to time required judicial action in wardship proceedings, occurs when a child needs urgent medical treatment against parental wishes. That it is appropriate for the court to use this order in such a context is evident from the ruling in *Re R (A Minor) (Blood Transfusion)*.[66]

PROHIBITED STEPS ORDER

This replaced the prerogative power previously available to the judiciary in wardship proceedings. It is defined by s 8(1) of the 1989 Act as follows:

> 'a prohibited steps order' means an order that no step which could be taken by a parent in meeting his parental responsibility for a child, and which is of a kind specified in the order, shall be taken by any person without the consent of the court.

Under s 10(4), the eligibility of applicants is as above for a specific issue order. All others may do so only with leave of the court. It may be made *ex parte.*

A prohibited steps order enables the court to place a veto against the exercise of specific aspects of parental responsibility, such as a threatened removal of the child in question from the jurisdiction,[67] from a particular school or prohibiting a specific medical operation. It replaces the traditional use of wardship to restrain contact between children and undesirable third parties. While the issue in question must relate to an aspect of parental responsibility, the order can be made against any person whether or not they are vested with such responsibility. It may, therefore, be made against an unmarried father or a former cohabitee to restrain that person from contacting the applicant. Under s 11(7), the court may attach conditions to a prohibited steps order.

There are limitations to the use of a prohibited steps order. It cannot, for example, be made in respect of a child in care. Unlike the range of powers available in wardship, a prohibited steps order, in common with all s 8 orders, may have to be buttressed by a separate application for an injunction where the offending matter or behaviour cannot be construed as strictly parental. Where the authority required is to prevent parents from contacting each other,[68] then an injunction rather than a prohibited steps order is appropriate. When one parent wishes to bar the other from their home then, as Sir Stephen Brown P pointed out, 'it is very doubtful whether a prohibited steps order could in any circumstances be used to "oust" a father from the

65 As in *Re D (A Minor) (Removal from the Jurisdiction)* [1992] 1 All ER 892, CA.
66 [1993] 2 FCR 544.
67 This was the type of activity instanced as the rationale for such an order by *Law Commission Report No. 172 Family Law Review of Child Law, Guardianship and Custody*, London, HMSO, 1988, para 4.20.
68 As in *Croydon London Borough Council v. A and Another* [1992] 1 FCR 522.

matrimonial home'.[69] Under s 9(5)(a), neither a prohibited steps order nor a specific issue order may be made where the objective is one which may be achieved by making a child arrangements order. The Court of Appeal[70] had cause to examine the relative merits of a contact order and a prohibited steps order as the means for providing a mother with the necessary authority to prevent a former cohabitee from contacting children in respect of whom he was considered to pose a risk. Butler-Sloss LJ, giving judgment for the court, held that a prohibited steps order would be more appropriate as liability for a breach would then lie against the cohabitee, whereas under a contact order it would lie against the mother.

Like the specific issue order, the prohibited steps order is a strictly limited legal means for giving effect to the welfare principle, and, unlike the residence order and contact order (both since subsumed into the child arrangements order), it continues to be available. It makes available a particular power, drawn from the wardship jurisdiction, to provide a narrowly defined authority for the protection of a child's welfare interests.

WARDSHIP ORDER

As is clear from its history (see, further, Chapters 1 and 4), the jurisdiction of wardship is based on safeguarding the welfare interests of a child and for centuries has done so through application of the paramountcy principle. The authority of the court when exercising the wardship jurisdiction is not quite the same as that vested in a parent. In some respects its scope is not so extensive. Authority for the adoption of a ward, for example, will not necessarily rest on judicial consent. However, when exercising its inherent and unlimited *parens patriae* jurisdiction (which encompasses wardship) its authority is more extensive than that of a parent. It may, for example, prohibit the publishing of information[71] concerning a ward, override the refusal of a parent or mature minor to consent to medical treatment,[72] override legal or professional privilege to obtain evidence[73] or attach a direction to an adoption order[74] requiring the Registrar General not to divulge certain information.

Wardship is rooted in private family law and is not governed by the restrictions on its use as listed in s 100 of the 1989 Act. However, the range

69 See *Nottingham County Council v. P* [1993] 3 All ER 815 at p 825b, CA.
70 See *Re H (Prohibited Steps Order)* [1995] 1 FLR 638, CA.
71 See, for example, *Re X (A Minor)* [1975] Fam 47, where it was held that in the particular circumstances of the case the interests of the ward should not prevail over the interests of freedom of publication. Note, also, that the court's inherent powers are buttressed by s 12 of the Administration of Justice Act, which makes it a contempt of court to publish any report of a wardship hearing.
72 See *Re W (A Minor) (Medical Treatment: Court's Jurisdiction)* [1992] 3 WLR 785, [1992] 4 All ER 627.
73 See *Barking and Dagenham LBC v. O and Another* [1993] 3 WLR 493.
74 See *Re X (A Minor) (Adoption Details: Disclosure)* [1994] 2 FLR 450.

and flexibility of orders, introduced under s 8 of the 1989 Act, had their intended effect of countering the attractions of wardship in private family law as an alternative to statutory proceedings.[75] As Waite LJ has stated:[76]

> the courts' undoubted discretion to allow wardship proceedings to go forward in a suitable case is subject to their clear duty, in loyalty to the scheme and purpose of the Children Act legislation, to permit recourse to wardship only when it becomes apparent to the judge in any particular case that the question which the court is determining in regard to the minor's upbringing or property cannot be resolved under the statutory procedures.

He went on to express the view that there has to be a special justification for giving a child 'the status – an exceptional status under the modern law as it must now be applied – of a ward of court'.

Although the annual number of private wardship applications has fallen since the 1989 Act came into effect, there have nonetheless been a significant number and range of cases where the jurisdiction has been exercised. Foremost in terms of growth has been that category of cases where medical practitioners seek the consent of the court in relation to the treatment needs of a child where their proposed action is being contested by a parent. The cases divide into two subcategories: those where a hospital wishes to deny treatment and those where it wishes to provide it.

In the first group, the cases of *R v. Cambridge District Health Authority ex parte B*[77] and *Re C (Medical Treatment)*[78] provide not untypical examples. The first concerned the well-publicised case of 10-year-old Jamee Bowen, who had leukaemia. Her wishes and those of her parents that certain expensive, painful and experimental treatment be provided was resisted by the medical authorities on the ground that it could not be justified as it was unlikely to lead to a successful outcome. The Court of Appeal approved the medical approach. The second case concerned a child aged 16 months, in intensive care, diagnosed with a fatal spinal disease and dependent upon a ventilator. The medical practitioners sought the consent of the court to withdraw the life support system against the wishes of the child's loving parents who, as Orthodox Jews, firmly believed that palliative care was sinful and that every effort should always be made to sustain life. Again, the court overruled parental objections and endorsed the medical approach. In the course of his judgment, Sir Stephen Brown P quoted with approval from caselaw in which

75 See *Re CT (A Minor) (Wardship: Representation)* [1993] 2 FLR 278 and *Re R (A Minor) (Blood Transfusion)*, op cit, for judicial views on the effect of restrictions imposed by the 1989 Act on access to wardship in private and public law, respectively.
76 In *Re CT (A Minor) (Wardship: Representation)*, op cit.
77 [1995] 1 FLR 1055.
78 [1998] 1 FLR 384.

the judicial view was expressed that the court would not force medical practitioners to adopt a treatment approach contrary to their clinical judgment.

In the second group, the religious beliefs of parents have often been a factor. For example, in *Re O (A Minor) (Medical Treatment)*[79] Johnson J ruled that the inherent jurisdiction was the most appropriate forum to authorise a blood transfusion for a child against the wishes of the child's parents, who were Jehovah Witnesses and caring, committed and capable people.[80] In *Re T (Liver Transplant: Consent)*[81] the court considered the case of a baby suffering from a life-threatening liver defect whose parents were opposed to treatment. Evidence was admitted which indicated that the prognosis for recovery following a transplant was good, whereas the child would die within 18 months without one. The parents, unmarried but in a stable relationship, and both healthcare professionals with experience in the care of sick children, maintained that it was not in their child's best interests to suffer the pain and distress of a major operation. The Court of Appeal agreed. The court held that it could not be in the child's best interests to order caring, well-informed parents to facilitate an operation with which they so profoundly disagreed. The legal significance of this decision lies in the judicial readiness to assimilate the welfare interests of a very dependent baby and those of a devoted, caring mother. This fusion of the legal interests of parent and child carries resonances of a judicial logic not dissimilar to that which last prevailed in the *In re Agar-Ellis*[82] ruling.

As Fortin has pointed out,[83] it is troubling that the court finds itself obliged to take decisions which place medical practitioners in a position of carrying out invasive treatment programmes which conflict with their clinical judgment. *Re T* may be an exception to this policy but perhaps it only indicates that a decision which does so conflict, but results in non-treatment, is not imposing any positive duties on medical practitioners and is therefore not a true exception. It is odd that the court would adopt such a policy in respect of the decisions of one specific professional group; it certainly would not regard itself as being so bound in relation to social workers and care orders, for example. Also troubling is the indication of a willingness to assimilate the interests of parent and child. If there has been one dominant trend in family law in recent decades it has been the painstaking untangling of their separate

79 [1993] 2 FLR 149. See also *Re R (A Minor) (Blood Transfusion)* [1993] 2 FLR 757.

80 See also: *Re B (A Minor) (Wardship: Medical Treatment)* [1981] 1 WLR 1421 and *Re S (A Minor) (Medical Treatment)* [1993] 1 FLR 376. However, subsequently, the practice has been to use specific issue orders to deal with less controversial issues, such as blood transfusions.

81 [1997] 1 WLR 242. For an authoritative dissection of the issues, see Michalowski, S., 'Is it in the Best Interests of a Child to Have a Life-saving Liver Transplantation? *Re T (Wardship: Medical Treatment)*', *Child and Family Law Quarterly*, 9(2) (1997), pp 179–190.

82 (1878) 10 ChD 49.

83 See Fortin, J., '*Re C (Medical Treatment)*: A Baby's Right to Die', *Child and Family Law Quarterly*, 10(4) (1998), pp 411–416.

sets of interests. It would seem important, particularly in issues where there could be a conflict, that the judiciary resist any return to an approach which aggregates the interests of parent and child.

Another area in which the judiciary have developed a use for the inherent *parens patriae* powers of wardship is where a child suffers from a condition which does not meet the definition of a recognised mental disorder under the Mental Health Act 1983, is judged not to have the competence to make a reasoned decision and whose veto of treatment is endangering his or her own welfare interests. There have been a small number of cases where wardship has been used to override the veto of an adolescent and authorise compulsory detention and treatment.[84] Arguably, for example, in *Re W (A Minor) (Medical Treatment)*[85] such behaviour could have been appropriately addressed by coercive proceedings under the 1989 Act, but instead the court chose to construe the circumstances as raising issues of private rather than public law. This use of wardship to substitute the court's views for the child's, on the issue of what is in the latter's best interests, has been questioned.[86] Of perhaps more fundamental significance is the question: who has authority to take decisions regarding the welfare interests of an adolescent?

From the judgments delivered, particularly in *Re W*, the answer would appear to be the child, the parent and any person or body (e.g. a local authority or court) vested with parental responsibility. Where parental responsibility rests with the court, as when the child has been warded, then its decision will override that of the child, and indeed that of the parent. Where the child is non-competent then a parent or other person or body with parental responsibility may decide. Where the child is *Gillick* competent then he or she may decide but so may a parent and, presumably, any other person or body with parental responsibility. It is not clear to whom a third party must look for a final decision on a matter affecting a child's welfare interests where the child, parent and/or other person with parental responsibility disagree on the best course of action.

There are also certain powers, such as protection from publicity,[87] which may on occasion require recourse to wardship. Although usually initiated by parents or guardians seeking injunctions to prevent unwelcome media attention being focused on their children, it may also be imposed by the court against the wishes of a parent.[88]

84 See, for example: *Re R (A Minor) (Wardship: Medical Treatment)* [1991] 4 All ER 177; *Re W (A Minor) (Medical Treatment)* [1992] 4 All ER 627; *Re K, W and H (Minors) (Medical Treatment)* [1993] 1 FLR 854; *A Metropolitan Borough Council v. DB* [1997] 1 FLR 767; *Re C (Detention: Medical Treatment)* [1997] 2 FLR 180.

85 Op cit.

86 See Downie, A., '*A Metropolitan Borough Council v. DB* and *Re C (Detention: Medical Treatment)*: Extra-statutory Confinement – Detention and Treatment under the Inherent Jurisdiction', *Child and Family Law Quarterly*, 10(1) (1998), pp 101–107.

87 This was the case in *Re M and N (Minors) (Wardship: Publication of Information)* [1990] Fam 211, CA.

88 See *Re Z (A Minor) (Freedom of Publication)* [1996] 1 FLR 191.

As was noted earlier (see Chapter 4), no order has been of greater value to the judiciary, in giving effect to the welfare principle, than wardship. The use of the paramountcy principle in the wardship jurisdiction has had the most far-reaching effects on the legal development of the meaning, role and weighting given to the welfare interests of children, which in turn have had profound consequences for all of family law. The unique feature of wardship has lain in its capacity to transcend thresholds of intervention and prescriptive rules regarding applicants' eligibility, grounds for orders, disposal options available, etc. The effect of a wardship order is to establish the welfare of the child as the overriding objective, to permit a broad exercise of judicial discretion in pursuance of it and to ensure that welfare is determined not by a brief adjudicative process but by ongoing and permissive judicial management.

Other orders and powers

In addition to the s 8 orders, the court had – and largely continues to have – other powers and orders available to it under the Children Act 1989. Some may be used at judicial initiative to supplement, or substitute for, the issue of s 8 orders. Others may be used in response to an application by a parent or other person with parental responsibility. In short, the court now has available to it a flexible array of orders and powers which it can employ on a 'pick-n-mix' basis to address the particular welfare interests of a child in contested private family law proceedings.

FAMILY ASSISTANCE ORDER

The court has the power to direct a local authority to carry out an investigation of the child's circumstances and may make orders for the financial relief of children. Under s 16 1(b) of the 1989 Act, in exceptional circumstances and with the consent of the relevant adult, the court may make an order directing the relevant local authority 'to make an officer of the authority available' to 'advise, assist and (where appropriate) befriend any person named in the order'. This may be coupled with a child arrangements order and be made for a period not exceeding six months.

The court may also make orders for the financial relief of children who are the subject of child arrangements orders, though not in favour of a parent or step-parent. Authority to do so is available under s 15 and Sched 1 of the 1989 Act.

WELFARE REPORTS

The discretionary judicial power to require a local authority to carry out an investigation of a child's circumstances has proved to be of great value as a means of identifying welfare needs of children undisclosed by the parties to private family law proceedings. Under s 7(1) of the 1989 Act:

> A court considering any question with respect to a child under this Act may –
> (a)ask an officer of the Service or a Welsh family proceedings officer; or
> (b)ask a local authority to arrange for –
> (i)an officer of the authority; or
> (ii)such other person (other than an officer of the Service or a Welsh family proceedings office) as the authority considers appropriate,
> to report to the court on such matters relating to the welfare of that child as are required to be dealt with in the report.

In any family proceedings, though most probably for contested s 8 orders, the court may issue a s 7 direction where it considers the arrangements to be questionable.

DOMESTIC VIOLENCE AND WELFARE INTERESTS

Part IV of the Family Law Act 1996, which came into effect on 1 October 1997, provided the civil remedies of proceedings for non-molestation orders and for occupation orders for victims of domestic violence. This legislation built on previous provisions, bringing together some caselaw developments and broadly giving effect to the recommendations of the Law Commission.[89] As the victims, directly or otherwise, are always any children involved, there can be no doubting the importance of these provisions for their welfare interests.

The two orders available, as under previous legislation, are the non-molestation order and the occupation order. Before making either order, the court must apply the 'balance of harm' test: the order must be made if it appears that the applicant or a relevant child is likely to suffer significant harm attributable to the respondent's conduct, unless either is likely to suffer greater harm if the order is not made.

Adoption

Adoption is the most radical of all family law orders. No other order so fundamentally changes the legal status of its subject on a lifetime basis. Its effect is to rewrite the relationships between three sets of legal interests with implications for the wider family circles of those involved, the consequences of which will be felt by subsequent generations. Perhaps for these reasons, the law has traditionally focused on status requirements as the threshold of entry of all parties to an adoption process: availability of child, consent of parent/s and eligibility of applicants.

Adoption has evolved to serve a range of social functions very different from the one it was initially designed to meet. Its long-established legal

89 See *Law Commission Report No. 207 Family Law, Domestic Violence and Occupation of the Family Home*, London, HMSO, 1992.

function[90] of 'providing homes for children who need them' with third-party applicants is dying out. As a consensual process for securing homes for indigenous healthy babies with unrelated applicants, it most probably has no future. However, until well into the latter half of the twentieth century, this legal process remained largely true to its traditional function, as governed by the Adoption Act 1976, though adjustments introduced by the Children Act 1989 were a precursor to more fundamental changes.

Welfare and the parties

The welfare factor in the statutory process of adoption has traditionally tended to be treated negatively, the court confining its considerations to ensuring that no consequences adverse to the child's welfare were likely to ensue as a result of it making the order. Until the turn of the century, the paramountcy principle had no bearing on the outcome of the process. Overall, this approach was not inappropriate when adoption was almost exclusively a private family law proceeding in which, typically, the care of a voluntarily relinquished child had been assumed by unrelated, agency-approved and -supervised adoption applicants. Then, the three sets of needs and legal interests neatly dovetailed.

Adoption, however, had greatly changed in the years since the introduction of the 1976 Act, having become much more complex due to issues arising from either the public law or step-parent contexts, which together generated the availability of by far the largest proportion of all children entering the adoption process. The role of consent as a threshold requirement was fraught with difficulty; its determining effect in the context of testing the rights of a birth parent could be as difficult to judge when withheld in the context of abuse as when freely given in the context of step-parent applications. Many children were of an age, and/or had needs so complicated by varying forms of disability, or by their foreign origin, as to require an in-depth professional and judicial examination of what constituted their particular welfare interests. Nevertheless, under the 1976 Act, the legislative role ascribed to the welfare principle continued to exclude a paramountcy weighting and to be essentially negative, serving as the final and relatively perfunctory test of process outcome after all formal status criteria had been satisfied.

The judicial role in relation to this principle had been broadened by the exercise of discretion to allow for the more frequent involvement of expert witnesses and for the increasing issue of contact orders to accompany adoptions. But exercises of judicial discretion to provide for welfare adjustments in determining the final outcome of adoption processes had not been matched

90 See *Report of the Departmental Committee on the Adoption of Children* (Houghton Report) (Cmnd 5107), London, HMSO, 1972, where the view is expressed that 'The child is the focal point in adoption; providing homes for children who need them is its primary purpose.'

by similar exercises of discretion in relation to the interpretation of threshold requirements at point of entry. Little use had been made of discretionary opportunities to employ the welfare principle to deal with the appropriateness of step-parent applications or to hold that agreement had been unreasonably withheld. The courts preferred to decide the issues almost exclusively in terms of threshold requirements. Welfare continued to be more a factor in, than the objective of, the adoption process.

The parties

Adoption traditionally bound the three parties – child, birth parent/s and adopters – into a process characterised by secrecy and stigma, the outcome of which was to be sealed permanently and exclusively. Of all orders affecting children, adoption was the most immutable in its legal consequences for all concerned. The future welfare of the child was thus predicated on legally sanctioned denial. Only in recent years has adoption acquired the characteristic of 'openness', allowing for a more flexible legal relationship to be shaped between the parties.

THE CHILD

The child is clearly the most important party. Both statutorily prescribed eligibility criteria and the rather more flexible availability criteria must be satisfied before a child can enter an adoption process. To be eligible for adoption a child must first be born,[91] be more than 19 weeks old but less than 18 years of age and, if related to the applicant or placed by an adoption agency, have been in the care of that person for at least 13 consecutive weeks prior to the order being made. In all other third-party applications (e.g. with foster-parents) the child must be at least 12 months old and have been with the applicants for at least the 12-month period immediately preceding the order. The 1976 Act continued the traditional requirement that the child is not and never has been married. Further, the fact that the child had previously been adopted was not a bar to his or her subsequent adoption. To be available for adoption, a child must also be resident within the jurisdiction, though neither domicile nor citizenship is necessary.[92]

Of the children now being adopted only a shrinking minority conform to the traditional stereotypical image of the healthy baby lovingly relinquished by an unmarried British mother to adopters able to afford a standard of care

91 It is not possible to adopt a foetus. However, as was apparent in *Re Adoption Application (Adoption: Payment)* [1987] 2 FLR 291, it is possible to contract in respect of a foetus to be carried to full term by a surrogate mother on behalf of a sperm donor in order that she may eventually be in a position to commence adoption proceedings.

92 Subject to the limitations imposed by the Hague Convention on Protection of Children and Cooperation in Respect of Intercountry Adoption 1993.

the birth mother is unable to provide. Then the threshold of access to the adoption process was set not by adopters' suitability but more by the child meeting eligibility criteria of 'adoptability'; the closer to the stereotype, the greater the probability of adoption and *vice versa.* This approach to adoption served the welfare interests of only a small proportion of the children available, the remainder of whom had to settle for options such as long-term foster care, institutional care in children's homes or benign transportation overseas. Now the majority of children entering the process have characteristics which do not conform to the traditional stereotype, and although far fewer orders are being made, they are being made in respect of children who are more likely to be non-nationals, from married parents, abused, older and/or suffering from a disability than was previously the case. Modern adoption practice has inverted the previous balance in the relationship between adopters and child: it is now the adopters' eligibility that must be established, and only a small proportion of them will be successful, while the remainder will have to explore alternative options, such as surrogacy. Adoption, at least in its third-party form, is now playing a key role in addressing the welfare interests of children who would otherwise remain in public care.

THE BIRTH PARENT/S

The parent or parents to whom the child is born are the parties with whom an adoption process begins. The mother of a non-marital child who wished to relinquish that child to a voluntary adoption society traditionally formed the primary set of needs around which adoption, as a legal process, was constructed. Over time, consenting mothers who wished to relinquish their children for adoption gradually became a dwindling minority of all parents engaged in the adoption process.

Consensual proceedings are now most likely to take the form of a birth mother making joint application with her husband to adopt the former's child born of a previous relationship. The consent of the mother is given for reasons precisely opposite to those that traditionally characterised her role in this process. Adoption is the chosen option of such a mother because it offers an opportunity legally to cement the child into her new marital family unit to the exclusion of any relationship claims which may be made by the child's birth father and/or any of his relatives. By the end of the twentieth century, most adoptions in England and Wales were step-adoptions involving children who would not otherwise have entered an adoption process.

Non-consensual adoptions have come to form an increasing proportion of the annual total of orders made. A birth mother is now likely to want to continue carrying care responsibility for her children but parental fault or default will cause her reluctant involvement with the adoption process. When such circumstances occur the judiciary place a heavy burden of proof upon her to show that she has made the necessary arrangements to secure a stable home environment for her child. Many such mothers are very young, which will not weigh in their favour as the standard of reasonableness required in relation to any proposed arrangements are those appropriate to a mature, reflective parent able to give objective consideration to a child's best interests.[93]

The *locus standi* of a birth father in adoption proceedings, though statutorily strengthened, remained marginal during most of the latter part of the twentieth century, affording him little direct opportunity significantly to affect the legal role of the welfare principle. As he did not have parental responsibility (though he could acquire it), he was not therefore accorded the same legal standing as a marital father. For example, in *Re C (Adoption: Parties)*[94] the court held that such a father did not even have to be made a respondent to an adoption or freeing application.

THE ADOPTERS

The eligibility of applicants is statutorily prescribed and forms a threshold for commencing adoption proceedings. Their suitability is largely determined by permissive criteria set by the adoption agencies (including reference to religion, maximum age, financial security, quality of relationships and lifestyle). Suitability criteria are in theory more discretionary and can permit a degree of flexibility which permits the matching of an applicant's attributes to the particular welfare needs of a child. The bearing of such criteria on the standing of the applicants differs according to whether they are first- or third-party applicants. In relation to the latter, the criteria set by agencies has at times been such as to leave them open to accusations of 'fettering their discretion' by imposing quite rigid rules (e.g. in regard to age, race and lifestyles) which have the effect of erecting a further threshold. The informal suitability threshold, ostensibly constructed around welfare indicators, has proved to be at least as formidable a barrier for a prospective applicant in adoption proceedings as the formal statutory threshold. In recent years the courts have demonstrated an alertness to instances where agencies have sought to introduce such unjustified suitability criteria and have been at pains to emphasise that while matters such as lifestyle, race, religion, etc. may be taken into

93 See the Court of Appeal decisions in both *Re V (A Minor) (Adoption: Consent)* [1987] 2 FLR 89 and *Re R (A Minor) (Adoption: Parental Agreement)* [1987] 1 FLR 391, where the court held that young mothers were being unreasonable in withholding consent when their conduct was viewed objectively.

94 [1995] 2 FLR 483. But see also *Re O (A Minor) (Custody: Adoption)* [1992] 1 FLR 77, where the court ruled that the custody of a child aged 15 months and placed at birth by its mother with an adoption agency should be granted to its natural father. It appears that the court took the view that neither the welfare interests of the child nor the marital status of the father should be determinative. See, further, Bainham, A., *Children: The Modern Law*, 2nd ed., Bristol, Family Law, 1998, pp 167–168, for evidence that the court will give weight to an application from a natural father where the contest lies between him and a third party rather than directly with the natural mother.

account, they cannot be permitted to prevail over the fundamental consideration of what is in a particular child's best interests (see below).

Statutory law and welfare interests

Adoption in the UK is very much a creature of statute. The legislative intent has always been to prescribe the criteria to be met if the status of a child is to be so radically and irrevocably changed. Although the welfare of a child is of central importance, under the 1976 Act it remained little more than one factor among several to be considered. The welfare requirement is positive and prognostic: that an order would merely be consistent with the child's welfare has never been sufficient grounds in itself for his or her adoption.

The principles governing the adoption process, as stated in s 6 of the 1976 Act, were:

> In reaching any decision in relation to the adoption of a child, a court or adoption agency shall have regard to all the circumstances, first consideration being given to the need to safeguard and promote the welfare of the child throughout his childhood; and shall so far as practicable ascertain the wishes and feelings of the child regarding the decision and give due consideration to them, having regard to his age and understanding.

This statement of the welfare principle, of central importance to the 1976 Act, did not make the welfare interests of a child the paramount concern. It was binding on both the court and an adoption agency 'in reaching any decision in relation to the adoption of a child'. In an important precedent,[95] 'any decision' was interpreted to mean that the principle did not apply to the issue of dispensing with agreement and, therefore, it continued to be excluded from determining that issue. Indeed, in relation to the role of the principle as a determinant of proceedings, it could be argued that satisfaction of the welfare requirement as part of the judicial function comes too late in the adoption process to be helpful to the child. Louis Blom-Cooper once rightly observed that 'the process of adoption is not essentially justiciable; the issues in adoption are hardly susceptible of solution by the application of legal concepts and rules of law'. There was also something of a philosophical conflict between the exclusiveness of an adoption order, with its presumption of severing all ties between a child and his or her family of origin, and the ethos of sharing parental responsibility, which underpinned the orders introduced under the 1989 Act.[96] Wall J acknowledged this when commenting: '[it is] logical that a

95 See the ruling of the House of Lords in *Re M (A Minor)* [1980] CYLB 1801, endorsing the judicial approach in *Re P (An Infant) (Adoption: Parental Consent)* [1977] Fam 25.

96 See *Re T and E* [1995] 1 FLR 581 for a case where the conflict was more than philosophical.

different test needs to be applied to the making of an order which extinguishes parental rights as opposed to one which regulates their operation'.[97] However, for the time being, the conflict existed largely on a philosophical level and adoption law remained relatively intact.[98] Nonetheless, the fact that adoption proceedings were designated family proceedings under the Children Act 1989 did carry some specific implications for the adoption process. It meant, for example, that the 'no-order' presumption applied, though it was open to a slightly different interpretation than the s 6 direction that 'the order if made be for the welfare of the child concerned'. The 'no-delay' rule similarly applied.

Adoption placement

Arguably, because of its capacity to determine future welfare, the most critical decision in the adoption process is the placement decision. Such placements were of two distinct types: third party and 'family'.

In relation to third-party placements, safeguards had been provided by the statutory requirement, mandatory in most circumstances, that they be subject to prior professional assessment. Indeed, one objective of the 1976 Act was to end the possibility (as graphically expressed by the Houghton Report) of a parent, or someone acting on their behalf, giving a child to a casual acquaintance, such as someone they had met in a launderette.[99] This objective was largely achieved by s 11, which prohibited a parent from either making a 'direct' adoption placement of their child with a 'stranger' or authorising a third party to do so. It did, however, permit a parent to place or make an arrangement to place a child with a proposed adopter who was a relative of that child. A third-party adoption placement would be legal only if made by a registered adoption agency, by authority of the High Court, by freeing order or with a relative of the child, though a third-party placement could – and increasingly did – arise from a foster-care placement.[100] A variant of third-party placements – those made in furtherance of inter-country adoption – grew in significance towards the end of the century.

A 'family' adoption usually resulted from one birth parent simply retaining care and possession after a breakdown in joint parenting arrangements. In

97 See *Re D (An Infant) (Adoption: Parent's Consent)* [1995] 1 FLR 895 at p 898, a view endorsed in para 7.1 of the 1992 *Review.*

98 In due course the findings of the Department of Health's *Review of Adoption Law: Report to Ministers of an Interdepartmental Working Group*, London, HMSO, 1992 and the subsequent White Paper *Adoption: The Future* (Cmnd 2288), London, HMSO, 1993 resulted in changes to adoption law which addressed the problem of harmonising the role of the welfare principle in child care and adoption.

99 See Houghton Report, op cit, para 81.

100 Interestingly, a foster-care placement made on the traditional basis of 'long-term with a view to adoption' was viewed as prohibited under the 1976 Act. See, for example, *Gatehouse v. Robinson* [1986] 1 WLR 18.

such circumstances the child is never actually 'placed' before an adoption application is made. The parent who has retained care responsibility then applies jointly with a new spouse to adopt the child. The welfare factor becomes susceptible to professional scrutiny only at a time chosen by the prospective adopters.

Both third-party and 'family' placements have, since the 1976 Act, been statutorily required to be professionally scrutinised, specifically for welfare assurance purposes, prior to the hearing of an adoption application.

PLACEMENT BY FREEING ORDER

The primary legislative intent behind the introduction of 'freeing' to the adoption process was to provide a mechanism for the consensual involvement of a birth mother allowing her to take an early decision to relinquish her child voluntarily for adoption and be spared any further legal role in that process. It was also thought that this would provide a means whereby the mother could be constructively involved, if appropriate, in the transfer phase until the child settled. Although only an adoption agency could apply for a freeing order, it was expected that applications would be made jointly by agency and parent/s. Initially, it was possible to make such an application in respect of a child in care on a voluntary basis,[101] but this was subsequently prohibited. Indeed, for various reasons, including changes made by the 1989 Act, freeing became and has continued to be very much a public law proceeding with applications being largely made on a non-consensual basis by adoption agencies in respect of children already the subject of care orders (see, further, Chapter 8).

Freeing without parental consent occurs when an adoption agency, as sole applicant, makes what is almost always a contested application in respect of a child in local authority care and the subject of a care order. In such cases the child is seldom a baby but usually under five years of age. However, before making application under ss 18–20 of the 1976 Act, an agency had to be sure that it could meet certain basic requirements. A preliminary issue for the court was whether the order, if granted, would satisfy the 'best interests' test of s 6.[102] There was also a clear expectation that the child concerned was either already placed with prospective adopters or about to be so placed. In the absence of parental consent, the applicant was required to satisfy the court that there was evidence that agreement to the making of an order should be dispensed with on a ground specified in s 18(2). Once made, the order operated to vest parental responsibility wholly in the adoption agency.

101 Research in England and Wales had shown that a high proportion of freeing orders (approximately 33 per cent in one study) were made in relation to children in care with parental consent. The Adoption Act 1976, s 18(2), (2A), as amended by the 1989 Act, Sched 10, para 6, had the effect of ending any possibility of the freeing process being used in respect of any child who was not the subject of a statutory care order.

102 See *Re D (A Minor) (Adoption: Freeing Order)* [1991] 1 FLR 48, CA.

Where a freeing order is made, an adoption process commences, which may or may not conclude in an adoption order. Unless the parent concerned has made a 'no further involvement' declaration then, 12 months later, the agency must inform that parent whether the child has or has not been placed for adoption and/or been adopted. In the event of no declaration being made and the child being neither adopted nor placed for adoption the parent has the right to apply for a revocation of the freeing order. If granted, revocation has the effect of extinguishing the parental responsibility vested in the agency, returning that responsibility to the parent/s and reviving any previous parental responsibility agreement, order or appointment of guardian but not reviving any order made under the 1989 Act.

The freeing process presented risks for the welfare interests of the child concerned. The process itself can be as time consuming as an application for an adoption order, which raises questions as to whether a lengthy two-stage process with accompanying uncertainty is always justifiable. Once granted, a freeing order consigns the freed child to what the *Adoption Law Review* once described as 'a legal limbo'.[103] The uncertainty regarding the legal status of such a child extends to doubt as to his or her succession rights. Finally, in the event of an adoption placement never being made or an adoption application failing, it seemed that all parental responsibilities vested by the freeing order in the agency remained so vested for the duration of the subject's childhood.

The welfare role of agencies and officials

Adoption legislation contains few objective criteria due to the fact that control over the adoption process is, in effect, delegated to adoption agencies. By the end of the century that process had both greatly contracted and at the same time become increasingly professionalised. The fewer children being adopted, many in the course of contested proceedings and bringing with them complicated legal and social problems, received attention from a new range of bodies and officials. Their bearing on the process differed according to whether an application was public or private.

A registered adoption agency is the key professional reference point in the adoption process. It has been defined as a 'body of persons whose functions consist of, or include the making of, arrangements for the adoption of children'.[104] Each agency is required to set up at least one adoption panel. This must take all referrals relating to whether: adoption is in the best interests of a particular child; a prospective adopter should be approved as an adoptive parent; and the home of a particular approved prospective adopter would provide a suitable placement for a particular child. The panel provides a vital

103 See *Adoption Law Review* (Discussion Paper No 2, London, HMSO, 1990, para 134.

104 Josling, J.F. and Levy, A., *Adoption of Children*, 10th ed., London, Longman, 1985, p 23.

and discretionary function by matching prospective adopters with available children. Although it makes recommendations rather than decisions for its agency, the latter – in practice, most often a local authority – is prevented from taking decisions in those areas without first inviting recommendations from the panel. As mentioned above, local authorities have a range of responsibilities in relation to adoption, including, for example, assessment and counselling services appropriate to the needs of all parties and supervisory duties in respect of 'protected' children.

GUARDIAN *AD LITEM*

Two officials – the guardian *ad litem* (GAL) and, to a lesser extent, the reporting officer (RO) – were assigned vital roles under s 65 of the 1976 Act in ensuring the welfare interests of a child in the adoption and freeing processes. The GAL and RO – being independent of the adoption agency involved in any particular application – were each appointed from panels established under the Children Act 1975. Once appointed, the GAL was required to carry out an exhaustive investigation into all the circumstances of the proposed adoption: interviewing all applicants and respondents, including, where feasible, the child and ensuring that any factor having a bearing on the welfare of the child was brought to the attention of the court. The role of both officers in safeguarding the welfare of children entering the adoption process was crucial: the GAL represented a child's welfare interests before the court while the RO was the child's legal representative and advocate for his or her views. The functional separation of roles, combined with their independent status, enabled a balanced picture of a child's particular needs to be brought before the court (see, further, Chapter 6). This particular balance in professional representation, providing separately for a child's welfare interests and legal rights, was very much in keeping with public family law proceedings (notably child-care cases) and very untypical of private family law proceedings.

REGISTRAR GENERAL

The Registrar General, another official whose duties have a bearing on the adoption process, though in effect tied to a post-adoption role, was obliged, by s 50 of the 1976 Act, to: maintain an Adopted Children Register; keep an index of this in the General Register Office; and ensure that records are kept providing a link between an entry in the Register of Births marked 'adopted' and the corresponding entry in the Adopted Children Register. This facilitated the registering of information sufficient to identify child, adopters, date and place in respect of every adoption order issued. Under Sched 10, para 21 of the 1989 Act, the Registrar General was and is required to maintain an Adoption Contact Register, which enables adopted persons and their birth parents who wish to contact each other to do so.

The welfare test

In the late twentieth century, much of the discussion on the policy of adoption legislation centred on the distinction between adoption and custody and the consequential functions of welfare in each process. Some of the most authoritative pronouncements in that regard are to be found in the judgments given by the House of Lords in *J v. C.*[105] Lord MacDermott then stated that 'custody and adoption orders are so different in concept, nature and legal consequences that one cannot validly argue from either of these jurisdictions to the other'.[106] Lord Upjohn commented: 'an adoption order, if made, is the antithesis of an order made in wardship proceedings'.[107] Lord Hailsham, in the debates on the Children Bill in 1975, argued that, while the paramountcy principle applied to 'care and control, custody and guardianship, it cannot be equally true of adoption'.[108] That debate continued for many years but the position remained that the welfare test in the context of adoption required only that the child's interests should be treated as the first consideration. Welfare interests were not of paramount importance.

WELFARE AND PRIVATE ADOPTIONS OF CHILDREN FROM THE PUBLIC CARE SYSTEM

The change of local authority policy, introducing non-consensual adoption for older and often abused or impaired children, rather than maintaining them in residential units or in long-term foster care, might not have been as successful if it had not coincided with both a dramatic decline in the availability of freely relinquished healthy babies and a continued increase in the number of childless couples wishing to adopt. This fortuitous convergence meant that when all prospects for safe rehabilitation had been exhausted, and the preference for a partnership approach between parents and local authority found not to be viable, then the principles and ethos of the 1989 Act gave way to professional decisions that adoption offered the best means of securing a child's welfare interests. The result was that very many children were given the opportunity of an upbringing in a normal family environment which they would not otherwise have had (see, further, Chapter 8). Not until the second decade of the twenty-first century would judicial pronouncements on the perceived undue readiness of local authorities to resort to the 'draconian' option of adoption, in respect of a child in care, have an adverse impact on the numbers being adopted annual.[109]

105 [1970] AC 668, [1969] 2 WLR 540, [1969] 1 All ER 788, HL.
106 Ibid, p 714.
107 Ibid, p 719.
108 See: https://api.parliament.uk/historic-hansard/lords/1975/feb/04/children-bill-hl-1.
109 Particularly *Re B-S (Children)* [2013] EWCA Civ 1146, per Sir James Munby.

WELFARE AND INTER-COUNTRY ADOPTIONS

Inter-country adoptions (ICAs) have given rise to concerns regarding abuses that may place the welfare of children at risk. These most often occur in the context of unauthorised payments,[110] unauthorised placements and proof of consents.

The first two represent the traditional legal abhorrence of 'trafficking' in children and were criminal offences under ss 57 and 11, respectively, of the 1976 Act. Improper payments (e.g. direct or indirect payments to the child's mother) would, if proven, prevent the court from making an adoption order,[111] though much depended on the circumstances and whether the child's welfare interests were otherwise impaired. Improper placements, which were viewed more seriously by the courts, were more likely to result in the refusal of an adoption order. The problems in relation to proof of consents are most often due to the difficulty in establishing, across geographical, cultural and language barriers, the legal status of parent and child and confirming that any consent was given freely and with full understanding of the consequences. Any one or combination of these issues may well complicate the court's ultimate application of the welfare test to a particular ICA application. However, as illustrated in *Re C (Adoption: Legality)*,[112] the fact that there were irregularities – in adopter approval, payments, matching and introduction of adopter and child – would not necessarily be sufficient to outweigh the fact that once the placement is made the passing of time steadily dictates the making of an adoption order as the best option available to the court.

Applying the welfare test to the child subjects of ICAs does of course give rise to some fundamental questions. It must be accepted that the circumstances of war and natural disaster governing the availability of many children are such that their welfare interests can only be improved by this modern 'child rescue' approach of adopters. This rationale, perhaps, lay behind the decision of the court in *Re K (Adoption and Wardship)*,[113] which concerned a five-year-old orphan who had been removed from Bosnia as an injured baby and then 'adopted' by her English rescuers. The court, when faced with a petition from the child's relatives, set aside the defective adoption order but rather than direct her return to her extended family and her country of origin ruled that she should remain with the English couple who had become her 'psychological parents'. However, for some children, their availability is conditioned by the social economics of their country of origin and it may be that the dislocation to family and culture resulting from adoption may prove in the long term not to be conducive to the promotion of their welfare interests.

110 See: *Re An Adoption Application* [1992] 1 FLR 341; *Re AW (Adoption Application)* [1992] Fam Law 539; and *Re C (A Minor) (Adoption Application)* [1992] Fam Law 538.

111 The court may, however, retrospectively authorise payments. See, for example, *Re WM (Adoption: Non-Patrial)* [1997] 1 FLR 132.

112 [1998] 1 FLR.

113 [1997] 2 FLR 230.

This line of reasoning prevailed in the decision of the Court of Appeal in *Re M (Child's Upbringing)*,[114] where it was held that preserving the Zulu identity of a ten-year-old boy, reared for seven years by white foster-parents, was sufficiently important to order his return to his birth parents in South Africa despite his strong wishes to the contrary. While it is admittedly difficult to reconcile the judicial rationales of these two cases, it may be that an ICA will satisfy the welfare test only where, as with other adoptions, rehabilitation in the family of origin has become impossible. The consent, or absence of dissent, of the child concerned must also be a factor in meeting that test.

WELFARE AND TRANS-RACIAL ADOPTIONS

Some of the same tensions present in ICAs exist in this context, too. The media-generated controversy surrounding trans-racial adoptions has tended to centre on adoption agencies' and local authorities' practice of making and breaking placements on the basis of whether or not there was a racial match between child and prospective adopters. There have been a number of cases where the propriety of this practice has been examined[115] and the emerging consensus is that, where possible, placement arrangements should reflect a child's ethnic background and cultural identity insofar as such considerations are compatible with the welfare interests of that child, which must always have priority. In particular, the courts have upheld the value of preserving established relationships as a key component of welfare interests in trans-racial as in all other kinds of placements, with the duration of current care arrangements and the age of the child being of crucial importance. In *Re N (A Minor) (Adoption)*[116] Bush J warned: 'the emphasis on colour rather than on cultural upbringing can be mischievous and highly dangerous when you are dealing in practical terms with the welfare of children'. The practice was subsequently addressed in a government White Paper on adoption.[117] The view then expressed was to the effect that a child's ethnic background and cultural identity should always be factors to be considered by agency staff when making adoption placements but not necessarily to be given greater consideration than other factors.

114 [1996] 2 FLR 441. See also *Re B (Adoption: Child's Welfare)* [1995] 1 FLR 895, which concerned an adoption application arising from the informal foster-care arrangement made for a Gambian child. In refusing the application, Wall J placed considerable importance upon the child's cultural inheritance as an integral aspect of its welfare.

115 See, for example: *Re P (A Minor) (Adoption)* [1990] 1 FLR 96; *R v. Lancashire County Council, ex parte M* [1992] 1 FLR 109; and *Re JK (Adoption: Transracial Placement)* [1991] 2 FLR 340.

116 [1990] 1 FLR 58 at p 63. See also *Re O (Transracial Adoption: Contact)* [1995] 2 FLR 597.

117 See *Adoption: The Future*, op cit, para 4.32.

WELFARE AND FAMILY ADOPTIONS

It has long been the case that an unmarried mother may adopt her own child,[118] as may an unmarried father.[119] However, the increasing recourse to adoption by mothers of non-marital children applying jointly with their husbands to adopt those children in order to legally seal the boundaries of their new family units eventually became contentious. The effect of an adoption order in such circumstances may be to marginalise not only the birth father but also his side of the family. In *Soderback v. Sweden*[120] the ECtHR accepted that such an adoption amounted to interference with the birth father's right to respect for family life as it totally and permanently deprived him of the opportunity to enjoy family life with his child. For almost all of the latter half of the twentieth century in this jurisdiction, there had been little evidence of suitability criteria being applied by the judiciary to refer uncontested step-parent applications to marital proceedings, despite a warning in the Houghton Report that an adoption order in such circumstances might prejudice rather than benefit the welfare of the child.[121] However, in the final year of the century, in a ruling[122] that went very much against the normal trend, the Court of Appeal did allow the appeal of a birth father against an adoption order made in respect of his child and in favour of the child's mother and husband on the grounds that the father had demonstrated the appropriate attachment, commitment and motive to be eligible for a parental responsibility order.

The Houghton Report also took the view that adoption by grandparents was not, as a rule, desirable.[123] This reservation rests on the significance of age differentials between adopter and adopted and echoes a much earlier warning issued by Vaisey J that 'they should be regarded as exceptional and made with great caution'.[124] There is little evidence that the availability of s 8 orders under the 1989 Act served to raise the suitability threshold for step-parent applicants to a significant extent.

Applications or petitions by birth parents, grandparents, relatives, foster-parents and others with an established relationship with the child were also apt to cause problems: a new legal relationship was being substituted for an existing legal and substantive relationship; purpose and motive became relevant. The use of adoption by family members was held to be unsatisfactory because it added a veneer to an existing legal status in the relationship between child and adopter which may obscure that relationship. The possible eliding of family relationships and potential loss of contact with significant

118 See *Re D (An Infant)* [1959] 1 QB 229 [1958] 3 All ER 716.
119 See *F v. S* [1973] Fam 203 at p 207, [1973] 1 All ER 722 at p 725, CA.
120 [1999] 1 FLR 250.
121 Op cit, paras 97 and 103.
122 See *Re G (Adoption Order)* [1999] 1 FLR 400.
123 Op cit, paras 111–114.
124 See *In re DX (An Infant)* [1949] 1 Ch 320 at p 321.

relatives were among the reasons why family adoptions were viewed as not necessarily conducive to promoting the welfare interests of the children concerned.

WELFARE AND SAME-SEX ADOPTIONS

At the end of the last century, the prospect of adoption by same-sex couples was highly controversial. The 1976 Act was silent on any such possibility; it was simply not within the ambit of legislative intent. The possibility of adoption by a single person was, however, and was duly provided for when the earlier statutory prohibition on adoption of a female child by a single adult male was removed. An adoption application by a single homosexual male or lesbian, where the applicant was living with a partner of the same gender, was therefore legally possible from 1976 onwards, but it did not become professionally or socially acceptable until considerably later, and it was not until the second decade of this century that it became illegal and discriminatory to deny same-sex couples, *per se*, the opportunity to adopt.[125] Judicial notice had been taken of research findings indicating that child-rearing by same-sex couples has not had any deleterious effects on the children concerned and led to the position where judgments began to emphasise that, providing such applicants satisfied the s 6 welfare test, then their sexual orientation was of little relevance. So, for example, in *AMT (Known as AC) (Petitioners for authority to adopt SR)*,[126] where the subject was a three-year-old boy and the applicant a male homosexual living with a long-term male partner, the court granted an adoption order. Similarly, in *Re W (Adoption: Homosexual Adopter)*,[127] an application for a freeing order was unsuccessfully opposed by a birth mother who objected to the local authority's placement of her child with two lesbian women who intended to adopt.

THE WELFARE TEST AND AN ADOPTION ORDER

Welfare is always the final threshold requirement to be met by applicants before an adoption order can be made. Under the 1976 Act, the principle was then given a 'first consideration' rather than a 'paramount' weighting. Lord Simon explained the distinction as follows: 'In adoption proceedings the welfare of the child is not the paramount consideration (ie outweighing all others) as with custody or guardianship; but it is the first consideration (ie outweighing any other).'[128] At the hearing (or earlier in freeing order proceedings) welfare was also present as a component in the threshold requirements to be satisfied by an adoption agency. The agency was then faced with

125 Following the introduction of the Marriage (Same Sex Couples) Act 2013.
126 Fam Law 8 and 225 [1997] 2 FLR 406.
127 [1997] 2 FLR 406. See also *Re E (Adoption: Freeing Order)* [1995] 1 FLR 382.
128 See *Re D (An Infant) (Adoption: Parent's Consent)* [1977] AC 602 at p 638.

the statutorily prescribed duty that it must provide evidence of the existence of either parental agreement or of grounds for dispensing with the necessity for it.

Parental agreement to adoption could be dispensed with only on the grounds stated in s 16(2) of the 1976 Act:

> the parent or guardian –
> (a) cannot be found or is incapable of giving agreement;
> (b) is withholding his consent unreasonably;
> (c) has persistently failed without reasonable cause to discharge his parental duties for the child;
> (d) has abandoned or neglected the child;
> (e) has persistently ill-treated the child; and
> (f) has seriously ill-treated the child but only where (because of the ill-treatment or for other reasons) the rehabilitation of the child within the household of the parent or guardian is unlikely.

The final two grounds were explicitly of a child-protection nature. Despite the opportunity they provided to base the rationale for an adoption on evidence of parental abuse of a child's welfare interests, these grounds were largely ignored. By far the majority of such cases proceeded on the grounds of parental unreasonableness. The test then was whether a reasonable person in the parent's position, being mindful of the child's welfare interests, would be justified in withholding agreement. As Lord Hailsham said in *Re W (An Infant)*,[129] 'welfare *per se* is not the test', or, as Lord MacDermott stated in the same case: 'the mere fact that an adoption order will be for the welfare of the child does not itself necessarily show that a parent's refusal to consent to that adoption is unreasonable'.[130]

The judicial role in adoption has always been essentially adjudicative. Adoption proceedings afford little scope for discretion and almost always end with a decision either to grant or not to grant the order sought. For an order to be made, evidence was required that the above s 6 test could be satisfied. Judicial interpretation of the welfare principle, in relation to the particular circumstances of the child, was then of determining significance. The comparative material advantages[131] offered by the prospective adopters have been held not to satisfy the welfare principle, as have reasons such as legitimation,[132] immigration[133] or simply the wish to change a child's name.[134] The granting of the proposed adoption order must, in the words of Davies LJ,[135] demonstrably further the

129 [1971] AC 682 at p 699.
130 Ibid at p 706.
131 See *Re D (No 2)* [1959] 1 QB 229.
132 See *CD Petitioners* [1963] SLT (Sh Ct) 7.
133 See *In re A (An Infant)* [1963] 1 WLR 34. See also *In re H (A Minor) (Adoption: Non-Patrial)* [1982] Fam Law 121, where an adoption order was granted in respect of an immigrant despite contrary advice from the Secretary of State.
134 See, for example, *In re D (Minors)* [1973] Fam 209.
135 See *In re P* [1977] Fam 25, CA.

welfare interests of a child by offering 'material and financial prospects, education, general surroundings, happiness, stability of home and the like'. While welfare was and is an important factor to be taken into account in all adoption applications, it remains insufficient in itself to justify an order.

Welfare may be interpreted as benefit, but this is not necessarily confined to benefits of a material nature as removal of the stigma of 'illegitimacy' has itself been considered a benefit. In the words of Josling and Levy,[136] 'the main benefit of adoption will be to give the child the social, legal and psychological benefits of belonging to a family'. However, even where an application would clearly safeguard and promote the welfare of the child, the order sought may still be refused, for instance if its purpose is to circumvent immigration policy,[137] or if the court construes it merely as a means by which the applicants are attempting to secure the benefits of education and a better standard of life for the child in question.[138] If a proposed adoption satisfies the welfare test in all other respects then the fact that the applicant is homosexual[139] or that the applicants and social worker have committed criminal offences in breach of ss 11 and 57 of the 1976 Act[140] will not necessarily provide grounds for rejecting the order sought. In *Re B*[141] Wall J commented that the interests of a child in being brought up in accordance with the religious beliefs of his birth parents would be displaced where his welfare interests required it. Under s 6 of the 1976 Act, there was an explicit requirement to consider whether the adoption order, if made, would promote the welfare of the child 'throughout his childhood'. This added a prospective dimension to the welfare test. So, for example, where the Court of Appeal upheld[142] an adoption order granted six days before the subject (who had a learning disability) attained his 18th birthday, it was held that in such circumstances the welfare consideration should extend beyond childhood. The similar requirement in s 6 to take into account whether the applicants can offer 'a stable and harmonious home' had the effect of raising a presumption in favour of adoption for long-term care arrangements, such as those provided by step-parents and foster-parents. This, perhaps, was the determining factor in *Re MW*,[143] where the court dismissed

136 Josling and Levy, op cit, p 5.

137 See: *Re A (An Infant)* [1963] 1 All ER 531, [1963] 1 WLR 231; and *Re R (Adoption)* [1963] 3 All ER 613, [1967] 1 WLR 34. However, see also *Re H (Adoption: Non-patrial)* [1966] 1 FLR 717 and *Re J (Adoption: Non-Patrial)* [1998] 1 FLR 225, where adoptions were allowed despite a breach of immigration rules. This factor was outweighed in importance by the welfare interests of the children concerned, which would be appropriately safeguarded by adoption.

138 See *Re B (Adoption Order: Nationality)* [1998] 1 FLR 965.

139 See: *AMT (Known as AC) (Petitioners for authority to adopt SR)* [1997]; *Re W (Adoption: Homosexual Adopter)* [1997] 2 FLR 406; and *Re E (Adoption: Freeing Order)* [1995] 1 FLR 382.

140 See *Re C (Adoption: Legality)* [1999] 1 FLR 370, 382.

141 [1995] 1 FLR 895.

142 See *In Re D (A Minor) (Adoption Order: Validity)* [1991] 2 FLR 66.

143 [1995] 2 FLR 759.

a surrogate mother's opposition to an adoption application by commissioning parents despite certain illegalities committed by the latter, as 'first consideration' had to be given to the welfare of the child, who by then had been cared for by the applicants for two and a half years.

WELFARE AND VIEWS OF THE CHILD

Under the second part of s 6 there was a requirement to 'ascertain the wishes and feelings of the child ... having regard to his age and understanding'. Following the *Gillick* ruling and the Children Act 1989, a certain amount of caselaw built up around the weighting to be given to a child's views (see, also, Chapters 6 and 7). For example, the decision of a court[144] to dispense with parental agreement was significantly influenced by an 11-year-old boy's views on adoption. This judicial approach was endorsed by an official recommendation[145] that the court should not be allowed to make an adoption order in relation to a child aged 12 years or over unless that child's consent had been obtained or the need for it had been dispensed with. In *Re I (Adoption Order: Nationality)*[146] the court attached considerable importance to the expressed consent of children aged 13 and 16 when approving their adoption despite opposition from the Home Secretary, who submitted that the application was a sham intended to circumvent immigration controls. The question of the importance of taking into account children's views has also arisen in the context of professional privilege. In *Re D (Adoption Reports: Confidentiality)* [147] the House of Lords considered a case concerning a contested adoption application in which the father and stepmother sought to dispense with the birth mother's consent on the grounds that it was being unreasonably withheld. The GAL had a number of interviews with the mother and children, some of the content of which was entered in his report. The wishes and feelings of the children were recorded in two sections of the report and the issue facing the court was whether these sections could be disclosed to the mother in accordance with her request. The decision of the court at first instance to veto disclosure was endorsed by the Court of Appeal but reversed by the House of Lords. In giving judgment, the House took into account: existing caselaw;[148] the differential in significance of disclosure in the context of proceedings in adoption, wardship and under the 1989 Act; and the lack of any

144 See *Re B (Minor) (Adoption: Parental Agreement)* [1990] 2 FLR 383. See also: *Re G (TJ) (An Infant)* [1963] 1 All ER 20, CA; *Re D (Minors) (Adoption by Step-Parent)* [1980] 2 FLR 103; and *Re B (A Minor) (Adoption)* [1988] 18 Fam Law 172.
145 See Department of Health's *Review*, op cit, para 3.
146 [1998] 2 FLR.
147 [1995] 2 FLR 687.
148 In particular: *Official Solicitor v. K* [1965] AC 201; *Re B (A Minor) (Disclosure of Evidence)* [1993] Fam 142, [1993] 1 FLR 191; and *McMichael v. United Kingdom* [1995] Fam Law 478.

similar differential in relation to the reports of a GAL, adoption agency or social services social worker. The ruling of the House, an important benchmark for welfare interests relative to professional privilege, was as follows:

1 It was a fundamental principle of fairness that a party was entitled to the disclosure of all materials which might be taken into account by a court when reaching a decision adverse to that party. That principle applied with particular force to adoption proceedings.
2 When deciding whether to direct that notwithstanding r 53(2) of the Adoption Rules 1984 a party referred to in a confidential report supplied by an adoption agency, a local authority, a reporting officer or a guardian *ad litem* should not be entitled to inspect that part of the report referring to him or her, the court should first consider whether disclosure of the material would involve a real possibility of harm to the child.
3 If it would, the court should next consider whether the overall interests of the child would benefit from non-disclosure, weighing the interests of the child in having the material properly tested against the magnitude of the risk that harm would occur and the gravity of that harm.
4 If the court was satisfied that the interests of the child pointed towards non-disclosure, the next and final step was for the court to weigh that consideration against the interests of the parent or other party in having an opportunity to see and respond to the material. In the latter regard the court should take into account the importance of the material to the issue in the case.
5 Non-disclosure should be the exception and not the rule. The court should be rigorous in its examination of the risk and the gravity of the feared harm to the child, and should order non-disclosure only where the case for doing so was compelling.
6 In the present case the judge had erred in approaching the question of disclosure in the manner of a pure discretion and in giving no weight to the strong presumption in favour of disclosure in adoption proceedings.

WELFARE, ADOPTION AND CONDITIONAL ORDERS

The future welfare interests of an adopted child may also be affected by the judicial power to issue an adoption order accompanied by a condition. Under s 12(6) of the 1976 Act, the court could attach such conditions as it considered necessary to an adoption order. For example, where a relationship already existed between the child and a birth parent or sibling, which may constitute a psychological bond and thus in itself be a determining factor of such welfare, then the courts might see fit also to issue a contact order when making an adoption. In the past the existence of such a meaningful bond has often been judicially viewed as vitiating the welfare ground for an adoption order, adoption and continued contact being seen as mutually exclusive.

The two factors that came to determine whether a contact order (or any other condition) should accompany an adoption order were the welfare of the child and enforceability. Both factors arose for consideration in a leading case[149] where the condition sought and granted was for sibling access. It was then held that a distinction could be meaningfully drawn between the legal standing of a parent and a sibling as regards the legitimacy of their respective claims that an access condition would be to the benefit of the child concerned. While the former would have had every opportunity to bring their claim before the court at the time the substantive issue of consent was being determined, the latter would not. However, once an adoption order had been made, the court would take a different view. In *Re S (Contact: Application by Sibling)*[150] the court refused an adopted nine-year-old child leave to apply for a contact order that would have enabled her to resume her relationship with her seven-year-old half-brother with special needs who had been adopted into a different family. The boy's adoptive parents resisted the application on the grounds that it would disrupt his life. The court held that the making of an adoption order was intended to be permanent and final, and issues such as contact should not be considered after that event except in the most unusual circumstances. Generally, however, in recent years the new flexibility permitted by the introduction of contact orders under the Children Act 1989, together with the tacit encouragement offered in a subsequent White Paper[151] to the practice of facilitating more 'open' adoptions and the concern expressed about step-adoptions, has led to a proliferation of adoption orders being accompanied by orders granting contact rights to birth family members.

Under s 8(4)(d) of the Children Act 1989, adoption proceedings are now defined as family proceedings. The court is therefore entitled, instead of granting an adoption order, to make any of the orders available under s 8 which may be more appropriate where the prospective adopter already has, in relation to the child, the status of step-parent, relative or foster-parent. For example, in a case[152] where an unmarried couple (then ineligible to adopt jointly) wished to adopt a five-year-old child whom they had been fostering for three years, an adoption order was granted to the foster-father despite opposition from the child's mother, and a shared residence order was granted to both foster-parents. The adoption order was considered appropriate as it placed the child on the same legal footing as the couple's other two children, and gave her the same surname. The residence order gave the foster-parent, who was the primary carer, a secure legal relationship with the child.

149 See *Re C (A Minor)* [1988] 1 AER 712h.
150 [1998] 2 FLR.
151 See *Adoption: The Future*, op cit.
152 See *Re B (Adoption: Joint Residence)* [1996] 1 FLR 27. For a judicial appraisal of the relative merits of a residence order and an adoption order, see the Court of Appeal judgment in *Re M (Adoption or Residence Order)* [1998] 1 FLR 570.

Conclusion

The legislative paradigm that construed the thresholds for child welfare and state intervention in family affairs as synonymous in matrimonial proceedings ended with the introduction of the 1989 Act. Thereafter, welfare no longer necessarily required state intervention. Marriage breakdown, the single most significant factor to affect the welfare interests of children in England and Wales, now largely occurs without any judicial scrutiny of proposals for their future care: only contested proceedings give rise to judicial appraisal; if uncontested, as is the case for the majority of proceedings, welfare falls to be cursorily noted on the papers by the parties' solicitors. Family law has conceded that the right of a parent to change his or her spousal status is not conditional upon first satisfying prescribed welfare criteria. Parent-initiated, consensual proceedings were essentially re-privatised and the welfare interests of the children concerned left to be assured by private rather than public scrutiny.

The state not only retreated from this field but reinvested authority in parents to answer for the welfare interests of children whether or not such proceedings were commenced. There was an absence of any legal requirement for a parent to consult with their child before taking a major decision affecting the latter's welfare interests.[153] Indeed, there was judicial authority for the view that, despite *Gillick*, a parent as well as or instead of their adolescent child may give a valid consent to a course of action by a third party on a matter affecting the child's welfare interests.[154] In the absence of child-protection concerns, the welfare interests of a child became subsumed within the legal concept of parental responsibility.

Adoption, and its capacity to respond to the welfare of children, also changed greatly in the latter part of the twentieth century. The role and statutory definition of the welfare principle broadened considerably as the Children Act 1989 amended the Adoption Act 1976 in order to accommodate the pressures generated by child-protection law and practice. It now no longer sits comfortably in either public or private law and its proceedings are as likely as not to be contested. It has become pivotal for all of family law, functionally distorted by legislative and judicial requirements that it respond to the pressures affecting the family in modern society. Understanding what is happening to adoption is key to understanding much of what is happening to the whole body of family law. The role played by the welfare interests of the child is crucial to any such understanding.

153 Unlike the situation in Scotland: see s 6(1) of the Children (Scotland) Act 1995.

154 See, for example: *Re R (A Minor) (Wardship: Medical Treatment)* [1991] 4 All ER 177; *Re W (A Minor) (Medical Treatment)* [1992] 4 All ER 627; *Re K, W and H (Minors) (Medical Treatment)* [1993] 1 FLR 854; *A Metropolitan Borough Council v. DB* [1997] 1 FLR 767; and *Re C (Detention: Medical Treatment)* [1997] 2 FLR 180.

Conclusion

By the beginning of the twenty-first century, the Council of Europe was able to declare that: 'Children are holders of rights, rather than just objects of protection. They are beneficiaries of all human/fundamental rights and subjects of special regulations, given their specific characteristics.'[1] This was clearly not always the case. Only relatively recently has the law deigned to treat children even as 'objects of protection'. For centuries. it had been concerned more with their control than their welfare: as noted in Chapter 3, on one day in 1814, five children aged between eight and twelve were hanged in England for petty larceny;[2] in the latter half of the nineteenth century and continuing well into the first half of the twentieth, tens of thousands of pauper children were consigned to the 'poorhouse' or transported – or trafficked – from England to its colonies.[3] When children were not safely within the patriarchal care, protection and control of a marital family their welfare was unlikely to attract sympathetic state intervention. Traditionally, only if their 'specific characteristics' included an entitlement to property did a child warrant legal protection. Currently, the treatment of trafficked and parentless young migrants[4] calls into question the reality – but not the worthiness of the aspiration – of children as 'holders of rights'. The journey towards the CoE's perception of children's legal status, as experienced in England from the Poor Laws until the end of the twentieth century – marked by the introduction of the Children Act 1989 and ancillary legislation – has been the subject of this book.

1 See Council of Europe, *Handbook on European Law Relating to the Rights of the Child*, 2015, at para 1.1.1: www.echr.coe.int/documents/handbook_rights_child_eng.pdf.
2 See Morris, A. and Giller, H., *Understanding Juvenile Justice*, London, Croom Helm, 1987, at p 6.
3 It has been estimated that Canada alone received some 80,000 children in the space of 50 years. See, further, Bean, P. and Melville, J., *Lost Children of the Empire*, London, Unwin Hyman, 1989.
4 In 2015 alone, for example, German child-protection services took into custody over 42,300 unaccompanied refugee children. See the Federal Statistics Office of Germany at: www.destatis.de/EN/Home/_node.html.

DOI: 10.4324/9781003268512-14

The principle of the welfare of the child – or, more accurately, the upgrading of its operational functions – has consistently provided the single most effective form of leverage in raising the salience of children's interests relative to all other considerations. This has been aided considerably by the influence of the many international treaties, conventions, protocols and rulings of the ECtHR and the UN Commission on Human Rights that have set expectations and standards for domestic legislators, judiciary and local authorities in terms of the priority weighting legally required to be given to the welfare interests of children.[5] So, to take just one example, in *Osman v. UK*[6] the ECtHR found that Article 2 of the ECHR implied a positive obligation on the authorities to take preventative measures to protect an individual whose life is at risk. Moreover, its decision – that a public body (the police) was not immune from challenge for negligence in its duty to afford such protection to the plaintiff – clearly suggests that a local authority is required to be proactive, and could be held to account for its failure, in respect of a similar duty to safeguard the welfare of children at risk of significant harm. This principle, if wholly accepted, would require local authorities to reverse their 'diagnostic inflation'[7] tendencies and ring-fence some support services (such as family centres and home help provision) for preventative intervention with children in need rather than allow such services to be siphoned off to ease pressures at the acute end with those confirmed as having suffered significant harm.

Indeed, the European Convention for the Protection of Human Rights and Fundamental Freedoms 1950 and the associated rulings of the ECtHR have been highly influential in shaping domestic law relating to child welfare. Additionally, by the end of the twentieth century, the UN Convention on the Rights of the Child 1989,[8] particularly its declaration that 'the best interests of the child shall be the paramount consideration', had become the gold standard to which decision-makers in the United Kingdom were being urged to adhere, while the Hague Convention on Intercountry Adoption 1993 was beginning to influence, if not regulate, the availability of children for international adoption. While it is difficult to judge the extent to which the law relating to the welfare interests of children in the United Kingdom has been influenced by international instruments and by principles developed in the related caselaw, it is highly probable that as a consequence of ratification, of assimilating such instruments into national legislation and of judicial notice being taken of ECtHR rulings on issues arising under Article 8, the domestic law has been nudged along more quickly and more radically than would otherwise have been the case. This direction of travel does, of course, bring

5 Including UN Standard Minimum Rules for the Administration of Juvenile Justice (the 'Beijing Rules') 1985, the Hague Child Protection Convention 1996 and the European Convention on the Exercise of Children's Rights 1996.

6 [1999] 1 FLR 193.

7 See Eekelaar, J. and Dingwall, R., *The Reform of Child Care Law – a Practical Guide to the Children Act 1989*, London, Routledge, 1990.

8 Ratified by the UK on 16 December 1991.

with it some in-built contradictions – most notably, the greater the legal emphasis placed on isolating the rights/welfare interests of children, the less capacity the law has to affirm family unity – which leaves the state somewhat compromised in balancing the consensual and coercive grounds for its intervention in family life.

The evolving interpretation of the principle of the welfare of the child and the greater legal weight assigned to it reflect the corresponding changes in the relationship between state and family: the balance between consensual and coercive state intervention; between criminal and civil jurisdictions; between the interests of parent and child; and, ultimately, between the child as the subject and as a full party to decisions affecting his or her welfare. These matters provide broad themes to be pursued in the following books that constitute the series *Children and the Law: From Welfare to Rights.*

Bibliography

Books and articles

Bainham, A., *Children: The Modern Law*, 2nd ed., Bristol, Family Law, 1998.

Bean, P. and Melville, J., *Lost Children of the Empire*, London, Unwin Hyman, 1989.

Bell, S., *When Salem Came to the Boro*, London, Pan Books, 1988.

Bettelheim, B., *Love is Not Enough*, Glencoe, IL, Free Press, 1950.

Blackstone, W., *Commentaries on the Laws of England*, 7th ed., vol 1, Oxford, Clarendon, 1775.

Bowlby, J., *Attachment*, London, Penguin, 1969.

Bowlby, J., *Child Care and the Growth of Love*, London, Penguin, 1972.

Brasse, G., 'A Tightly Run Procedure? Interim Care Orders under Strain', *Family Law*, 24 (1994), pp 261–264.

Bromley, P.M., Bromley's Family Law, 8th ed., London, Butterworths, 1992.

Carpenter, M., *Reformatory Schools for the Perishing and Dangerous Classes and for the Prevention of Juvenile Delinquency*, London, Routledge, 1969 (first published 1851).

Corby, B., *Working with Child Abuse*, Milton Keynes, Open University Press, 1987.

Dingwall, J., Eekelaar, J. and Murray, T., *The Protection of Children: State Intervention and Family Life*, Oxford, Basil Blackwell, 1983.

Downie, A., 'A Metropolitan Borough Council v. DB and Re C (Detention: Medical Treatment): Extra-statutory Confinement – Detention and Treatment under the Inherent Jurisdiction', *Child and Family Law Quarterly*, 10(1) (1998), pp 101–107.

Eekelaar, J., *Family Law and Social Policy*, London, Weidenfeld and Nicolson, 1984.

Eekelaar, J. and Dingwall, R., *The Reform of Child Care Law – a Practical Guide to the Children Act 1989*, London, Routledge, 1990.

Eekelaar, J., Dingwall, R. and Murray, T., 'Victims or Threats? Children in Care Proceedings', *Journal of Social Welfare Law*, 4(2) (1982), pp 68–82.

Fortin, J., *Children's Rights and the Developing Law*, London, Butterworths, 1998.

Fortin, J., 'Re C (Medical Treatment): A Baby's Right to Die', *Child and Family Law Quarterly*, 10(4) (1998), pp 411–416.

Fox Harding, L., *Perspectives in Child Care Policy*, London, Longman, 1997.

Frost, N. and Stein, M., *The Politics of Child Welfare*, London, Harvester Wheatsheaf, 1989.

Gabler, I. and Aldridge, J. (eds) *In the Best Interests of the Child: Culture, Identity and Transracial Adoption*, London, Free Association Books, 1994.

Goldstein, J., Freud, A. and Solnit, A.H., *Beyond the Best Interests of the Child*, New York, Free Press, 1974.

Goldstein, J., Freud, A. and Solnit, A.H., *In the Best Interests of the Child*, New York, Free Press and Collier Macmillan, 1986.

Gough, D., *Child Abuse Interventions*, London, HMSO, 1993.

Hayes, M., 'The Proper Role of Courts in Child Care Cases', *Child and Family Law Quarterly*, 8(3) (1986), pp 201–216.

Hester, M. and Radford, L., 'Domestic Violence and Child Contact Arrangements in England and Denmark', *Journal of Social Welfare and Family Law*, 14(1) (1992), pp 57–70.

Hoggett, B., *Parents and Children*, 4th ed., London, Sweet and Maxwell, 1993.

Holdsworth, W.S., *History of English Law*, 7th ed., London, Methuen & Co, 1996.

Holmes, J., *John Bowlby and Attachment Theory*, London, Taylor and Francis, 1993.

Josling, J.F. and Levy, A., *Adoption of Children*, 10th ed., London, Longman, 1985.

Kellmer-Pringle, M., *The Needs of Children*, London, Hutchinson, 1980.

Kempe, C., Silverman, F., Steele, B., Droegmueller, W. and Silver, H., 'The Battered-Child Syndrome', *Journal of the American Medical Association*, 181 (1962), pp 4–11.

Lowe, N. and White, R., *Wards of Court*, London, Butterworths, 1979.

Maidment, S., *Child Custody and Divorce*, London, Routledge, 1985.

Manton, J., *Mary Carpenter and the Children of the Streets*, London, Heinemann, 1976.

Macpherson, W., *A Treatise on the Law Relating to Infants*, London, Maxwell & Son, 1842.

Michalowski, S., 'Is it in the Best Interests of a Child to Have a Life-saving Liver Transplantation? Re T (Wardship: Medical Treatment)', *Child and Family Law Quarterly*, 9(2) (1997), pp 179–190.

Morris, A. and Giller, H., *Understanding Juvenile Justice*, London, Croom Helm, 1987.

Morris, A., Giller, H., Szwed, E. and Geach, H., *Justice for Children*, London, Macmillan, 1980.

Murch, M. and Hooper, D., *The Family Justice System*, Bristol, Jordan Publishing, 1992.

O'Halloran, K., *The Welfare of the Child: The Principle and the Law*, Aldershot, Arena/Ashgate Publications, 1999.

O'Halloran, K., *Children and the Law: European Perspectives on Welfare and Rights*, Abingdon, Routledge, forthcoming.

O'Halloran, K., *Children and the Law: Shaping the Modern Welfare Principle in the British Isles*, Abingdon, Routledge, forthcoming.

Parker, H., *Receiving Juvenile Justice*, Oxford, Blackwell, 1981.

Pinchbeck, I., 'The State and the Child in 16th Century England', *British Journal of Sociology*, 7(4) (1957), p 72.

Pinchbeck, I. and Hewitt, M., *Children in English Society*, vol 2, London, Routledge & Kegan Paul, 1973.

Platt, A., *The Child Savers*, Chicago, University of Chicago Press, 1969.

Plotnikoff, J. and Woolfson, R., *The Pace of Child Abuse Prosecutions*, London, DoH, 1995.

Pollock, F. and Maitland, F.W., *The History of English Law*, 2nd ed., vol 2, Cambridge, Cambridge University Press, 1968.

Rowe, J. and Lambert, L., *Children who Wait*, London, British Association of Fostering and Adoption, 1973.

Rutter, M., *Maternal Deprivation Reassessed*, London, Penguin, 1972.

Salmond, J., *Jurisprudence*, London, Sweet & Maxwell, 1947.

Schechter, M. and Roberge, L., 'Sexual Exploitation', in Helfer, R. and Kempe, C. (eds), *Child Abuse and Neglect*, Cambridge, MA, Ballinger, 1976, pp 127–142.

Thompson, F.M.L., *The Rise of Respectable Society: A Social History of Victorian Britain*, Oxford, Oxford University Press, 1988.

Tizard, B., *Adoption: A Second Chance*, London, Open Books, 1977.

Reports

A Child in Trust: The Report of the Panel of Inquiry into the Circumstances Surrounding the Death of Jasmine Beckford, London, London Borough of Brent, 1985.

Adoption Law Review (Discussion Paper No 2), London, HMSO, 1990.

Adoption: The Future (Cmnd 2288), London, HMSO, 1993.

Booth, Dame M., *Avoiding Delay in Children Act Cases*, London, Lord Chancellor's Department, 1996.

Child Protection: Messages from Research, London, HMSO, 1995.

Crime, Justice and Protecting the Public (Cmnd 965), London, HMSO, 1990.

Department of Health, *Family Support, Day Care and Educational Provision for Young Children*, vol 2, London, HMSO, 1991.

Department of Health, *Review of Adoption Law: Report to Ministers of an Interdepartmental Working Group*, London, HMSO, 1992.

Department of Health and Social Security, *Review of Child Care Law*, London, HMSO, 1985.

Department of Social Security, *Report of the Committee of Inquiry into the Care and Supervision Provided for Maria Colwell*, London, HMSO, 1974.

Gibbons, J. *et al.*, *Operating the Child Protection System: A Study of Child Protection Practices in English Local Authorities*, London, HMSO, 1995.

Home Office, *Report of the Committee on Child Adoption* (Cmnd 1254), London, HMSO, 1921.

Home Office, *The Child, the Family and the Young Offender* (Cmnd 2742), London, HMSO, 1965.

Home Office, *Children in Trouble* (Cmnd 3601), London, HMSO, 1968.

Home Office, *Report of the Advisory Group on Video Evidence* (Pigot Report), London, HMSO, 1989.

Home Office, *Crime, Justice and Protecting the Public* (Cmnd 965), London, HMSO, 1990.

Home Office, *No More Excuses – a New Approach to Tackling Youth Crime in England and Wales* (Cmnd 3809), London, HMSO, 1997.

Home Office, *Strengthening Punishment in the Community* (Cmnd 2780), London, HMSO, 1995.

Law Commission Report No. 91 Review of Child Law: Guardianship, London, HMSO, 1985.

Law Commission Report No. 172 Family Law Review of Child Law, Guardianship and Custody, London, HMSO, 1988.

Law Commission Report No. 207 Family Law, Domestic Violence and Occupation of the Family Home, London, HMSO, 1992.

Levy, A. and Kahan, B., *The Pindown Experience and the Protection of Children*, Stafford, Staffordshire CC, 1991.

Lord Chancellor's Office, *Improvements in the Arrangements for Care Proceedings*, London, HMSO, 1988.

Lord Chancellor's Office, *Children Act Advisory Committee Final Report*, London, HMSO, 1997.

Murch, M., Hunt, J. and Macleod A., *Representation of the Child in the Civil Courts: Research Report for the Department of Health, Summary of Conclusions and Recommendations*, Bristol, Socio-legal Centre for Family Studies, University of Bristol, 1990.

Report of an Unofficial Committee of the Society for Investigating the Causes of the Alarming Increase in Juvenile Delinquency in the Metropolis, London, J.F. Dove, 1816.

Report of the Care of Children Committee (Curtis Report) (Cmnd 6922), London, HMSO, 1946.

Report of the Commission of Inquiry into the Circumstances Surrounding the Death of Kimberley Carlile, a Child in Mind: Protection of Children in a Responsible Society, London, London Borough of Greenwich Social Services, 1987.

Report of the Committee on the Age of Majority (Latey Report) (Cmnd 3342), London, HMSO, 1967.

Report of the Committee on Child Adoption (Hopkinson Report) (Cmnd 1254), London, HMSO, 1921.

Report of the Committee on Children and Young Persons (Ingleby Report) (Cmnd 11910), London, HMSO, 1960.

Report of the Departmental Committee on the Adoption of Children (Cmnd 9248), London, HMSO, 1954.

Report of the Departmental Committee on the Adoption of Children (Houghton Report) (Cmnd 5107), London, HMSO, 1972.

Report of the Departmental Committee on Children and Young Persons (Cmnd 1191), London, HMSO, 1960.

Report of the Departmental Committee on the Treatment of Young Offenders (Cmnd 2831), London, HMSO, 1927.

Report of the Inquiry into Child Abuse in Cleveland 1987 (Cmnd 412), London, HMSO, 1988.

Report of Interdepartmental Group, DoH, Review of Adoption Law, London, HMSO, 1992.

Report of the Royal Commission on Marriage and Divorce – Report 1951–1955 (Morton Report) (Cmnd 9678), London, HMSO, 1956.

Report on Children and Young Persons (Scotland) (Kilbrandon Report) (Cmnd 2306), London, HMSO, 1964.

Utting, D., *Family and Parenthood: Supporting Families, Preventing Breakdown*, York, Rowntree Foundation, 1995.

Utting, Sir W., '*Putting Children First*', NFM Lucy Faithfull Memorial Lecture, 13 November 1997.

Waterhouse, R., *Lost in Care: Report of the Tribunal of Inquiry into the Abuse of Children in Care in the Former County Council Areas of Gwynedd and Clwyd since 1974*, London, HMSO, 2000.

Whose Child: Report on the Death of Tyra Henry, London, London Borough of Greenwich, 1987.

Working Together under the Children Act 1989: A Guide to Arrangements for Inter-agency Co-operation for the Protection of Children from Abuse, London, HMSO, 1991.

Index

FSC
www.fsc.org
MIX
Papier | Fördert gute Waldnutzung
FSC® C083411

Kolibri 360 GmbH
Ferdinand-Jühlke-Straße 7
99095 Erfurt, Deutschland
produktsicherheit@kolibri360.de